This provocative new book takes up and de
of rationality and irrationality in Jon Elster
purposes are threefold. First, Elster shows ho...
erence formation in the realm of politics are shaped by social
and political institutions. Second, he argues for an important
distinction in the social sciences between mechanisms and theories. Third, he illustrates those general principles of political
psychology through readings of three outstanding political psychologists: the French classical historian Paul Veyne, the Soviet
dissident writer Alexander Zinoviev, the great French political
theorist Alexis de Tocqueville.

As with all Elster books, the style is succinct and readable
ensuring that it will be fully accessible to graduate students and
teachers in philosophy, political science, and the history of ideas.

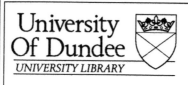

POLITICAL PSYCHOLOGY

University
Of Dundee
UNIVERSITY LIBRARY

Date of Return		

Political
Psychology

JON ELSTER

CAMBRIDGE
UNIVERSITY PRESS

Published by the Press Syndicate of the University of Cambridge
The Pitt Building, Trumpington Street, Cambridge CB2 1RP
40 West 20th Street, New York, NY 10011-4211, USA
10 Stamford Road, Oakleigh, Victoria 3166, Australia

Cambridge University Press 1993

First published 1993

Printed in Canada

Library of Congress Cataloging-in-Publication Data

Elster, Jon, 1940–
Political psychology / Jon Elster.
p. cm.
Includes bibliographical references and index.
ISBN 0–521–41110–6 (hardback). – ISBN 0–521–42286–8 (paperback)
1. Political psychology. I. Title.
JA74.5.E47 1993
320'.01'9 – dc20   92–17779
                                                                  CIP

A catalog record for this book is available from the British Library

ISBN 0–521–41110–6 hardback
ISBN 0–521–42286–8 paperback

CONTENTS

Abbreviations   *Page vi*
Preface   *vii*

Introduction: Why Political Psychology?   1
1 A Historian and the Irrational: A Reading of
   Bread and Circuses   35
2 Internal and External Negation: An Essay in
   Ibanskian Sociology   70
3 Tocqueville's Psychology I   101
4 Tocqueville's Psychology II   136

References   192

Index   199

v

ABBREVIATIONS

The following abbreviations are used in this book:

AP   *Archives Parlementaires. Série I: 1789–1799*, Paris 1875–1888, vols. 8–30.

PC   Paul Veyne, *Le pain et le cirque*, Paris: Editions du Seuil 1976.

BC   Paul Veyne, *Bread and Circuses* (abridged translation of the above), London: Allen Lane 1990.

DA   Alexis de Tocqueville, *Democracy in America*, New York: Anchor Books 1969.

FC   M. Farrand (ed.), *Records of the Federal Convention*. New Haven: Yale University Press 1966, vols. I–II.

YH   Alexander Zinoviev, *The Yawning Heights*, New York: Random House 1979. On a few occasions I have modified the translation somewhat, on the basis of the generally superior French translation (*Les hauteurs béantes*, Lausanne: L'Age d'Homme 1977).

RF   Alexander Zinoviev, *The Radiant Future*, New York: Random House 1981.

PREFACE

Ten years ago I published earlier versions of Chapters 1 and 2 of this book, in the form of a study of Paul Veyne in *Informations sur les Sciences Sociales* (1980) and a critical note on Alexander Zinoviev in *Archives Européennes de Sociologie* (1980). In the first article I showed that Veyne had been profoundly influenced by Hegel and Tocqueville, and went on to say that:

> To these two internal reference points within the book there is to be added a third, which both illuminates it and is illuminated by it: Alexander Zinoviev's *The Yawning Heights.* The affinities and contrasts between authoritarian, democratic and totalitarian societies will enable us to rebuild political sociology on new and solid foundations with Veyne, Tocqueville, and Zinoviev as permanent references.

In the introductory note to the second article I said much the same:

> By a happy coincidence, I read Zinoviev's work at the same time as *Bread and Circuses,* when I was also rereading *Democracy in America.* From time to time I shall have the opportunity of pointing out some of the many points at which the three books converge, a subject to which I hope to be able to devote a separate study later.

I often thought of carrying out the project, but it was not until 1989 that I had the chance to do so. With my colleague Stephen Holmes, of the University of Chicago, I was invited by the CREA of the Ecole Polytechnique (Paris) and the Institut Raymond Aron to give a series of lectures on Tocqueville. I chose as my topic "Tocqueville's psychology," which is the subject of Chapters 3 and 4 of this book. I then had the idea of taking up the articles on Veyne and Zinoviev, to see whether they had worn well enough to merit inclusion, along with the more recent text on Tocqueville, in a small text in political psychology. On rereading them, I found some obscure passages and an occasionally grandiloquent style that set my teeth on edge, but there were also sounder elements on which, I thought, something could be built. It needed many revisions before I finally felt that they were acceptable. I added an introductory chapter, in which I try to explain why political psychology, long neglected and to all intents and purposes nonexistent as an intellectual discipline, offers an especially fruitful means of understanding the great historical events and movements of both the past and the present.

The book has been quite extensively revised for the English translation, mainly for the same reasons that led me to revise the original articles. It turned out that various arguments, which to my imperfect pitch sounded plausible and even compelling when stated in French, did not survive the translation into sober English. While not exactly flaky, they owed too much to my desire to be terse and elegant in a language that I did not fully master. In addition, I made extensive changes to reduce the overlap with my other English books. I apologize for the overlap that remains. It could not, I felt, be eliminated without upsetting the balance of the book.

INTRODUCTION: WHY POLITICAL PSYCHOLOGY?

T HE following four chapters present the case for seeing political
psychology as important and relevant. It is in the details of
these analyses that the answer to the question raised in the title
has to be sought. The aim of this Introduction is to provide some
preliminary clarification by describing the role and scope of the
discipline, setting out the central question it raises, providing
some examples, and explaining the method I have opted for.

THEORIES VERSUS MECHANISMS

I shall start with the last of these. Why would it seem useful,
when explaining a theoretical approach, to concentrate on writers
rather than on the theory itself? Although Veyne, Zinoviev, and
Tocqueville are brilliant writers, may not their splendid style be
a hindrance to any systematic exposition of a coherent theory?
Does one have to be a genius to be a practitioner of political
philosophy?

My reply is that the choice of these three writers itself ensures
a degree of coherence, even if it is largely accidental and post
factum. From Aristotle to the present political theorists have
proposed innumerable typologies of political regimes. Each has
its advantages and drawbacks, and none can claim any special
status or any particular close relationship to the nature of things.
Choosing Veyne, Zinoviev, and Tocqueville suggests a division
of political systems into authoritarian, totalitarian, and democratic
regimes. If we ask whether such a three-way split is exhaustive,
or whether the categories are mutually exclusive, the answer

1

in both cases must be no. The Italian city-states, for instance, do not fall neatly into any of the categories. According to Tocqueville, democracy not only contains the germ of an ubiquitous and intrusive totalitarianism (however gentle and protective it may also be), but also entails the risk of creating an industrial aristocracy that could produce a new kind of authoritarianism – tendencies that could develop within the democratic framework rather than replacing it. Historical regimes form an infinitely more richly shaded mosaic than that offered by the threefold division suggested.

It would of course be possible to provide a pseudosolution to this pseudoproblem by introducing mixed regimes, rather as Marxism introduced the notion of a social formation to get around the rigid distinction between modes of production. This would allow us, for instance, to see set historical regimes within a triangle having the three "pure" regimes at the angles. It is not worth taking the idea any further. The reason why the distinction between authoritarian, totalitarian, and democratic regimes seems to me a fruitful one is that it both takes in a large proportion of historical regimes and makes it possible to identify and analyze the psychological mechanisms at work in *all* regimes. In other words, these three types of regime provide enough diversity and variety to cover also those that have different institutions. A typology of *regimes* is a fragile and artificial construction serving only limited purposes. A catalogue of *mechanisms* is a sounder and more helpful tool.

Mechanism: This is the key word. It will figure very largely in this book. In my view, progress in the social sciences does not lie in the construction of general theories such as historical materialism, Parsonian sociology, or the theory of economic equilibrium. The aim of such theories – to establish general and invariable propositions – is and will always remain an illusory dream.[1] Despite a widespread belief to the contrary, the alternative to nomological thinking is not a merely descriptive or narrative

1 Earlier arguments to this effect are Veyne (1984) and Boudon (1986). See also, ch. 1 of Elster (1989a).

ideographic method. Between these two extremes there is place and need for the study of mechanisms. I do not propose a formal definition, but shall only provide an informal pointer: A mechanism is a specific causal pattern that can be recognized after the event but rarely foreseen. Some examples will clarify this proposal.

In Chapters 1 and 4 I examine the mechanism of the "sour grapes syndrome," in which desires are adjusted in accordance with the means of achieving them. The opposite mechanism can also be seen, for sometimes we want what we cannot have, precisely because we cannot have it. If we consider the behavior of the citizens in totalitarian regimes, we can see that those who condemn Western freedom and stress the evils of Western society are very like the fox in La Fontaine's fable. Among those taking the opposite view, there will be some who want the freedoms they lack because they are worth having in themselves, and no doubt others who want them simply because they cannot have them. There is no a priori reason why the three character types should not all exist at the same time, and no way of knowing in advance to what degree they will all be observable.

In Chapter 4 I discuss the formation of beliefs and tastes as a result of a desire to conform – not to the external situation, but to the beliefs and tastes of others. Here too the opposite mechanism – the formation of beliefs and tastes as a result of an (unconscious) desire to be different – can also be observed. This phenomenon, which should not be confused with mere indifference to others (see Chapter 2), can exist alongside with conformity in a constantly shifting relationship. Electoral behavior, for instance, has been analyzed in these terms, with some voters tending to favor the candidate tipped to win (the "bandwagon effect") and others to identify with the one tipped to lose (the "underdog effect").[2]

A third example involves the fine grain of altruistic motivation.[3] Some people are unconditionally altruistic, in the sense that

2 Simon (1954).
3 This is discussed at greater length in ch. 5 of Elster (1989b).

their contribution to charities is in no way dependent on how much others give. In the case of conditional altruists, there are those who subscribe to a norm that prevents them giving less than their peers. Others adopt a utilitarian approach leading to the opposite result: Large contributions from others make the beneficiaries better off, and hence (assuming declining marginal utility of money) an extra contribution less effective, which makes them less inclined to give. Here too, elections provide an example. As a high turnout at the polls can be seen as a public good, in the absence of which democracy might crumble, an individual vote may be seen as a gift to the community. For some, the obligation to cast one's vote is deemed to be more compelling when the average propensity to do so is high, whereas for others it is stronger when the latter is falling.

A final example is taken from the psychology of envy, further discussed in Chapter 4 below. The definition of targets of envy can be governed by either of two mechanisms. On the one hand, there is a *spillover effect* by which the habit of envy tends to spread. According to Plutarch, once the habit of envying enemies is established "it sticks; then from habit we start hating and envying friends."[4] On the other hand, there is a *compensation effect*: If envy is denied one outlet, it will seek another. (For more about these two mechanisms, see Chapter 4 below.) Plutarch, again, argues that to the extent that "envy is a fact of life, unload it on enemies, who will render you pleasanter to your friends in their prosperity by draining your potential for envy."[5] Instead of concluding that Plutarch was contradicting himself, we may interpret him, more charitably, as implying that either mechanism can operate, on different occasions.

Anyone stating two opposite general propositions is in fact contradicting himself. We cannot at the same time maintain that men prefer what they have to what they cannot have and that they prefer what they cannot have; that they think like others and the opposite to others; that they give more when

4 Walcot (1978), p. 36.
5 Ibid.

4

others give more and that they give more when others give less; and that envy of one's enemies both strengthens and weakens the tendency to envy one's friends. If one of the propositions is true, the other is necessarily false. But we *can* maintain, without fear of contradicting ourselves, the existence of two contrary mechanisms. The distinctive feature of a mechanism is not that it can be universally applied to predict and control social events, but that it embodies a causal chain that is sufficiently general and precise to enable us to locate it in widely different settings. It is less than a theory, but a great deal more than a description, since it can serve as a model for understanding other cases not yet encountered.

Moving from a plurality of mechanisms to a unified theory would mean that we should be able to identify in advance the conditions in which one or the other mechanism would be triggered. In what circumstances do people give more when others give more? Or, alternatively, what are the characteristics of those who give more when others are doing the same? My own view is that the social sciences are currently unable to identify such conditions and are likely to remain so forever. Using experimental procedures, one can often establish general propositions of the following type. In conditions C_1, C_2 ... C_n, we observe mechanism M_1. In conditions C'_1, C'_2 ... C'_n, we observe mechanism M_2. In the real world, however, the number of possible permutations of conditions is too great for us to be able to establish the characteristic mechanism operating in each of them. That is why experimentally based social psychology is both indispensable and insufficient. It is indispensable because it can foster in their pure state mechanisms that would otherwise have passed unnoticed, and insufficient because it has very little predictive power outside the laboratory.[6]

Identifying mechanisms can also be helpful in another respect. The correlations that social scientists can identify between different patterns of behavior tend, even when they are statistically sig-

6 Useful introductions to experimental social psychology are Nisbett and Ross (1980) and Aronson (1988).

nificant, to be quite weak. In such cases, we might ask whether the weak correlation does not really mask two strong correlations, one positive and the other negative.[7] Imagine, for instance, that we found that there is a weak tendency for people to donate more to charity when others donate more. This tendency might well be the net effect of the two opposing mechanisms that I discussed above, with the norm of reciprocity being somewhat stronger (guiding the behavior of more people or guiding people's behavior more of the time) than the utilitarian reaction.

Or take another, nonhypothetical example: Walter Mischel's celebrated finding that the crosssituational consistency in behavior tends to be quite weak.[8] People can be aggressive at the workplace and mild-mannered at home; selfish in one setting and altruistic in another. In terms of the present approach this finding could be understood in two ways. On the one hand, one might see the setting as the trigger of a mechanism. On the other hand, however, we might postulate the existence of two different kinds of individuals. To anticipate on the discussion in Chapter 4, some persons might be subject to a *spillover effect*, so that, for instance, the ability to delay gratification in one arena creates a general habit of doing so in all walks of life.[9] Weightwatchers might find it easier to give up smoking. Other individuals might be subject to a *compensation effect*, so that drives denied an outlet in one arena will seek one in another. Weightwatchers might find it more difficult to quit smoking if they need to give themselves a break from time to time and to reward themselves for the strict dieting.[10] In such cases, a weak aggregate correlation might mask the presence of strong opposite correlations on a less aggregate level.[11]

A final comment on mechanisms. It might appear, from the examples given, that mechanisms are essentially psychological.

7 For a similar point, see Lewis (1982), p. 32.
8 Mischel (1968).
9 Ainslie (1992) offers impressive evidence to this effect.
10 For findings to this effect, see Nisan (1985).
11 See also the comments in note 13 below.

However, we can use psychological mechanisms as building blocks in the construction of sociological ones. In the discussion below of revolutionary behavior I indicate, for instance, how heterogeneous motivations may interact to create a snowball effect that none of them would have produced taken by itself. In Chapter 4 I show how some of the psychological mechanisms identified by Tocqueville can interact so as to account for large-scale social phenomena. Like the individual-level mechanisms themselves, these interactive structures are largely contingent. We cannot tell in advance when the mix of individual motivations needed to generate aggregate phenomena will turn out to be present.

METHODOLOGICAL INDIVIDUALISM

The importance of political psychology is linked to the postulate of methodological individualism, a much criticized but, if properly understood, essentially trivial doctrine.[12] It implies neither an atomistic perspective (it grants that relations between individuals are not always reducible to their monadic predicates), nor egoism (it is compatible with any specific set of motivations), nor rational choice (here again it is perfectly neutral), nor the innate or "given" character of desires (it is consistent with the view that desires are shaped by society, that is, by other individuals), nor finally with political individualism (being a methodological doctrine, it is compatible with any political or normative orientation).

It does, however, answer guilty to the charge of reductionism, by its claim to explain the complex by the simple – the principle that has brought about scientific progress in the face of all kinds of holistic obscurantism.[13] Like any kind of reductionism, it is

---

12 I have written more about this in Elster (1989c).
13 This is the place to comment on a possibly confusing aspect of my terminology. In earlier work (Elster 1983a), reductionism was also characterized as a search for *mechanisms*, but not in the sense in which that term is used here. According to this earlier argument, the difference between theory and mechanism is one of fineness of grain. A theory is a lawlike "If, then" statement relating an antecedent state to a subsequent one. A mechanism provides

sometimes applied prematurely and overenthusiastically, given the scientific tools available. Thus Pascal's criticism of Descartes was not that he embraced atomism, but that he wanted to implement it: "We must say summarily: 'This is made by figure and motion,' for it is true. But to say what these are, and to compose the machine is ridiculous. For it is useless, uncertain, and painful." (*Pensées*, 79.)

This being said, we must beware of confusing the substance of a doctrine and the abuses to which it has been subjected. We may agree that many "economic" explanations of revolutions are ridiculous, and yet it has to be stressed that the actors on the revolutionary stage are men, not classes. (Later in this Introduction we shall see how the development of a revolution can be understood in the perspective offered by methodological individualism.) Nor can we talk of social institutions as if they were monolithic, since essentially they are collections of human beings. If they were not, how could we explain their corruption and the erosion of their authority? And if their instability needs explanation at the level of individuals, should not the same type of explanation be offered for their stability?

Methodological individualism tells us to study the individual human action as the basic building block of aggregate social phenomena. In a general way, any action can be explained by the motivations and beliefs of the actors.[14] (This is not an im-

the causal chain that mediates between the two states. In the absence of a mechanism, the law is a mere black box (but see Suppes 1970, p. 91 for the point that "one man's mechanism is another man's black box"). In the present exposition, theories and mechanisms differ in level of generality rather than in fineness of grain. In my earlier terminology, going from theory to mechanism is to go from "If A, then always B" to "If A, then always C, D, E, F and B." On the view set out here, going from theory to mechanism is to go from "If A, then always B" to "If A, then sometimes B." However, I also urge the further move to "If A, then sometimes C, D, E, F and B."

14 In Chapter 4 I formulate this somewhat differently, saying that any action can be explained by the (subjective) desires of the actor and the (objective) opportunities at his disposal. Often, the two come to more or less the same thing, because in the first place what the actor does is explicable in terms of what he thinks he can do and in the second place what he thinks he can

plication of methodological individualism, but a truism that follows from the definition of action, as distinct from mere behavior.) A central and very important case is when an actor chooses the action which for good reasons he sees as most likely to achieve his aims, that, is, the case of rational choice.[15] In a number of cases, however, psychologists and decision theorists have shown that action does not conform to that paradigm. Sometimes the beliefs underlying it are less than fully rational (see below). Sometimes there is a discrepancy, with the action actually taken being different from what would be dictated by the motivations and beliefs of the actor. Two major cases are weak and excessive will, discussed in Chs. 4 and 1, respectively.

There is a wide and varied range of motivations: substantive and formal, conscious and unconscious, self-regarding and non-self-regarding, forward-looking and backward-looking. I argue in Chapter 4 that the most important motives are advantage (or interest), passions and social norms. These are all, as it were, substantive motivations. They fit into a framework of formal motivations, which include attitudes to risk, uncertainty and the distant future. What often determines the behavior of an actor in the political field is not so much what he desires and how strongly he desires it as his aversion to risk or his preference for the present moment rather than the future. The "decision value" of an experience may, for these reasons (among others), differ from its inherent value.

Motivations can be conscious or unconscious. As further explained in Chapter 1, one should beware of ascribing to unconscious impulses properties that are only appropriate to conscious desires. However, it would be equally wrong to deny the

do is largely explicable in terms of what he can in fact do. There are, however, many exceptions to the second statement. Some of them are explored in later chapters. Although the desire−opportunity model could probably be restated so as to take account of these exceptions, I shall not try to do so. The model is offered as a mechanism (or a set of mechanisms), not as a theory.

15 For a more detailed examination of the theory of rational choice, see Elster (1986a; Elster 1989d, ch. 1).

existence of unconscious motivations, although their precise mode of operation remains a mystery.

Moreover, motivations may be classified by the way in which they take into account the effects of an action on other people. For purely logical reasons, we have to give pride of place to selfish motivations.[16] This does not rule out, of course, that in the real world altruism and envy (see Chapter 4) may be just as important.

Finally, we can distinguish between rational motivations, which are orientated toward the future, and those that carry the past with them. A rational actor is one who is willing to let bygones be bygones. He does not, for instance, seek revenge unless the reputation of being someone who gets even is likely to be useful to him in the future.[17] Those who are unable to shed the past may be subject to a cognitive mechanism often called "the sunk-cost fallacy" or (by reference to some phenomena that embody it) the "Concorde effect" or the "Vietnam effect." Or they may be in the grip of a social norm that tells them to return good for good and bad for bad, regardless of the consequences.

Cognition similarly varies both in its substantive objects and in its modalities. Human opinion is directed toward individual facts (what does my opponent intend to do?), toward general causal connections (what will reduce inflation?) or toward the future (what will the dollar exchange be in a year's time?). Among modalities, we must first distinguish between certainty and what is believed to be more or less likely and then, more

---

16 See also Elster (1989b), pp. 35–6 for an argument that rational action is also methodologically prior to irrational action.

17 Of course, having that kind of reputation may be useful even if it is not the outcome of the rational pursuit of reputation. The following comment on Robert Moses illustrates the point: "If Moses was indulging his enjoyment at hurting people not in order to help him with his aims but simply because he liked hurting, the indulgence nonetheless helped him achieve his aims. As Judge Jacob Lutsky puts it, 'If you know that every time you get in a guy's way, he's going to kick you in the balls, you make pretty damn sure you don't get in his way – right?' " (Caro 1974, p. 507)

subtly, between what is unreservedly accepted and what is only half believed (see Chapter 1). We may also differentiate between strong and deep convictions, where the former are characterized by their ability to shape action and the latter by their ability to remain stable in a turbulent environment.

The realm of error, sophism, and fallacy is a particularly rich source for political psychology, and one to which I shall return again and again. The most important instances in the present book are the microeconomic and micropolitical illusions (Chapter 1), the tendency to confuse the absence of desire for X and the desire for X to be absent (Chapter 2) and the tendency to confuse partial and general equilibrium (Chapter 3). Also worth mentioning is the "everyday Calvinism" underlying "everyday Kantianism."[18] The latter (a form of unconditional altruism) is a normative attitude, compactly summarized in the persuasive question, "What if everyone did that?" The former is a cognitive fallacy, viz. that of confusing the diagnostic and the causal values of an action. If a person believes that his choice between, say, giving and not giving to a charitable cause is not only diagnostic of whether others will give, but actually has an impact on whether they will give, he is more likely to be swayed by the Kantian question.

THE FORMATION OF BELIEFS AND DESIRES

Political psychology cannot limit itself to tracing the effects of beliefs and desires on individual actions and thereby on social processes. It also has to concentrate on the mechanisms by which desires and beliefs are formed. In these mechanisms, causes as well as effects can belong either to the order of motivations or to that of cognitions, giving four distinct cases. In the following, I am mainly concerned with mechanisms that

---

18 The following draws on Quattrone and Tversky (1986). See also Leff (1976), pp. 167ff and ch. 5 of Elster (1989b).

distort desires and beliefs, broadly defined as those whose operation would be unacceptable to the subject were he aware of it.[19]

In the first place, the formation of motivations can itself be explained with reference to mechanisms that are of the order of motivations. Here, I am not talking about conscious and motivated character planning as advocated in Stoic, Buddhist, or Spinozistic philosophy,[20] but of the operation of unconscious motivations or drives that have as their end result a conscious motivation.[21] Among these, the most important one is the *reduction of cognitive dissonance* (Chapter 1). Despite the term, the phenomenon is motivational rather than cognitive. The organism seems to have a need for interior tranquillity, which makes it adjust its desires to its beliefs (or vice versa[22]) until they are relatively consonant with each other. Although being in the grip of this mechanism makes for loss of autonomy, it does at least create some, even if perhaps merely temporary, contentment.[23] (See Chapters 3 and 4 for comments on Tocqueville's discussion

---

19 The following repeats some of the analysis in Elster (1983b), ch. 1, and Elster (1989d), ch. 1, but with a view to laying the groundwork for the discussions in later chapters.
20 See notably Kolm (1982).
21 For a critical discussion of the distinction between character planning and "sour grapes" (an important special case of the distinction made in the text) see Bovens (1992).
22 Often we can observe that a given situation of dissonance induces different individuals to go different ways. Thus in his analysis of Chinese reactions to the West at the beginning of this century, Levenson (1968) distinguishes between two types of response. Some saw Western technical development as an option that China had contemplated and rejected long ago (sour grapes). Others thought it might be possible to keep the essence of things Chinese and reject only the Western function (wishful thinking). In other words, the latter wanted to take the techniques they thought would be useful to them without the cultural and political concomitants. However, as Tocqueville observed with regard to a similar problem, "these things hold together, and one cannot enjoy the one without putting up with the others" (DA, p. 589).
23 The contentment can be permanent if the adjustment operates on the desires. If it operates on the beliefs, by making them correspond to the desires rather than to reality, there will usually be a penalty to pay down the road. See also Chapter 1 below.

of such cases.) Sometimes, however, it is possible to observe mechanisms that *create* dissonance, such as one sees with case-hardened pessimism or the tendency to tire very quickly of the very thing that had been desired and chosen. These are doubly counter-productive, because they subvert both the autonomy and the happiness of those subject to them.

Secondly, desires can be formed under the influence of cognitive-type mechanisms. The relative attractiveness of two options can change when they are described differently, even if logically the two descriptions are equivalent. I may be ready to pay two dollars for a glass that is half full, but no more than $1.50 for one that is half empty. There is by now a long list of phenomena of this kind.[24] In a way, they are akin to cognitive illusions, with the difference that in some cases there is no way of telling which of the alternative evaluations is the correct one. We know that in reality the stick in the water is not broken, but no test will tell us whether $2 or $1.50 is the right price for the glass of water. Some of the phenomena discussed in Chapter 2 also fall under this heading, as does the link between everyday Calvinism and everyday Kantianism.

Third, beliefs and opinions can be formed by "hot," that is, motivated, mechanisms. Self-deception and wishful thinking are as uncontrovertibly real as they are paradoxical. On the one hand, anyone who refuses to admit his own occasional or frequent tendency to believe that the world is as he would like it to be is thereby providing an example of what he is denying. On the other hand, analysis suggests that in the case of self-deception, the same proposition is both affirmed and denied. In itself, there is nothing paradoxical about that (Chapter 2). It is paradoxical only insofar as self-deception seems to offer an example of a seemingly impossible phenomenon, namely intentional and motivated denial.[25] If someone told us that on his way to work he always takes great care not to see any cats, we would wonder

---

24 Some recent surveys are in Thaler (1991, 1992).
25 See Pears (1984) and Davidson (1986) for attempts to make sense of this phenomenon.

whether he doesn't have to catch at least a glance of them in order to avert his eyes.

A largely ignored but very significant phenomenon for the study of political life is that of beliefs arising from a need for *meaning*. I believe we can identify several needs of this kind. First, there is the need to find a purpose – an end, a function – even in the tiniest things. This may give rise to a theoretical functionalism or to psychoanalytical conjectures (Chapter 1), but also to eminently practical consequences, as in the Stalinist notion of "objective complicity." Second, there is the need to find justice in the universe, as elaborated in "just world" theories.[26] Misfortune is translated into blame and guilt, even when it is manifestly random in origin (as in the draft lottery). Even in authoritarian societies, the citizens need to justify the order under which they live (Chapter 1). Thirdly, human beings seem to have a deep need to have sufficient reasons for what they do, and an equally deep aversion to situations in which reason gives no clear answer.[27] They often need a belief – some belief or other – more than they need a correct belief. Even in situations in which they do not have the necessary information to form a sensible opinion, they are reluctant to admit their ignorance or agnosticism (Chapter 2). It ought to be an important task for the social sciences to examine this need for meaning and its consequences. Instead, they have to a large extent served as tools for realizing this need. Functionalism and psychoanalysis have, as I said, invented meanings where none exist. Decision theory, notably of the Bayesian variety, has told us how to give reasons for decisions that are essentially incapable of rational justification.

Fourth, beliefs can also be formed – or distorted – by means of "cold" mechanisms, that is, cognitive processes so rigid or naive that they systematically lead people into error. I have

26 See for instance Lerner (1980).
27 Elster (1989d), ch. 2. See also Chapter 2 below.

already mentioned a number of false reasonings of this type.[28] Although the usual approach to political psychology is more concerned with mechanisms that have motivations either as their input or their output,[29] I argue in Chapter 1 below that important aspects of ideology fall in the doubly cognitive character.

THE POLITICAL PSYCHOLOGY OF REVOLUTIONS

I shall conclude by giving two instances of applied political psychology: the dynamics of revolution and of constitution making.[30] It is sometimes said that to make a revolution a streak (or more) of irrationality is needed.[31] I shall try to separate out what is rational from what is irrational in revolutionary movements. In writings on constitution making, it is sometimes asserted that *ideas* and *interests* – rational argument and strategic thinking – are the two dominant factors.[32] While not denying this view, I shall offer what I believe to be some important modifications.

In this subsection I indicate how, in an unstable political situation, interaction between subjects and subjects, and between subjects and the ruler, can snowball and destroy the existing regime. The tale I tell will be half factual and half invented,

28 For case studies see Kahneman, Slovic, and Tversky (1982) and Bell, Raiffa, and Tversky (1988).
29 Thaler (1983) is a rare exception.
30 Both examples are transparently inspired by the great events in France and the United States at the end of the eighteenth century (Elster 1991b) and by the recent waves of revolution (Elster 1990b) and constitution making (Elster 1991c) in Eastern Europe. The exposition will, however, be kept in a stylized form.
31 Tocqueville (1970, p. 22) has this to say: "I have always thought that in revolutions, especially democratic revolutions, madmen (not those metaphorically called such, but real madmen) have played a very considerable political part. At least it is certain that at such times a state of semi-madness is not out of place and often leads to success."
32 With regard to the Federal Convention in 1787, see references in note 52 below. For a contemporary example, see the discussion in Rapaczynski (1991) of the constitutional debates in Poland.

borrowing features from the great revolutions of the past and the present without however coinciding with any of them. First I shall consider the situation potential revolutionaries find themselves in, and their motives.

Briefly stated, we can say that they are faced with an n-person Prisoner's Dilemma.[33] Slightly less briefly, their situation is defined as follows. A successful revolution would establish a public good, that is, a good that could not be restricted solely to the militants themselves. Although it is possible to refuse social justice or political freedoms to those who have actively fought against the revolution, it would be impracticable to deny them to those who had taken no action or joined the movement only shortly before its final victory. The consequences of a failed revolution would be severe punishment for those supporting it, and even if it succeeded it would do so only after a prolonged struggle in which the lives, the health and the fortunes of those taking part would be at risk. The rational conclusion seems obvious: There would be everything to gain and nothing to lose by abstaining from any revolutionary strategy. Abstention, in fact, is a *dominant strategy*, since whatever others may do it is in the interest of the individual to stay on the sidelines. If they commit themselves, he can plough his own furrow and benefit from their efforts. If they do not, the risks he himself would run if he joined are enough to dissuade him.

Yet revolutionary movements have been known to come into being and sometimes even to succeed. If all else failed, we could account for them on the basis of the irrationality and madness of those engaging in them. Before doing so, however, we need to find out whether there are any other explanations still falling within the bounds of rational behavior that could show how they develop. One suggestion would be that the revolutionaries, having nothing to lose but their chains, are acting quite rationally in taking up arms against the existing regime. Historical examples show that things are seldom so simple. Over the centuries Chinese

33 Taylor (1987, 1988).

rebels knew very well that if they were captured by the Imperial Army, they would die the death of a thousand cuts, to which any existence or even any other death would be preferable.[34] Moreover, abject poverty tends to reduce both motivation and the range of means available, the former as a result of resignation or adaptation (Chapters 1 and 4), and the latter simply because the poorest seldom have the necessary resources to take one step backward in order to take two steps forward (Chapter 4).[35] In Vietnam, it was the middling rather than the poorest peasants that headed the revolutionary movement.[36] Tocqueville's famous analyses in *The Old Regime and the Revolution* are slightly ambiguous from this point of view, since he cites both living standards and their rate of change as independent variables. A high standard of living provides resources and the means of revolutionary action, whereas a rapid rate of change frees men from their "adaptive preferences."

There is a further rationalistic interpretation which holds that revolutionaries are prompted by selective incentives in the form of either rewards or punishments.[37] Revolutionary leaders, in fact, are able to offer several types of encouragement. They can tempt peasants that associate with the movement not only with immediate benefits such as education or help with the harvest, but also with the promise of a privileged place in the post-revolutionary society or, in Islamic revolutions, in a future life. Conversely, they can announce that those who do not support the revolution will be punished, either immediately or after it.

34 Tong (1988).
35 Elsewhere (Elster 1985a, pp. 352–3) I have argued that in a revolutionary situation, motivations and opportunities are inversely correlated (see also Oliver and Marwell, forthcoming). The very poor do not have the resources needed to engage in revolutionary activities (they are too busy just surviving), and the very rich do not have the motivation to do so. Drawing on Veyne and Tocqueville, I am now claiming that the poor may be low on both motivation and opportunities.
36 Popkin (1979).
37 Olson (1965). In his study of the Vietnamese revolution Popkin (1979) stresses positive incentives, whereas negative incentives are emphasized in Chen (1986).

This analysis, like the preceding one, turns out not to be very satisfactory, chiefly because it does not explain the behavior of the leaders. Why should it be in their rational interest to offer selective incentives? In particular, will it really be to their advantage, once the revolution has succeeded, to keep their promise to punish opponents and reward militants? For a rational actor, the only reason to keep his word is the need to build up a reputation for honesty that is likely to be useful in the future, but revolutions rarely occur twice. This problem of *credibility* is a thorny one for any revolutionary movement.[38]

The incentives that can be offered while the revolution itself is going on raise problems of a different kind. Because the potential members of the revolutionary movement are at the same time under intense pressure from the existing regime, the level of rewards and punishments easily tends to escalate. Because revolutionaries usually have fewer resources than the government, they may be tempted to use the stick rather than the carrot. Against this, it must be borne in mind that the strategy of punishment can have negative psychological effects. It is far from clear, under these conditions, which incentives rational revolutionaries should offer.

For some, participation is its own selective incentive. Some people see the revolution as a holiday, a happening or a feast, and its instrumental efficiency as purely secondary or even irrelevant. The problem of the free rider no longer arises once involvement brings benefits rather than costs.[39] Individuals thus motivated could not, however, account for the bulk of a revolutionary movement. At the very most, all they are useful for is to swell the ranks of a movement that as a whole is inspired by different and more serious motives. With their impatience and lack of the requisite revolutionary ability to wait,[40] they may even delay the revolution's coming.

38 For recent discussions see Elster (1989b), pp. 272–87, and Dixit and Nalebuff (1991). Both are heavily indebted to Schelling (1960).
39 See Hirschman (1982) for this line of argument.
40 This phrase ("revolutionäre Attentismus") is used by Groh (1973) in his study of German Social Democracy at the time of the 2nd International. He

So far I have limited myself to rational, self-interested motivations. Contrary to a widespread misunderstanding, however, rationality does not rule out altruism. If the revolutionary takes the consequences of his action for other people into account, the large number of such people may make up for the limited effect on each of them. In principle, nothing rules out the product of these two quantities being greater than the costs and risks of individual involvement, which in such a case would be perfectly rational. Whether such is actually the case depends on the circumstances. During the initial stages of a revolution there is a great deal of risk and no certainty of effective action, and even the most thorough-going utilitarian would hesitate to get involved. Nor would he take part in the final phase, when success already looks a matter of course but the personal risk involved is still not negligible. (Even then, however, he might want to join the movement, in order to "shorten and lessen the birth-pangs." But he would probably have been more effective had he joined earlier.) It is mainly in the intermediate phase that utilitarian motivations are likely to be at all effective.

If we are to explain the initial phase of revolutions as well as recruitment beyond the point at which success looks certain, we must widen the spectrum of motivations still further by also taking into account nonrational motivations.[41] If we rely on the idea that rationality is defined by instrumental efficacy and orientation toward the future, we can distinguish between two types of nonrational behavior. First, there are the unconditional participants who do their duty without worrying about the efficacy

uses it, however, as a pejorative phrase, to characterize the attitude of Social-Democratic leaders like Kautsky for whom the time somehow never was ripe for a revolution. (But see Gilcher-Holtey [1986], pp. 219ff, for strong arguments against this view of Kautsky.)

41 This is a generally applicable procedure. To explain a given phenomenon, the actors are initially assumed to have rational, self-interested motivations. If their behavior cannot be explained on this minimal basis, altruistic (although still rational) motivations are introduced. If the explanation is still inadequate, nonrational motives are admitted. In the last case, it is important to indicate the specific kind of irrationality we have in mind. Using the irrational as a residual category merely names the problem without solving it.

of their action, thus differing from the utilitarians in that they get involved right from the start without waiting for others to commit themselves. Although they take no account of consequences, their behavior can nevertheless have very desirable consequences. Such frequently admirable behavior must, however, be considered irrational, partly because it has its roots in magical thinking (everyday Calvinism) and partly because it may work against its own ends. Unilateral participation may produce an effect that is *worse for all* than general nonparticipation. The worker facing up alone to his employer or the authorities may give them an excuse for repressing the group of workers as a whole.

Second, we have to take into account that some participants may be motivated by a norm of fairness. They become involved if, and only if, a sufficient number – which can vary from individual to individual – of others do so too. Like the utilitarians, they will never be present at the creation, but unlike them they will continue to be involved beyond the point at which their participation is no longer efficacious. The idea of duty is not the unconditional one of the Kantian, but the notion that they should share the sufferings of others rather than remain on the sidelines. Like the Kantians, however, they disregard any form of future-oriented, instrumental thinking. They take their cue from the past (how many individuals have already joined) rather than from the future.

Such is the catalogue of motivations of actual and potential revolutionaries. To go further, we also need to understand the choice presented to the leaders of the existing regime. In a situation of actual or potential discontent, they have essentially five options – preemptive action, inaction, partial reform, repression, or diversion of attention toward an internal or external enemy.[42] Recent political history, from the fall of the Shah of Iran to the Soviet reforms and the revolutions in the countries of Eastern Europe, suggest that in the long run only preemptive

42 I am grateful to Carlos Weizman for suggesting that I add this last category.

moves can succeed.[43] As Tocqueville noted, partial, symbolic or tactical reforms merely inflame the opposition without satisfying it.[44] Repression, although often successful in the short term, entails two serious risks for rulers. On the one hand, it can strengthen opposition to the regime by making it look even more odious than before.[45] On the other hand, it often provides a source of information for the opposition (Chapter 2) by showing it that resistance is more widespread than it had imagined. Prior to the age of opinion polls, the reaction of the regime was the main indicator for the opposition of its own strength. Inaction, in these situations, tends to be interpreted as either arrogance or weakness. Either perception will have destabilizing effects. Diversion, finally, cannot work indefinitely. Although some of the Communist regimes in Eastern Europe exploited anti-Semitic feelings to create a lightning rod for discontent, the diversion worked only for a while.

I have tried to identify the major elements at work in the great historical revolutions. They are only elements or, in my language, mechanisms, and their effects and importance may vary from one situation to another. What they lead to will depend on the precise mix of motivations or, more precisely, on the interaction of the actors thus motivated.[46] The little tale I am about to unfold shows only one (hypothetical) combination among others.

43 See Tocqueville (1955), p. 165, for a suggestion that Louis XVI might have preempted the revolution had he listened to the advice of his minister, de Machault. He adds, however, that "such steps are rarely taken on another's advice; only a man who is himself capable of conceiving such ideas is disposed to put them into practice." Successful cases of preemption include Bismarck's social reforms and, on a smaller scale, wage increases for the purpose of blunting the inducement of workers to unionize.
44 Tocqueville (1955), pp. 145, 153.
45 In Roemer (1985) this is embodied in an axiom intended to capture "the psychology of tyranny."
46 Needless to say, the outcome will also depend on financial, military, and other constraints within which the battle of minds is played out. Stone (1972), which seems to me to be a model of its kind, neglects neither constraints nor motivations. Scocpol (1983) attaches a too exclusive importance to constraints. *The Old Regime* perhaps goes too far the other way.

Let us then suppose that in the beginning there is a small nucleus of revolutionaries fired by the vision of a better society. Their actions cannot be explained in terms of the adequacy of their means to that end or the desire for individual gains. It matters little whether they are mad, irrational, Kantians or men of principle. The essential fact is their commitment to a non-instrumental value. As the revolution progresses, they will be indispensable from several points of view. At first, they bring it through the most difficult trial by providing an influx of participants in the early stages when more prudent men are reluctant to commit themselves. Later, they are the only ones that can act effectively as leaders, because their proven integrity means that they can make promises or utter threats which in the mouth of others would lack credibility.[47] Their standing also helps them to economize on the costs of communication, by replacing a large number of exchanges within the rank and file by a smaller number of bilateral ones between themselves and their followers.

At the second stage, there is an influx of individuals spurred on by diverse motives. Some are swayed by the promise of immediate help or leading positions in the postrevolutionary society. Others, more concerned with the cause the movement has adopted than with personal profit, become involved once the first-comers have taken the movement beyond the threshold at which the action can begin to be instrumentally efficacious. Yet others join in because the revolution offers the promise of a feast or a release from everyday ties and responsibilities.

At this point the existing regime begins to notice the new phenomenon. It will have either to grant concession or engage in brutal repression or – as is usually the case – do both. The effects will be as already indicated. On the one hand, the demand for reform enjoys increased legitimacy; there is more intense resistance to the regime and more reliable information about the extent of that resistance. On the other hand, the costs of

---

47 Popkin (1979), p. 261, points out that the leaders of the Vietnamese Communist Party owed their credibility to their Spartan and austere life style.

joining the opposition go up. The net effect on the movement will depend on the precise combination of stick and carrot chosen by the regime and on the distribution of the various types of motivation in the population.

Let us suppose that the net effect is to encourage more people to join the movement. A snowball effect can then get started. For specificity, let us assume that a percentage **s** of the total population is moved by the norm of fairness. Of that group, a percentage p_1 becomes involved once a percentage r_1 of the total population has done so. There will then be a percentage p_2 whose threshold of commitment lies between r_1 and $(r_1 + s \cdot p_1) = r_2$. Similarly, there will be a percentage p_3 with a threshold between r_2 and $(r_2 + s \cdot p_2) = r_3$, and so on. The process can continue until the whole population has joined the movement, or stop before that point. We must also take into account the fact that the movement tends to lose adherents at the same time it is recruiting. For some, involvement ceases alongside the instrumental efficacy that justified it. For others, the revolution as a happening and a holiday is undermined by the inevitable increase of bureaucracy in a mass organization. Unlike the Kantians who get involved at the beginning and remain so, these individuals *only* want to be present at the creation. Because of these changing dynamics the movement may never reach a stable membership, as individuals of different types attract and repel each other in an endless saraband.

At each point of the process the reactions of the existing regime also come into play, in the forms we have seen. The complex nature of the relationships cuts short any hope of a theoretical explanation. In any given historical case, the most one can do is to provide a post factum identification of individual motivations and the ways in which they interact to produce the final outcome. The very idea of creating a general theory of revolutions that would enable us to predict or, for that matter, manipulate the behavior of the masses is absurd. Yet, as I have been at some pain to emphasize, rejecting theory in this sense does not imply that we are doomed to mere description (or at most to what Clifford Geertz calls "thick description"). Political psychology can, I believe, help us to identify the mechanisms that we can expect to see at work in any revolutionary situation, thus offering an intermediate degree of generality. I do not claim to have provided an exhaustive list, but neither do I think that the catalogue of motivations can be extended indefinitely.

THE POLITICAL PSYCHOLOGY
OF CONSTITUTION MAKING

Constituent assemblies can be momentous occasions, in which the framework of political life for generations is laid down. There is a strong pressure to adopt impartial argument: Interest-group pluralism won't work when most of the affected parties are generations yet unborn. They can also be very dramatic, due to the fact that they often take place in turbulent circumstances, in the wake of a revolution or in the midst of a crisis. Hence constituent assemblies are often more polarized than ordinary law-making bodies. They are not engaged in politics as usual, but oscillate between what Bruce Ackerman calls "higher law-making"[48] and sheer appeal to force. As Tocqueville said, in times of crises the political actors either rise above the normal or fall below it (DA p. 199).

In constituent assemblies (and in other fora for collective decision making) we encounter two main types of speech act: arguing and bargaining.[49] In argument, speakers make statements with a claim to validity.[50] In bargaining, they utter *threats* and promises with a claim to *credibility*.[51] To this distinction between the types of statement made in the constituent assemblies we may add a distinction among three kinds of motive that may animate the framers: interest, passion, and reason.[52] Impartial

48 Ackerman (1991).
49 For the theory of speech arts, see Searle (1969, 1979).
50 For elaborations, see Habermas (1984/1989, 1990).
51 For elaborations, see the works cited in note 38 above.
52 For a discussion of this trio of motives among the American founders, see White (1987), pp. 102ff. For a discussion in a different constitutional setting,

argument presents itself as based on reason. (In reality, it may well proceed from self-interest, but that is a complication I ignore here.[53]) Bargaining is usually based on overt self-interest or group-interest. The role of passion in constituent assemblies is closely linked to that of rhetorical persuasion, a phenomenon that I will neglect because I do not understand it very well.[54]

Threat-based bargaining is a relatively well-understood phenomenon.[55] I shall not expand on it here, except to mention

see Whitaker (1992). More frequently, the ideas are opposed to each other in pairwise fashion. David Hume, when addressing the relation between *passion and reason*, argued that the latter was and ought only to be the slave of the former (Hume 1960, p. 415). Roughly speaking, he meant that there could be no rational deliberation about ends, only about means. Albert Hirschman (1977) has considered the changing attitudes toward *passions and interests* in the eighteenth century, arguing that the dominance of interest over passion in a commercial society constituted "a political argument for capitalism before its triumph." In many discussions of the debates at the Federal Convention, *reason and interest* are believed to exhaust the motives of the framers (Jillson, 1988, pp. 193–4 [citing Madison, Hamilton, and Tocqueville to the same effect] and *passim*). See also Rakove (1987).

53 In debates over electoral systems, for instance, the following pattern is found over and over again. Small parties argue for proportional representation on the grounds that it is more respectful of democratic rights (and not because it improves the chances of small parties). Large parties argue for single-member districts on the grounds that this system enhances governmental efficiency (and not because it improves the chances of large parties). Elster (1991b), pt. VI, explores such strategic uses of argument in greater detail.

54 For a useful introduction, see Nash (1989), especially ch. 6 ("Images of argument"). For an application to constitutional debates, see Fink (1987). For a brilliant study of selling and marketing as rhetoric see Leff (1976). If we apply the interest-reason-passion distinction to the audience in constitutional debates, rhetoric may perhaps be defined by the feature that it appeals to the passions of the audience rather than to their reason or self-interest. The question needs much further exploration, however. In some debates, reason speaks to reason; in others, interest to interest; in still others, passion to passion. But other constellations also occur. Moreover, as we shall see, constitutional debates usually involve a third party, viz. the future generations for whom the constitution is written. Hence a typical constitutional speech act is one in which an orator (speaking from specific motives) addresses an audience (with specific motives) about the proper institutional response to the specific motives he imputes to future legislators.

55 For a nontechnical exposition, see Elster (1989b). For a semitechnical exposition, see Sutton (1986).

that a great deal of bargaining took place in the two constituent assemblies that will provide most of my illustrations here, the Federal Convention in Philadelphia in 1787 and the Assemblée Constituante in Paris in 1789–91. In Philadelphia, the main bargaining episodes concerned the representation of the states in the Senate and the maintenance of the slave trade.[56] In Paris, the royal veto and the issue of bicameralism were objects of explicit bargaining within the revolutionary elite.[57] My focus in the following, however, will be on constitutional arguing. In trying to identify some important features of the reasoning of the framers I shall assume (with one exception) that they were motivated by impartial concerns. However, I shall take account of the fact that the framers imputed more complex motives to those for whom they were legislating.

First, the constitution making process can be viewed as one in which rational impartial framers try to contain the passions of future generations. This idea has two aspects, related, respectively, to the machinery of constitutional amendment and the ordinary machinery of legislation. By making it hard to amend the constitution, the framers can restrain passionate majorities who might want to suppress the rights of minorities. By slowing down the ordinary legislative process, through bicameralism and executive veto, the constitution can reduce the dangers of reckless and fickle majority legislation. Madison's argument (FC I, p. 421) that the Senate is needed to protect the people against its predictable "fickleness and passion" falls in this category.

By and large, the records from the Federal Convention give little evidence that the framers were concerned with the passions of future generations. They were much more concerned with their tendency to pursue myopic or partisan interests. They assumed, by and large, that motives are always and everywhere

---

56 Jillson (1988) is an excellent overview of the issues, but with exclusive emphasis on voting rather than bargaining.
57 Egret (1950) is the best modern discussion. Mounier (1789) offers a participant's perspective.

self-interested. The assumption was probably adopted for prudential reasons, not because it was believed to be literally true. According to Hume, "It is . . . a just *political* maxim, *that every man must be supposed to be a knave*; though, at the same time, it appears somewhat strange, that a maxim should be true in *politics* which is false in *fact*."[58] Steeped as they were in Humean thinking, the framers naturally adopted the same outlook.[59]

In the Assemblée Constituante, the assumptions made about human nature were both nastier and loftier than the ones adopted at the Federal Convention. Although Hume's assumption of universal knavishness is often thought to represent a worst-case scenario, there are worse things than self-interest.[60] Foremost among them are envy, spite, pride, and vanity. Although there are a couple of arguments (FC I, pp. 72, 176) at the Federal Convention that may be read as if the framers imputed envy to those for whom they were legislating, the passages are ambiguous and atypical. In the Assemblée Constituante, however, arguments from pride and vanity, *amour-propre*, played a considerable role. One should never place an agent in a situation in which his vanity might lead him to act against the public interest. Twenty-five years later Benjamin Constant remained concerned with "the problem of *amour-propre*, a peculiarly French flaw," and argued that "institutional devices" were needed to counter it. He advocated, for instance, the British system that forbade written speeches in Parliament.[61] Tocqueville, too, constantly emphasized this character trait of the French, explaining how as the Foreign Minister of Louis Napoleon he got his way by flattering the *amour-propre* of his opponents while riding roughshod over their interests.[62]

In the Assemblée Constituante, Bergasse repeatedly argued the need to accommodate the vanity or pride of the agents

58 Hume (1963), p. 42.
59 For the influence of Hume on the framers, see White (1987).
60 Hirschman (1977); Holmes (1990).
61 Holmes (1984), pp. 139–40.
62 Tocqueville (1970), p. 233.

whose behavior will be regulated by the constitution (AP 9, p. 115). The prosecutor, he says, should not also serve as judge, because if the functions are combined, the *amour-propre* of the magistrate might bias him toward the guilt of the accused (AP 8, p. 443). If the legislature accuses a minister of misconduct, he should not be judged by an ordinary court, as it might make this an occasion to "humiliate the pride" of the legislative body (AP 9, p. 111). A suspensive veto for the king will not have the intended effect of making the assembly reconsider, because its *amour-propre* will prevent it from backing down (AP 9, p. 116). Malouet (AP 8, p. 591) discussed a similar argument that had been advanced against the proposal to give a veto to the senate which could only be overruled by a two-thirds majority in the lower house. In his reply, Malouet did not deny the operation of *amour-propre*, but argued that it would be limited to those who had initiated the law and not extend to everybody who voted for it.

A subtle instance of such reasoning arose over the duration of the suspensive veto of the King. Could the next legislature overrule him, or could the veto be repeated until a third legislature? In his letter to the assembly (AP 8, p. 612 ff.)[63] Necker argued that the King's right to two consecutive vetos was essential, as it allowed him to yield to the assembly's wishes in the second legislature *without appearing to be forced to do so*.[64] Only in this way could the King's dignity and majesty be upheld. Arguing for the same proposal (which was eventually adopted), Clermont-Tonnerre (AP 9, p. 59) also referred to the need to conserve the royal dignity. Although dignity is hardly the same as *amour-propre*, they belong to the same family of motives. It is hard to

---

63 An alliance between the partisans of an absolute veto and the patriots who disliked any ministerial interference blocked the reading of the letter to the assembly (Egret 1950, pp. 154–5).

64 Necker's preferences (AP 9, p. 615) were for (i) suspensive veto for two periods, (ii) absolute veto, and (iii) suspensive veto for one period. Neither (ii) nor (iii) would ever be used (although for different reasons), but (ii) would at least leave the King with the appearance of majesty.

imagine a similar argument being made about the presidency at the Federal Convention.

Second, the reason of the framers can try to control and harness the self-interest of future legislators. Public choice theory was well represented at the Federal Convention, where the framers constantly based their arguments on the incentive effects of various schemes. Let me cite three examples, all from Madison. He was worried about requiring landed property for members of Congress. Looking back, he observed that "It had often happened that men who had acquired landed property on credit, got into the legislatures with a view of promoting an unjust protection against their creditors" (FC II, p. 123). Another instance of incentive-effect reasoning occurred in his comments on a proposal that in voting for the president, each elector should have two votes, one of which at least should be cast for a candidate not from his own state. Madison "thought something valuable might be made of the suggestion. . . . The only objection which occurred was that each citizen after having given his vote for his favorite fellow citizen would throw away his second vote on some obscure citizen of another State, in order to ensure the object of his first choice" (FC II, p. 114). A final argument is less convincing. Arguing against selection of the executive by the legislature, Madison asserted that "the candidate would intrigue with the legislature, would derive his appointment from the predominant faction, and be apt to render his administration subservient to its views" (FC II, p. 109). But it is not clear that a candidate's promise to favor his electors would be credible. Unless the executive can stand for reelection, we would rather expect the legislature to become subservient to its creature.[65] The kingmaker, in fact, should beware of the king.

---

65 This was apparently the typical outcome in the power struggles between the Roman Senate and the Emperor it elected; see PC, pp. 714ff, and the discussion in Chapter 1 below. Although the elected Polish kings were more tightly constrained, they were bound not by electoral promises (except for the election in 1576) but by standing constitutional rules. (Davies 1982, vol. I, p. 331 ff).

The last example raises a more general issue. Bargaining turns crucially on the credibility of threats and promises. Now, constitution makers might, in legislating impartially for the future, take account of the possibility of threat-based bargaining in later legislatures, and discourage or encourage it by acting on the elements that lend credibility to the threats.[66] At the Federal Convention Gouverneur Morris applied such reasoning on two occasions. Arguing against the proposal that all bills for raising money should originate in the first branch, he referred to the following scenario: "Suppose an enemy at the door, and money instantly and absolutely necessary for repelling him, may not the popular branch avail itself of this duress, to extort concessions from the Senate destructive of the constitution itself?" (FC I, p. 545) The argument is dubious, because the threat of the popular branch to withhold money would hardly be credible. On a later occasion a proposal was made to have a census at regular intervals for the purposes of adjusting representation. According to Madison's notes, "Mr.Govr. Morris opposed it as fettering the legislature too much. Advantage might be taken of in time of war or the apprehension of it, by new states to extort particular favors" (FC I, p. 571). This argument also seems implausible, for similar reasons.

The argument that the assembly could derive bargaining clout from its power to withhold taxes was also discussed in the Assemblée Constituante. In defending the absolute veto for the King, Mirabeau (AP 8, p. 539) argued that the assembly could always overrule the veto by the threat of refusing to vote taxes. A number of delegates then responded that in refusing to vote taxes, the assembly would be cutting off its nose to spite its face. "To cease payment of taxes, would be like cutting one's throat in order to heal a wound in the leg" (AP 8, p. 588; see also AP 8, p. 547). The threat, in other words, would not be credible.

Third, rational framers can try to create the conditions under which future legislatures, too, will be able to exercise their rea-

---

66 This might be a reason, for example, to keep the right to secession out of the constitution in federally organized states (Sunstein 1991, pp. 648ff).

soning powers. At the Federal Convention, this idea was never mentioned. In the French assembly it was central. In some respects, as I said, the members of the Assemblée Constituante thought more highly of their successors than did their American counterparts. They believed that an assembly existed to effectuate the transformation of preferences through rational discussion, going well beyond a simple process of aggregation. In the best-known statement of his view Sieyès argued (AP 8, p. 595) that the *"voeu national,"* the desire of the nation, could not be determined by consulting the *cahiers* of complaints and wishes that the delegates had brought with them to Versailles. Bound mandates, similarly, could not be viewed as expressions of the national will. In a democracy (a term that was used pejoratively at the time), he said, people form their opinions at home and then bring them to the voting booth. If no majority emerges, they go back home to reconsider their views, once again isolated from each other. This procedure for forming a common will, he claimed, is absurd because it lacks the element of deliberation and discussion. "It is not a question of a democratic election, but of proposing, listening, concerting, changing one's opinion, in order to form in common a common will." In the debates over the revision of the constitution, d'André (AP 30, p. 68) and Barnave (AP 30, p. 115) similarly claimed that the idea of constitutional convention with bound mandates from primary assemblies would be a betrayal of the representative system in favor of democracy. In Barnave's phrase, "a personal wish or the wish of a faction, which is not illuminated by a common deliberation, is not a real wish *(un voeu véritable)*."

This view had several other implications. Although he was opposed to bicameralism, Sieyès believed that for purposes of discussion the assembly might usefully be divided into two or even three chambers (AP 8, p. 597). After separate discussions and votes, the outcome would be decided by adding up the votes in all three chambers. In this way one would achieve the benefits of rational discussion while avoiding "error, haste or oratory seduction" stemming from a common cause. As observed by Condorcet, the argument is specious. If the sections of the assembly were large, there would still be room for eloquence and demagogy in each of them, perhaps in favor of opposite opinions.[67] A more compelling application was made by Mirabeau (AP 8, p. 299) in a discussion of the voting rules in the assembly. Replying to a proposal that the quorum should be set at half of the total number of the delegates, he said that this would amount to giving a veto to the absent. "However, this kind of veto is the most fearsome and the most certain. While one can hope to influence and convince individuals who are present, by the use of reasons, what influence can one have on those who reply by not appearing?" One cannot argue with the absent.

Turning finally (this is the exception mentioned earlier) to the motives of the framers themselves, we may consider the possibility of an *imperfectly rational* concern with the public good. Imperfect rationality – being weak, and knowing it – can induce actors to take steps to forestall predictable, undesirable behavior in the future.[68] The members of a constituent assembly can seek to structure their own proceedings so as to minimize the scope of passion and self-interest. Both eighteenth-century assemblies created institutional devices for this purpose.

At the Federal Convention, the sessions were closed and secret. As Madison said later (FC III, p. 479), "had the members committed themselves publicly at first, they would have afterwards supposed consistency required them to maintain their ground, whereas by secret discussion no man felt himself obliged to retain his opinions any longer than he was satisfied of their propriety and truth, and was open to the force of argument." Presumably, the fear was that the pride and vanity of the delegates, as well as pressure from their constituencies, might prevent them from backing down from an opinion once they had expressed it. (However, Madison did not consider another effect of secrecy – that of pushing the debates away from argument and toward bargaining.)

---

67 Condorcet (1847), p. 345.
68 For the notion of imperfect rationality, see Elster (1984), ch. 2.

Unlike the Federal Convention, the Assemblée Constituante functioned also as an ordinary legislature. That arrangement, however, may be undesirable. A main task of a constituent assembly is to strike the proper balance of power between the legislative and the executive branches of government. To assign that task to an assembly that also serves as a legislative body would be to ask it to act as judge in its own cause. A constitution written by a legislative assembly might be expected to give excessive powers to the legislature.[69] In the abstract, this problem could be solved by means similar to the ones used in legislative bodies, by checks and balances. A royal veto over the constitution might, for instance, have kept the legislative tendency to self-aggrandizement in check. The Assemblée Constituante adopted another solution, by voting its members ineligible to the first ordinary legislature. It was Robespierre (AP 26, p. 124), in his first great speech, who won the assembly for this "self-denying ordinance."[70]

Although sometimes viewed by posterity as a disastrous piece of populist overkill,[71] Robespierre's solution did correspond to a genuine problem. If framers have both the motive and the opportunity to write a special place for themselves into the constitution, they will do so.[72] At the Federal Convention, the motive may have been lacking. Although the framers were guided by the idea that future voters and politicians had to be assumed to be knaves (see

69 An analogous problem arose in recent debates over the role of the Senate in the Polish constitution. That body, which was created as part of the Round Table Talks compromise, had little justification after the fall of Communism. However, as the Senate will have a vote on the new constitution, it cannot be expected to abolish itself (Rapaczynski 1991, p. 615).

70 Thomson (1988), pp. 134ff.

71 Furet (1988), p. 104.

72 As shown by White (1987), the motive–opportunity distinction was central in the arguments of the *Federalist*. To ensure checks and balances, one ought to deny the branches of government either the motive or the opportunity to extend their sphere. At the same time, they should have both the motive and the opportunity to resist encroachments. With respect to the prevention of factious majorities, large electoral districts will prevent both the formation of factious motives and the opportunity to act on such motives. For a discussion of similar arguments in Tocqueville, see Chapter 4 below.

above), they viewed themselves as moved by loftier motives.[73] More importantly, perhaps, the opportunity was lacking. It was a given fact, outside the control of the delegates, that the Convention would be dissolved forever once the constitution had been written. In the Assemblée Constituante, by contrast, the founders had to take active steps to remove the opportunity to give themselves a privileged place in the constitution.

These two case studies of revolutions and constitutions have little in common beyond showing, as if it needs showing, that motivations and beliefs matter. The immediate motivations of the political actors matter, as do the assumptions they make about the motivations of others. In a revolutionary situation, the motivations of the actors can be rational or irrational, self-interested or not. Whether they join the ranks of the revolution will depend not only on their own motivations, but also on their beliefs about those of others. In a constitutional moment, the actors must not only form beliefs about each other, but also about the motives of later generations. While arguing and bargaining with each other, they are also trying to adjust to – or even shape – the attitudes of voters and legislators in the future.

In later chapters I try to exhibit some of the finer grain of desires and beliefs in the political arena, using the writings of Veyne, Zinoviev, and Tocqueville as my vehicle. In doing so, I also pursue two other tasks. On the one hand, the book is a running argument for the importance of mechanisms, as opposed to general theories. On the other hand, I offer some exegetical comments on the three writers, and notably on Tocqueville. Given this multiplicity of aims, readers are entitled to feel a bit confused about exactly what is going on in any given part of my argument. My hope, nevertheless, is that they will end up having the same experience as I had, that these various approaches facilitate and enhance each other instead of interfering with each other.

73 White (1987), pp. 114, 249; Lovejoy (1961), p. 52.

1

A HISTORIAN AND
THE IRRATIONAL:
A READING OF
BREAD AND CIRCUSES

I first read Paul Veyne's *Le Pain et le cirque* a summer on the Côte d'Azur when, along with *Nice Matin*, it was my only intellectual nourishment for a month.[1] I had the hallucinating experience of seeing both sets of reading matter, which are not self-evidently similar, merge into one. Basically, *Nice Matin* devotes its pages to two kinds of news items: reports of the activities of local gangsters and accounts of the meetings of the Rotary Club, the Lions Club, the Chamber of Commerce, and the like. It is fairly easy to read between the lines and realize that there is a link between the two worlds, and that the wealth so generously displayed and distributed to benevolent associations sometimes comes from sources that would not stand up to close scrutiny. The Rotary Club is of course merely a secondary form of euergetism (PC, p. 26) and gangsterdom is not the same thing as the *Gelegenheitsunternehmungen* of the notables of antiquity (PC, pp. 121, 511). Nevertheless, sociological kinship and geographical proximity were enough to fuse them into a single Mediterranean institution: the effect was like traveling backwards in a time machine.

Bread and Circuses, dazzling in both its entirety and its details, offers at least four viewpoints to the reader. First – and this is its explicit subject – it is a history of euergetism, a form of

---

1 Let me point out once and for all that I know virtually nothing about ancient history, so there will be no question of arguing about historical facts or interpretations.

patronage that was regularly practiced by notables, senators, and emperors of classical antiquity. It is also – and this is perhaps what it is really about – an overall view of the ancient world, particularly with regard to relationships of political authority. Moreover, it weaves a network of comparisons and contrasts that make it a never-ending source of hypotheses and counterexamples for historical and comparative sociology. Finally, it offers a philosophical anthropology that is full of historical learning and a close knowledge of the social sciences, without any of the aprioristic approach that is the besetting sin of the genre.[2] On the basis of a few assumptions – the need for any superiority to justify and express itself and for any inferior to justify the order he submits to – Veyne sets out to explain, in astonishing and usually convincing detail, the behavior of rulers and ruled in the ancient world.

The multitude of notes in the book cite thousands of writers and texts, all of them very well chosen as far as can be judged from the areas in which I have first-hand experience. And yet Veyne never, or scarcely ever, quotes the two authors who quite obviously provided the essential elements of his conceptual framework, Hegel and Tocqueville. We have to go to the back

2 Here we can see a curious development in Veyne's thought. In his first book, *Writing History*, he states that the historian should invoke science only to analyze unintended consequences. History appeals to science, natural or social, only when its "discoveries make it possible to account for a gap between the intentions of agents and the results" (Veyne 1984, p. 209); all the rest is story, plot, and extension of the repertoire of mechanisms. In *Bread and Circuses*, Veyne takes up once more the analysis of unintended effects, as in the brilliant pages on the Keynesian effects of euergetism (PC, pp. 1152ff), but now also argues that a scientific analysis of the *formation* of intentions and beliefs is possible. As I show below, he also suggests and uses classical-type macrosociological generalizations. In my Introduction above I have explained why I prefer Veyne's earlier views to his later methodological views. However, I must say that I find both infinitely more interesting than his most recent ones, those of the Veyne who wrote the postface "Foucault revolutionizes History" to the second edition of *Writing History* or *Did the Greeks believe in their myths* (1983). Here he defends a cognitive relativism that is astonishingly simplistic in such a subtle writer. Gauchet (1986) offers a robust rebuttal of these views.

cover of the book to find out that, following the *Phenomenology of Mind*, Veyne sees politics as the "internal struggle of minds." Although often deployed in specific analyses, this Hegelian idea is never explicitly set out. For a graduate of the Ecole Normale Supérieure in the fifties, the age of Sartre, Hyppolite, and Merleau-Ponty, it probably went without saying. More surprising is the almost total absence of references to *Democracy in America*, from which Veyne seems to have borrowed not only a great number of observations of detail, which I shall indicate later, but also the central idea that "nothing comes more natural to man than to recognize the superior wisdom of his oppressor" (DA p. 436).[3] While drawing on the insights of Tocqueville, Veyne also takes his place at his side; I can think of no greater praise.

THREE STAGES OF EUERGETISM

The history of euergetism falls into three parts: that of the notables in the Hellenistic cities, that of the republican oligarchy in Rome, and that of the emperor. The essential features of the phenomenon is the same in all cases, even if its concrete forms and the reasons behind it may differ.

Euergetism was a form of patronage that the patron was in no way obliged to engage in, except by his own inner promptings and the informal expectations of the public. It was aimed at the citizens as such rather than at the poor, with no economic or political function: It was neither charity, nor redistribution of wealth, depolitization or taxation. Sometimes it was comparable to a gratuity, sometimes to conspicuous consumption, sometimes to an expression of majesty. It may occasionally have been useful but was never motivated by utilitarian considerations. Euergetism enabled rulers and ruled to live in peace with themselves, but that does not mean that it was indispensable to the political system. In one sense, it was a marginal phenomenon, rather like a "margin of charity" (BC, p. 33), but more of a "disdainful

3 In Chapter 4 I return to this point at some length.

marginal of solidarity" (PC, p. 691). It was not aligned to the interests of the rulers, but neither was it opposed to them. As people believe only what they have no interest in *not* believing (BC, p. 28), they do only what they have no interest in not doing, which was the case of euergetism.[4]

Veyne summarizes his analysis of Hellenistic euergetism in the following terms: "Any direct democracy tends to become a government of notables, and any community governed by notables is likely to seek the resources it needs in euergetism unless there is already a tradition of taxation" (PC, p. 228).[5] Markedly less optimistic in his analysis of Greek democracy than, for instance, Moses Finley,[6] Veyne believes it was bound to fail because it had been set up as an emergency measure and demanded from its citizens a degree of participation that could not be maintained (BC, p. 85). There was a shift to a regime of notables, whose natural need for self-expression encountered the economic needs of the city. The result was euergetism, first free and subsequently constrained by informal expectations before it finally became a formal obligation linked to certain political functions. Thrown

---

4 Belief and action do not of course have the same relationship to interest. We could say that, according to Veyne, we believe neither in accordance with nor against our interests, but on the other hand, we often act in accordance with them (PC, pp. 320ff). The distinction between not thinking in terms of self-interest and thinking against self-interest falls under the distinction between external and internal negation examined at greater length in Chapter 2. The fact that many actions or beliefs are neutral insofar as self-interest is concerned, even when they are of some importance to us, allows a refutation of crude functionalism. Its more sophisticated version will be considered later.

5 These are two examples of the sweeping generalizations the author of *Writing History* might have rejected as totally devoid of interest. We might call to mind his sarcastic commentary (Veyne 1984, p. 198) on the attempt to provide nomological explanations of Louis XIV's impopularity. Starting from the generalization that "any king imposing excessive taxes becomes impopular," we would soon have to modify the statement by making exceptions, the cumulative effect of which would be that we had "reconstituted a chapter of the history of the reign of Louis XIV with the amusing feature of having been written in the present and the plural" rather than in the past tense and the singular.

6 Finley (1973).

out from the door, free euergetism came back through the window once it was informally expected that the notables should go beyond the legal minimum. This led to the notables outdoing each other's gratuities, but also to some of them attempting to shrug off a burden that was primarily a collective necessity. "It was . . . in the interest of each notable not to sacrifice himself to the ideal, and to let others shine in his stead" (PC, p. 325). If they nonetheless stood fast, it was because of "the precise fear of vague sanctions and the vague fear of precise sanctions which the future might have in store" (BC, p. 139), as Veyne puts it in one of his innumerable luminous remarks.[7] Two apparently minor facts show both the paradoxical way in which euergetism developed and the gradual deterioration of public life: In the end, people paid in order to avoid honorable offices (BC, p. 188–9), while being a "councillor free of charge" was the ultimate honor (BC, p. 142).

The euergetism of Hellenistic cities was linked to their relative lack of political power. "The autonomy of the cities, which was not enough to make them a political battlefield . . . *was* enough to clothe municipal offices with a prestige that the rich did not want to abandon to others" (BC, p. 154); however the snobbery attached to municipal dignities was not compatible with the exercise of real power (BC, p. 120). In Rome the senators played the game of politics on a world-wide scale, engaging in a serious undertaking that was infinitely more elevated than the caperings of provincial notables. This inevitably meant that the euergetism

---

7 By the former he means the pressure exerted by ubiquitous and diffuse social norms. A vague fear of precise sanctions would be the risk of seeing what one had not given willingly be seized by the crowd (BC, pp. 222–3). What is sketched here is the basic structure of the Prisoner's Dilemma: The collective interest favors euergetism, whereas individual interest favors abstaining from it. If euergetism nevertheless occurs, it is because defection is made impossible or dangerous by loss of face in the eyes of peers or by fear of inferiors. Although euergetism was not instituted as a concession to the masses, abolishing it would have been felt as an insult to the people (BC, p. 153). This asymmetry between exit and entry is a major theme of the book, and one to which I shall return.

of the Roman oligarchs took different paths and sprang from different motives. To take the paths first: The notables offered entertainment and buildings, whereas the senators provided games and distributed grain to the citizens, money to the voters, and, as generals, bounties to the soldiers. There is a ready explanation for some of these euergetic actions: They were symbolic gifts, setting the seal of a client relationship that existed in addition to the hierarchical ones, a dualism that constituted the "sociological uniqueness of Rome" (PC, p. 414). Others, such as the more or less free distribution of grain to citizens, owe their origin to accidents without much further meaning. We are left with the games – the "circuses" of Veyne's title – and "electoral corruption." The games were a regular institution, paid for by certain functionaries who were, it seems, ready to bankrupt themselves in order to do so without receiving any specific return. The explanation is that the function was a necessary stage in any political career aiming at a consulship, and that magistrates made a virtue of necessity in grasping this occasion for popularity. Why "necessary"? Veyne provides hardly any answer, except in the form of a dubious functional explanation (see below) to the effect that the games constituted a financial barrier to political life by excluding anyone who was not rich (PC, p. 400).

Electoral corruption, in the form of "extraordinary" shows to treat the electorate or in straightforward handouts of money, was aimed not at the plebs but at a minority of rich proprietors. The latter probably sometimes saw vote selling just as another kind of *Gelegenheitsunternehmung* (PC, p. 425), but that does not explain why they let themselves be influenced by the shows. In any case they did not allow themselves to be too obviously bought; they were courtesans rather than prostitutes (BC, p. 226). They did not vote out of an interest in the outcome, firstly for the always applicable reason that a single voter has no more than an infinitesimal chance of influencing the final result, and secondly for the specifically Roman reason that the result was of virtually no interest to them.[8] In that case, why vote at all? And why be influenced by shows in making a political choice? The latter question is answered by the "evidence theory" (PC, p. 773): when excellence is seen as one and indivisible (BC, p. 45–6), someone who does one thing well will do another equally well, even if the qualities required are quite different.[9] Scarcely any answer is provided to the former, but we might assume that for the "handful of rich electors who controlled the agricultural shows" (PC, p. 425) elections were certainly pleasant and possibly profitable social occasions not to be missed. That does not rule out the possibility that the decision to vote could be made by a self-interested calculation, with the electors wondering what people would think of them if they abstained. But then we would also have to ask why "people" should run the risks involved in expressing their disapproval of others. Any social norm, including that of taking part in an election, ultimately presupposes disinterested behavior, either in those obeying the norm or in those forcing them to do so.[10]

The last magistrates of the Republic were already the forerunners of the emperors, and the euergetism of Caesar, Octavius and Agrippa was a manifestation of their supreme majesty rather than part of their politicking. The emperor's benefactions fell

---

8 Concerning the first reason, see Barry (1978) and ch. 5 of Elster (1989b) for discussions of the voting paradox that continues to baffle those who try to explain voting in terms of rational, self-interested choice. In modern societies, it is easy to understand why a voter prefers one party to another and votes for it once he has made up his mind to go to the polling booth. The problem is the original decision to make the effort. In the case of the Romans, it is difficult to explain not only why they made a choice, but also the choice they made. In both cases, it is hard to escape the idea of a disinterested attitude (PC, p. 425). I should add that the second reason is not quite specifically Roman. Langholm (1984) shows, for instance, that the same was true of limited suffrage elections in nineteenth-century Norway, where it was a matter not of choosing a policy, but of honoring a man by elevating him to a public function.

9 For discussions of stereotyping, see Jones (1977) as well as Chapter 2 below.

10 Elster (1989b), ch. 3.

into three largely unrelated areas: those connected with his function, the apparatus of the cult of the king, and public games. In the first place, the emperor was "the cause of what was good, but not responsible for what was evil" (BC, p. 305). He was the source of all that was good in the empire, since it was because of him that there was a society rather than nothing (BC, p. 305). This attitude did not emanate from propaganda from above, as in modern dictatorships.[11] In Rome, it came from below, from the people who, with a fine disregard for consistency, loved the king while denouncing his policies or his counsellors. If only the king knew! There was also the divinization of the emperor and the cult surrounding him, a phenomenon that gives rise to some of the finest pages in the book. Veyne is an agnostic (PC, p. 586), which is perhaps why he so subtly and successfully disentangles the relationship of the divine to the divinities. The declaration of the divinity of the emperor was, like many a *euergesia*, the result of a combination of a popular need – not to believe but to feel governed by a good master – and the royal need to display and express majesty. Veyne does not deny that there was also hegemony and symbolic force, but sees them as secondary and marginal. Finally there is the question of the public games, of particular importance during the empire, with the ruler and spectators spending a quarter or a third of their time together at the shows (BC, p. 400). Veyne sees in this the expression of a complex triangular relationship between the emperor, the senate and the plebs.[12] In the end Rome became

11 See Chapter 2 below. However, in Zinoviev's picture of Soviet society, the myth propagated by the authorities has no takers, a state of affairs conforming to Veyne's observation that "apologetics is not a rational form of behaviour: very frequently it fails in its effects" (BC, p. 380).

12 Elsewhere (BC, pp. 334ff), there is a long analysis of the relationship between the Senate and the praetorian guard in the nomination of the emperor, adding a fourth pole to this balance of power. According to March (1966), the notion of power can be analyzed according to one of two slogans: "Let the king beware of the kingmaker" or "Let the kingmaker beware of the king." It would seem that for Veyne the first held good for the emperor's relationship to the praetorian guard and the second for his relationship to the Senate (PC, pp. 685–6). On the one hand, "the guard murdered Emperors

the emperor's court and the plebs his clientage. The senate despised the plebs and kept its distance from the emperor, who for his part loved to see himself loved by the plebs and would not allow the senatorial kingmakers to have the slightest hold on him. In that hidden and silent struggle he depended on the plebs, who had good grounds for fearing a senate hegemony.

AUTHORITY IN THE ANCIENT WORLD

The framework for these historical analyses is a general conception of political authority in the ancient world. In broad terms, Veyne distinguishes between three sources of authority, namely delegation, absolute right and "the nature of things." The last is both the one to which he attaches most importance and his most original contribution. It is not unlike charisma, but goes beyond it into traditionalism.

The authority of the Greek notables was originally a power by delegation, which tended irresistibly to transform itself into the natural ascendancy that belongs to all superiors. The power of the emperor tended toward absolute and divine right without, however, reaching the same degree as in oriental despotism. Between these two extremes, each of which was tempered, modified, or attracted by the center, the power of the senators represented the intermediate and so to speak normal position. One was born an oligarch, as one was born poor or a subject, and politics was at once the art of dividing up offices among the former and – in a more or less high-handed way – humoring the sensibilities of the ruled. The latter function was all the more effective (and less machiavellian) as politics was also expression, display and radiance.

who were too senatorial" (BC, p. 336), but on the other, "the plebs liked to see the bad Emperors humiliate the nobles" (BC, p. 415). In addition the senators themselves preferred not to put too much pressure on their creature, so as to avoid having to confess their impotence. The solution was "to proclaim that Caesarism was bad but the reigning Emperor was good" (BC, p. 413).

One of Veyne's constant themes is the great debate among the ancients about the nature of authority and the danger to rulers involved in the pleasures of those they ruled. Polybius and Cicero embody the totalitarian position, in which authority is either total or nonexistent. The Gracchi and the demagogues whom Polybius opposed sought to maximize not obedience but discipline and social peace, in the belief that the latter demanded a minimum of concessions to the people. Hence the great argument: "Euergetism can be interpreted in two ways: as an act of oligarchy skillfully moderating itself or as a corruption of true oligarchy" (PC, p. 465).[13] According to Veyne, there was scarcely any justification for the fears of Cicero and Polybius; their attitude is explicable not in terms of a rational analysis but of a natural human tendency to go to the limit, which often means going too far (PC, p. 708). It would, however, be just as wrong to see euergetism as a manipulative instrument of the elite. Abolishing the games would perhaps have had undesirable consequences, but it does not necessarily follow that that form of *euergesia* was introduced specifically to avoid them. Pleasures are not given to the populace; it is allowed to have them. Hence there is no contradiction when Veyne (PC, p. 787) invokes the "Tocqueville effect" – a harsh regime is never more threatened than when it begins to become more liberal. Granting a concession is one thing, not withdrawing a traditional entertainment is another.

In such societies, which were traditional and authoritarian rather than despotic or totalitarian, the established order was like a landscape within which one lived, sought out one's niche, and adapted a little to make it more bearable, but did not dream of changing radically. That there is authority and order goes

13 In a few brilliant pages, Veyne (BC, pp. 246ff) sorts out the confused idea that luxury and elegance lay behind the fall of the republic. The thesis can be taken to be either that luxury softened the people or that wealth corrupted the aristocracy. In its turn the first idea can also be split in two: In the "democratic version," luxury wiped out civic spirit, and in its oligarchic counterpart, it made the people less docile. The second, too, can be split: Either wealth gave rise to parvenus or it eroded the old nobility itself, insofar as it refused to open its ranks to new men.

without saying; the modalities of power alter little, except for the picturesque surface of things, a matter that was neither negligible nor important. Seeing euergetism as an element of a social contract or compensation for a transfer of power would delight exchange theorists but misrepresent historical experience; insisting on the opportunity to resist authority is a philosopher's notion that ignores the real distinctions of lived experience. Nevertheless, not all authority is respected, and the established order is not always seen as legitimate. There *are* upheavals, and we need to understand the conditions in which they occur. In Veyne's view, the macrosociological fact of inequality does not cause the microsociological fact of envy (PC, p. 307), and even if there is envy, it gives rise to an irritating sense of impotence rather than revolutionary feeling (PC, p. 308), to which must be added that a "bookish" knowledge of inequality is hardly likely in itself to arouse revolution (BC, p. 241).

If neither wholesale nor retail injustice has the effect of mobilizing opinion, what has? In what circumstances is dissonance reduction, that major stabilizing mechanism in traditional societies, rendered inoperative? To Veyne's mind, the greatest danger for authoritarian societies is a universalistic system of social mobility in which promotion is by merit rather than by chance (PC, p. 314).[14] Chance outcomes cannot also be possible outcomes; unforeseeable and accidental promotion is a thunderbolt that increases the sense of powerlessness with regard to the "landscape society" mentioned above. Like Tocqueville,[15] Veyne compares upward mobility in traditional societies to a lottery (PC, p. 314). Unlike him, however, he does not see it as a stabilizing element. For Veyne, the transformation of the regime of the notables into a formal order eliminates the lottery without increasing frustration in the process (PC, p. 315). Here, I think he is right and Tocqueville

14 Tocqueville argued that in democratic societies, stability requires an effort to "banish chance, as much as possible, from the world of politics" (DA, p. 549). Veyne makes the inverse argument for authoritarian societies: Here undeserved promotion is intolerable, whereas promotion by merit is not.
15 Tocqueville (1952), p. 46.

wrong. It is true that anyone *can* win the jackpot, but what does it mean to say that anyone *can* get into an elite group, independently of his efforts and merits? For Veyne, if I have understood him correctly, the effect of chance is not to raise the hope of winning in everyone, but to eliminate the envy we would otherwise feel for the winner.[16]

COMPARATIVE SOCIOLOGY

I have canvassed two systematic aspects of Veyne's book, the history of euergetism and the analysis of authority in classical antiquity. I now turn to the use of the book as a pool of ideas for comparative sociology, not merely with respect to patronage or authority but in all the areas covered by the author's reading and reflection. This aspect clearly does not lend itself to interpretation or summary; some examples will have to do.

The sociology of oligarchy

The interests of the oligarch, like those of any man, are many: money, power, and prestige. A multiplicity of interests means a conflict of interests, a fundamental theme in the book. Among the Greek notables there was, as indicated above, a contradiction between the personality of the individual oligarch, who was personally little disposed to generosity, and the demands of the oligarchical regime; however, "a little pressure helps him to take the difficult and decisive step, after which he is quite happy to have done what he hesitated to do" (PC, p. 231–2). Among the Roman senators, there was also a contradiction between

16 On the one hand, mobility may have a destabilizing effect, by increasing subjective frustration. Instead of replacing (destabilizing) frustration with (stabilizing) hope, upward mobility accentuates frustration, since ambitions both increase faster than the means of achieving them (Boudon 1982) and arouse envy in others when they are achieved (Hirschman 1973). On the other hand, mobility may stabilize society by two objective mechanisms: It provides fresh blood for the ruling classes and weakens the potential for revolt in the oppressed classes by depriving them of their most gifted members.

the short-term self-interest of the oligarchs as men of property and their political advantage (PC, p. 476). The agrarian law of Tiberius Gracchus was in this respect the equivalent of the nineteenth-century English Factory Acts, that is, the defense of the interests of a class at the expense of those of its members, the only difference being that the Roman senators could not allow themselves to be forced by another class to act in their own interest. "The first propertied class not to have ruled will have been the bourgeoisie" (PC, p. 117), a fact that has been variously interpreted as desperate calculation, a confession of impotence or a sign that the accumulation of roles became too great a burden for the actors (BC, p. 117).[17] The relationship between prestige and money, or between *euergesia* and investment, may be one of contradiction, complementarity or neutrality (BC, p. 59), depending on the relationship between the notables and the populace and on that between the notables themselves.[18]

The sociology of public goods

Euergetism was doubly a matter of public goods. On the one hand it constituted a public good for the ruling class (see above), and on the other hand it sometimes provided public goods for the city. Concerning the first aspect, Veyne explains that it "was in the interest of the whole body [of notables] that the obligation to distribute largesse form a barrier and restrict social superiority to as narrow a group as possible, but that it was in the interest of each member to increase the number of notables in order to

17 For the other interpretations, see ch. 7.1.4 of Elster (1985a).
18 For a different type of case, see Elster (1976) commenting on the work of Eugene Genovese on American slavery. Here, the relationship is not neutral. The socially necessary expenditure is not proportional to "whatever surplus one happens to be left with" (PC, p. 163), but to the *gross* product of the estate. A great lord owes it to himself to spend in accordance with his activities. The more slaves he uses, the greater his prestige, provided he also spends a proportional amount on pure consumption. Hence the possibility – so disturbing for neoclassical economists – of including luxury consumption under the heading of production costs.

47

spread the burden over as many men as possible" (PC, p. 325).[19]
With regard to the *euergetes* providing collective goods in the
more traditional sense (buildings, spectacles), Veyne distinguishes
on the one hand between the useful and the agreeable, and on
the other hand between the durable and the momentary, suggesting that the first preference of the benefactor was for the
durable and then for the useful, whereas the people ranked the
momentary first and the agreeable second. As a symbol of his
majesty, the emperor would plump for a column whose fine
details were all but invisible to the naked eye (BC, p. 381);
aqueducts were built to last forever (BC, p. 364–5) when there
were certainly other and more pressing needs. As Veyne subtly
notes, such pointless or pointlessly elaborate constructions "reflected a class psychology without serving class interests" (BC,
p. 148–9). I shall return to this key idea later.

Social psychology

In addition to the more general anthropological ideas to be
examined later, Veyne offers insights into the social psychology
of the ancient world, of which the following are a few examples.
Honor: the honor of the medieval lord was automatically assumed
unless there was proof to the contrary, whereas a Roman's

---

19 This is, once again, the free-rider problem discussed in Olson (1965) or
Hardin (1982). Veyne is not absolutely clear on this point. From the point
of view of the individual oligarch, increasing the number of notables would
have not only the positive effect indicated in the cited passage, but also the
negative one of reducing the prestige of the oligarchs, and it would be hard
to tell in advance what the net effect would be. It would seem more correct
to say that for each individual oligarch it would be preferable (for a given
number of peers) to refuse class obligations, as the consequent loss of prestige
would be far outweighed by the corresponding reduction of expenditure.
However, that assertion presupposes, perhaps implausibly, that prestige was
really a public good created by the behavior of oligarchs in general and thus
enabling each of them to behave parasitically, rather than a local phenomenon
making individual prestige depend on individual behavior (see the preceding
note and Elster 1978, pp. 215–16).

"dignitas" was acquired, preserved, and enhanced (BC, p. 205).[20] *Attitude to time*: because they saw the future as closed, the men of the ancient world were unable to understand that techniques and preferences are necessarily subject to change.[21] *The micro-economic illusion*. This illusion (PC, p. 149–50) goes hand in hand with a micropolitical illusion (BC, p. 302 ff.): since luxury created jobs and the *princeps* order, a society without luxury or emperor would sink into unemployment or chaos, as if nothing or no-one could replace the former or the latter.[22] *Philanthropy*: in the ancient world, "philanthropy was noble only if it relieved elevated misfortunes" (BC, p. 31). *From sacrifice to festivity*: from the point of view of the gods it mattered little whether believers

20 This theme could be pursued more systematically (for a beginning, see Elster 1990b). In Montenegro until quite recent times, many feuds were caused by acts undertaken with the knowledge that a feud might ensue and undertaken only because a feud might ensue, although not for the purpose of causing a feud. These were acts of brinkmanship – insults carried to the point at which there was a real risk that the offended party might retaliate. "The exchanging of insults, then, was a very delicate art that involved ultimate risk taking. Decisions as to what to say next were potentially matters of life and death, since simply to maintain one's honor one had to take at least some small risks of being killed" (Boehm 1984, p. 146) The same observation applies to actions that might lead to a duel in sixteenth-century Italy. According to a contemporary writer, "giving [insults] pertains to the nature of man; because everyone seeks distinction, one mark of which is to offend fearlessly" (Bryson 1935, p. 28). These ideas of honor seem to belong more to *dignitas* than to the medieval variety.

21 Tocqueville, by contrast (see Chapter 4), showed how the Americans anticipated and internalized changes of techniques and preferences, to the point of not making investments that might be pointless when they came to fruition. On the rationality of taking future changes of preferences into account, see Cyert and de Groot (1975); for an application, see Goodin (1978). On the rationality of taking future changes in techniques into account, see Henry (1974); for an application, see Elster (1979).

22 Veyne quite rightly sees the "ancient praise of luxury" (PC, p. 149) as similar to mercantilism. It could also be seen as akin to certain typical errors in the counterfactual analysis of history (Elster 1978, pp. 211–12) or the "spontaneous ideologies" created by everyday life (Elster 1985a, pp. 652–6). Tocqueville's analysis of marriages of inclination (Chapter 3 below) is based on the same logic.

consecrated precious objects to them, or sacrificed to them a day (a "holy day") and what they would have earned by working on that day" (BC, p. 210). The list could go on indefinitely, had not the point of making it been to induce the reader to look up the original.

VEYNE'S THEORY OF CHOICE

The last aspect of Veyne's book is what I called his philosophical anthropology, which I shall read here through the grid of the theory of rationality. Are choices conscious or unconscious? Are they rational, irrational, or perhaps functional? Are beliefs rational, in the threefold sense of being well-grounded, coherent, and efficacious? If rational behavior does not achieve its aim, must we insist on the rationality of the irrational? Can one rationally adopt the same attitude toward a thing, another human being, and oneself? Veyne's exposé, which is steeped in Hegel, dissonance theory, and modern economics, suggests answers to such questions without, however, explicitly posing them.[23] This means it needs a structure, and I intend to propose one as follows. First, I examine Veyne's idea of individual choice.[24] Next, I argue that he was both a victim and a critic of functionalist explanation. Third, I state his path-breaking theory of beliefs and ideology. I finish on a Hegelian note: the fight for recognition and paradoxical behaviors.

Our current understanding of rational choice is based on the idea of an optimal relationship between means and ends. Veyne subjects this conception of instrumental rationality to two criticisms. Firstly, it is seen as overemphasizing instrumental as compared with expressive action, and secondly as neglecting a

23 Compare my comments in Chapter 3 below on Tocqueville and the arrogance of the historian.
24 Let me repeat here what I said in the Preface to Elster (1983b), viz. that the core chapters of that book (chs. II and III) owe essential insights to these pages of *Le pain et le cirque*. The present essay is nothing more than a small repayment of this debt.

certain number of subtle and important phenomena tending to change the means–end relation into a dynamic whole in which the composite elements are barely separable. We shall look at the two objections, but first it should be noted that Veyne also offers an analysis of instrumental rationality in the more conventional sense, seen, that is, as "the realization of a universal tendency that encourages us to do all things rationally, whether in war, government, sport or chess" (PC, p. 130). That attitude belongs to every time and place, although it has been wrongly restricted to capitalist undertakings.

Veyne discusses the problem of economic rationality in the ancient world at length (PC, pp. 139, 178, 183; BC, p. 57–8), but to my mind this is one of the least satisfying parts of the book. Contrary to what his text implies, it is possible to "optimize" without investing much, depending on the preferred combination of present and future consumption. Initially, he rejects the distinction between the routine management of the patrimony and the capitalist method of undertakings (PC, pp. 139, 179) stating that methodical conservation leads to growth through "learning by doing." But not all economic growth or technical change is incremental. Sometimes we need to take one step backward to take two steps forward, which requires a very different attitude.[25] Yet later that same distinction is defended, when he suggests that there are two types of societies, those which "follow routine and are satisfied with what they have" and those which optimize, invest, and grow (PC, p. 160 ff.).

A constant theme in the book is Veyne's criticism of the excessive rationalism of our contemporaries, who always see intention, design, strategy, or planning when the true situation is marked rather by expression, radiance, or accommodation. Veblen, for instance, confused the display going with prestige and its perversion. Display is when a certain splendor has to be exhibited in order not to lose face with others who expect no less; it is perverted when "a man behaves admirably in order

25 Elster (1984), ch. I; Elster (1983a), ch. 5.

to be seen as admirable" (PC, p. 99). The following key passage sums this up:

> There is something paradoxical about expression and how it is adopted to its ends. If it is too rational, it fails to achieve them. When a man delights in himself and his greatness, he takes little heed of the expression to be produced on others and is careless in calculating it. Those others, moreover, know this. They know that authentic expression ignores spectators and does not seek to match the effects to them. Self-important men, who calculate too much, do not see the smiles behind their backs. Spectators have doubts about a carefully thought out expression. Would true greatness not take a greater delight in itself alone? Only an expression not seeking to achieve an effect can achieve one. (PC, p. 679)

The last sentence suggests the idea of states that are essentially by-products,[26] or states that can only be achieved unintentionally or by using indirect strategies like Pascal's attempt to create belief by pretending to believe.[27] Some things we seek slip away when we try to grasp them and fall into the hands of those who turn away from them, provided that this is not why they have done so. The paradigm of such states is sleep, to which we could add forgetfulness, belief, sincerity, self-respect, dignity, innocence, spontaneity, faith, salvation, as well as the respect, admiration, gratitude, or love of others.[28] The attempt to achieve such states by the will alone is a *hubris* that mankind has always known, even if it is perhaps more manifest today.[29] We may refer to it, perhaps, as *excess of will*, and contrast it with the better known idea of *weakness of will* (Chapter 4).

In terms of moral psychology, the most significant cases are those in which an actor seeks to produce a state that is essentially a by-product in himself. With regard to political psychology,

26 Elster (1983b), ch. II.
27 Elster (1984), ch. II.3.
28 As I show in Chapter 4, Tocqueville was well aware of this phenomenon.
29 See notably Farber (1976) on "willing what cannot be willed" and Watzlawick (1978) on impossible injunctions such as "Be spontaneous!" or "Don't be so obedient!" Veyne, similarly, refers to the "bad emperors" who tell their subjects, "Adore me!" (BC, pp. 382, 405).

the effort to create such states in others may be more important. In a sense, this phenomenon is less paradoxical. If the intention to obtain X by doing Y is incompatible with a state in which X obtains, one can achieve it only by hiding from oneself that that is the reason for doing Y. But, as Sartre says, self-deception itself is essentially a by-product: "One puts oneself in bad faith as one falls asleep."[30] There is, however, nothing so overtly paradoxical about trying to deceive others, since we can hide our intentions from them without deceiving ourselves. Nevertheless, says Veyne, we rarely succeed in doing so: "man merkt die Absicht und wird verstimmt." There is no sure formula for creating either the appearance of unconcern (see Chapter 2), an impression of spontaneous generosity, or a reputation for irrationality,[31] because the use of a formula would leave a pattern that would suggest to the intelligent observer that behind the apparently spontaneous behavior there lies a subtly calculating intention.

A first premise, then, is that a certain kind of behavior, such as ostentation or generosity, produces a certain effect in other people. A further premise is that the effect is useful, agreeable, or desirable to the actor. Two mistakes can then occur. One is to see the effect as the motive for the action, even when it is essentially a by-product. The other is to declare the effect to be the function of the action (and to explain the action by that function). Veyne inveighs very heavily against the first error, saying that "the bourgeois believes that the romantic artist lived as an artist in order to shock the middle classes" (PC, p. 98), whereas in reality artists are artists as the rich are rich and lions are lions (PC, p. 99), that is, when and only when they are unreflectingly themselves.[32] But to me he seems not sufficiently on guard against the second error, as when he states, for instance, that the function of ostentation is to raise a barrier (PC 1976,

30 Sartre (1968), p. 68.
31 Much has been written recently about the rationality in investing in such a reputation (e.g., Kreps and Wilson 1982). But as Schelling (1960), pp. 36, 38, pointed out long ago, the best way to look irrational is to be irrational.
32 The wrongness of Veblen's analysis of conspicuous consumption is glaringly obvious when one drives past the houses of the rich in France or the United

p. 400).[33] I shall return to this point. Underlying both mistakes is an obsession with the instrumental meaning of the action, as if every action must have one, and an automatic presumption that *cui bono?* offers a favored answer.[34]

Toward the end of the book (PC, p. 706 ff.) Veyne summarizes in a few, excessively compact pages his theory of "heterogeneous options and their paradoxes." The most important idea is that of endogenous changes in preferences, mainly by the mechanism of dissonance reduction. "Once a choice has been made or accepted, the interests it satisfies will become more than proportionally important" (PC, p. 709). By the same token the interests it does not satisfy become proportionally less relevant (the "sour grapes" syndrome). We shall see in Chapter 4 that long before Festinger,[35] the authority quoted by Veyne, Tocqueville had the same idea and deployed it in numerous specific analyses.

In general terms, the theory of cognitive dissonance states that men tend to match their desires and beliefs to their means so as to avoid the intolerable situation of wanting what they cannot have or finding inescapable circumstances undesirable. Veyne adds that such adjustment is never perfect: Authoritarian societies induce their subjects to *over-adapt* to the constraints they impose on them[36]:

> Men do not make equality and justice indispensable
> conditions; they match their aspirations to what is possible.

States. Far from displaying themselves to the world, they hide from it, behind either unsurmountable walls or acres of lawns.

33 Bourdieu (1979) makes the same error (see Elster 1983b, pp. 69–71, 106).

34 As explained in the Introduction, there is a third error that often arises in such cases, that of seeking the meaning of the action in the unconscious desires of the actor. When explanation in terms of intentions breaks down, one can take refuge in the area just short of the conscious intention (the unconscious) or just beyond it (unintended effects). Sometimes we use psychoanalysis to make functionalism work, and sometimes as a substitute when it doesn't work.

35 Festinger (1957, 1964).

36 Tocqueville (1953), p. 331, made a similar observation: "The Frenchman behaves licentiously in everything, even when practising servility. He loves to do more than he is ordered to do; as soon as he has entered the spirit of servility, he goes beyond it."

The relative stability of societies, somewhere between the idyllic and the chaotic, is not the result of some just equilibrium they have achieved between men, but of the fact that humanity does not raise problems unless it can resolve them. The Hellenistic regime lasted not because of euergetistic redistribution, but because, in the face of economic inequality, the crowd of scattered plebeians, with their own internal inequalities, were just as incapable of forming a coalition as a crowd of unorganized and unequally-threatened peasants is of throwing off its age-old passivity when a river burst it banks. They refuse to struggle for the land the catastrophe has overwhelmed and – significantly – even stick to the area a little inside the flood limits. (PC, p. 312)[37]

Why should men over-adapt and make do with less than they could have had? Veyne's answer is linked to his idea that they prefer going to extremes rather than settle for the middle ground.[38] According to Veyne, this tendency accounts for the cult of mono-lithic authority (PC, p. 466), and for the fact that in Christian theology it is not only necessary to renounce dangerous pleasures but also to give up some licit ones (BC, p. 482). Even economic investment can be seen as a flight forward of this kind (PC, p. 139). However, this tendency to go to extremes is itself in need of an explanation. Sometimes an explanation is suggested in terms of an irrational attitude to risk (PC, pp. 92, 139), but more often than not we have the impression that to Veyne's mind the tendency is a universal and basic fact, to be accepted rather than explained. However, I think it may be possible to do better.

According to Festinger and Veyne, preferences tend to change once a choice has been "made or accepted." But the phenomenon is more general, for sometimes preferences change *before* a choice

37 Note the profound incidental observation that the obstacle to collective action is that the actors are under a *different degree of threat* from their social or natural enemy. In such cases, collective action means not only that the actors must overcome the free-rider problem, but also – and this is a great deal harder – that they must manage to negotiate the distribution of tasks among themselves (see Elster 1989b, ch. 4).
38 Again, there is a forerunner in Tocqueville: "Our nature . . . is often reduced to choosing between two excesses" (DA, p. 43).

is made, so as to make the decision easier and the risk of regretting it lower. When two options are of more or less equal value, there often occurs a mental shift toward making one look distinctly more attractive than the other.[39] Indeed, this mechanism might offer an explanation of our tendency to go to extremes. Preferences that dovetail too neatly with what is possible may well, in an uncertain world, create too many grounds for regret. To be on the safe side, I may turn the flaws of the preferred option into virtues, in addition to the routine devaluation of the good sides of the rejected one.

Another possible explanation of the tendency to go to extremes is simply that it may be difficult to stop in time: "the autonomous dynamism of such an energetic psychic position and the powerful mental inertia of the effort already carried out to negate some value propel resentment toward a final movement consisting of the affirmation that that is a counter-value."[40] I may begin envying you a promotion; then I decide that promotion is not worth having; and I end up by thinking that promotion can only be attained through disreputable means.

Another explanation in terms of internal psychic dynamics is related to the mechanisms for self-control.[41] Ideally, I would like to be able to take an occasional drink without worrying too much about it. When, however, I learn that any drinking I do tends to get out of hand, I may impose strict rules on myself to limit or even eliminate my intake of alcohol. The trick is to strengthen the motivation by raising the stakes: The smallest breach of the dam will lead to a flood. To raise them even further, I may create a link to rule-governed behavior in other walks of life. A failure to get out of bed at 6 a.m. to do my physical exercises will not only predict further failings of the same kind, but also spill over to my resolve to abstain from drinking. (See Chapter 4 below for more about such spillover effects.) To protect the first defense against the impulses we build a second, and so

39 Shepard (1964); Elster (1989d), ch. II.
40 Mora (1987), p. 72.
41 Ainslie (1992).

on until nothing is left of the personality but an elaborate system of defenses.

A final possibility is canvassed in Chapter 2 below: We go to extremes because we are incapable of admitting the possibility of neutral states. Whoever is not for me is against me; for the believer, the agnostic is simply an atheist. As suggested in the Introduction, this cognitive deficiency may have a motivational basis in our need for meaning. Objectively, we ought to prefer a situation in which we are uncertain whether another person is our enemy or simply a neutral bystander, over the certainty that he is against us. Subjectively, we often feel more at home in a universe where everyone is either a friend or an enemy.

The ideas I have been discussing – the problem of by-products, the phenomenon of adaptive preferences, and the tendency to go to extremes – all move in the same direction, that of clouding the simplistic expositions of the economics textbook. "That is why sociologists and historians are to be pitied. When they have to decipher the motives for our action, they are faced with a doubly unclear text, for the solution we have chosen never coincides with the rationality we might suppose it has, and the importance of our various motives seems to have been modified by the constraints of the solution" (PC, p. 708). I am fully convinced that this observation is an extremely fruitful one, and that economists need to broaden their conceptual framework in order to accommodate it. Veyne's method seems to me to be exactly right: to understand economics through social psychology, and social psychology through history.

VEYNE AS CRITIC AND VICTIM
OF FUNCTIONALISM

The paradigm of functionalist explanation exercises a powerful attraction even on the best minds, in spite of its inherent flaws.[42]

---

42 Functionalism is best set out and defended in Merton (1957), Stinchcombe (1968), and especially, in chs. 9 and 10 of Cohen (1978). I state my own objections in Elster (1983a), ch. 2.

Veyne does not, in my opinion, completely avoid falling into its traps. To be sure, he devotes a great number of pages to refuting certain functionalist interpretations of euergetism. It was neither the functional equivalent of taxation (BC, p. 99– 100), nor an "element of the social and political machinery" (BC, p. 152), nor did it serve to "maintain the relations of production" (BC, p. 153). Nevertheless, in his discussions of euergetism we often encounter characteristically functionalist phrases, referring to actions that can be traced back to no actor and intentions that do not seem to be those of any identifiable subject.

By a functionalist explanation I mean any attempt to account for a formal institution or a regular pattern of behavior in terms of effects that are (1) beneficial for a certain group (which may or may not be the same as the group of actors that produce these effects) or for some more abstract feature of social life; (2) not intended by the actors; and (3) not recognized by the beneficiaries. Thus for Marx, the upward mobility of workers is explicable in terms of its stabilizing impact on the capitalist relations of production; for Bourdieu and Passeron the freedom given to teachers in the French educational system is a means of perpetuating class relationships; for many anthropologists feasts are a means of assuaging envy; and so on, ad infinitum and sometimes ad nauseam.[43] Such explanations rest on an abuse of an often fruitful question, *cui bono*? On the one hand, functionalist writers find it hard to admit that there can be such a thing as an accidental (or at least nonexplanatory) benefit. On the one hand, they are notoriously unwilling to produce the *mechanism* by which the benefits are supposed to explain their own causes.[44]

---

43 Marx (1981), pp. 735–6; Bourdieu and Passeron (1970), p. 159; Walcot (1978), p. 59.
44 Some nuances must be added. Cohen (1978) offers a powerful argument to the effect that functional explanations rest on laws rather than on mechanisms. However, garden-variety functionalism fares no better in producing laws that in offering mechanisms. Stinchcombe (1976), van Parijs (1981), and Faia (1986) do offer mechanisms of varying degrees of applicability

A Historian and the Irrational

Perhaps the clearest example of such dubious functionalism in Veyne is to be found in his analysis of the Roman *collegia*.[45] If I have rightly understood him, he starts from two premises: (1) Everyone needs festivities, and (2) festivities lose their meaning if they include everyone. From this he deduces the emergence of "small groups whose size could be artificially limited by an official purpose in accordance with which members would be selected" (PC, p. 293). These were the *collegia*, whose manifest function was no more than an arbitrary selection "in order to" facilitate the latent function of allowing people to have a good time. I can well believe that the *collegia* had this effect as an unintended, unrecognized and agreeable consequence – but how could that consequence explain the institution? The uneasy use of the functionalist paradigm is evident in the revealing use of a verb with no subject: "how to fight the erosion" (PC, p. 293) that would threaten an over-large group?

This may be the clearest example, but others, some of them already mentioned, are more important. The function of euergetism was to set up a barrier to keep the less well-off out of politics, just as the Chinese mandarins kept the system of examination going "in order to perpetuate themselves" (PC, p. 400). "In order to" implies an intentional subject – who is the subject here? I do not readily see how that explanation differs from the functionalist interpretations rejected by Veyne and referred to above. Of course euergetism was a barrier of money, but not the only possible kind, and in any case such barriers are not of money only, as the Chinese example proves. To my mind, the explanation of euergetism in terms of the

and generality. However, it is a rare functionalist explanation that could plausibly be supported in any of these ways.

45 Although Veyne does not cite Tocqueville on this point, the analysis may have been inspired by the observation that, in democracies, "a multitude of artificial and arbitrary classifications are established to protect each man from the danger of being swept along in spite of himself with the crowd" (DA, p. 605). It is hard to tell whether this embodies the fallacy of by-products or the functionalist fallacy.

asymmetry between entry and exit is more convincing than this explanation based on latent functions.

Another passage hesitates, in characteristic fashion, between the appeal to the collective unconscious and to latent functions: because delegated charisma "exalts a leader as chief . . . public opinion will adore him *in order to* remove from itself the right to remove the representative it has given itself" (PC, p. 577–8: my italics). To whom is this calculation imputed?[46] The Roman oligarchs "made presents to an allegedly sovereign people *in order to* show that they owed it nothing" (PC, p. 489: my italics); elsewhere they "instituted the privilege of prerogative *in order to* make it the equivalent of drawing lots" (PC, p. 422: my italics). Other examples, not all of them equally clear-cut perhaps, might be quoted. Their overall impact is to create a conceptual unease in the reader, or in one reader.

IDEOLOGY

In the analysis of ideology, several of the book's major themes come together: the multiplicity of the beliefs held by a single person, the need to justify and be justified, and an expressivity that is neither intentional nor functional.

The idea of a peaceful coexistence of contradictory beliefs is introduced in one of the many bravura numbers in the book, Veyne's analysis of attitudes toward death:

> At one and the same time an octogenarian can plant a tree for his great-nephew, believe in the immortality of the soul, wish to go to Paradise as late as possible, die with the resignation of a poor man, hope to live in the memory of posterity, order a beloved object to accompany him to his last resting-place, make sure that his funeral will be marked by all the splendour

---

46 I fully agree with Veyne that "the unconscious cannot contain rules unless it is conscious, for rules are representations . . . and a representation cannot be unconscious" (PC, p. 140). It also follows, I believe, that the unconscious can never calculate, at least in the strong sense required by the ability to take one step backward in order to take two steps forward. When a choice is made in terms of the future effects of the alternatives, those effects have to be represented at the time of choice.

due to his rank, show in his will an unselfishness that was
unknown when he himself had enjoyment of his possessions,
never mention the dead without an abundance of *litotes*, and
yet talk to those around him, with no embarrassments on
either side, about his latest testamentary dispositions and the
richness of his tomb, be afraid or unafraid of death (he may or
may not spend the night after the death of a relative without a
lighted lamp in his room) depending on whether or not he is
deeply imbued with the feeling that death means a passage to
a better state. (PC, p. 248)

The topic of contradictory beliefs falls into three parts, which
Veyne to my mind does not adequately separate. Firstly there
are those that raise no problem, because they belong to different
and always separate areas. If they chance to come into contact,
one of them disappears. For instance, as a child (and even later)
I had two contradictory ideas about how we got hot water into
the house. I held a practical belief that told me quite clearly and
convincingly that in the basement there was a hot water tank
holding limited quantities (not everyone could take a bath in
the morning), whereas a more bookish belief pictured parallel
networks of hot and cold water pipes running under the streets.
One day I was struck by the absurdity of the latter notion, and
it never recovered from the shock.

Secondly, there are contradictory beliefs that coexist not because
they are far apart but because their modalities are not the same.
Even as children, we do not believe in Father Christmas in the
same way as we (also) believe that our presents come from our
parents (PC, p. 699). Thus, in a striking analysis, Veyne explains
that the cult of the emperor was not really or fully a religion,
since when serious matters were concerned recourse was had
to quite different gods. The conception of the divinity of the
emperors was a religion without believers, and existed so to
speak only in the minds of those who did not believe in it –
the Christians (PC, p. 589).[47] I return to this idea at some length
in the next chapter.

47 On this point one may consult Pruyser (1974), writing in the tradition of
   William James. Veyne, although often very close to James, does not seem

Thirdly, there may be a contradiction not so much between ideas as within one and the same idea, as, for example, when an individual "cannot think through his own annihilation, which his experience of corpses nevertheless proves to him: he goes on thinking that after his death he will suffer from being dead and forgotten, although reason tells him that this thought is contradictory" (PC, p. 249). In this stance, the person sees himself simultaneously as *en-soi* and *pour-soi*, thing and consciousness. We might well say, in fact, that for the Sartre of *Being and Nothingness* man is defined by the contradictory project of hearing his own funeral oration, and that human existence could be summarized in this adventure of Tom Sawyer and Huck Finn.[48]

According to Veyne, one key to ideology is found in contradictions of the second kinds, with the subjects both believing and not believing in the divinity of the sovereign. Their belief is sufficient to give them a little peace of mind as subjects, but not deep enough for them to think about it at moments of crisis in their lives. At the same time, the ideology meets the prince's need to express and justify himself and to gain their love. The divinisation of the emperor was the coming together of two needs rather than the manipulation of one by the other. In his reflections on this phenomenon Veyne offers us a series of propositions that are clearer and more forceful than any other recent writings in the field, even if the ideas are occasionally more dazzling than illuminating.[49]

First proposition: An ideology is not a system of ideas, but the justificatory use that can be made of certain ideas. We can "put truth to edifying and advantageous use" (PC, p. 671). More generally, "a society that does have an ideology in the sense

to have read him. He may, however, have been inspired by Tocqueville (1955), p. 149: "False and objectionable as they may have been, the religions of antiquity never encountered vigorous or widespread antagonism before they were challenged by Christianity. Until then they had been gradually dying out in an atmosphere of skepticism and indifference."

48 See Elster (1978), ch. 4, for an analysis of contradictory thoughts from the viewpoints of Hegelian dialectic and modal logic, as well as Chapter 2 below.
49 Elster (1983b), ch. IV, is largely inspired by these analyses.

that it has a morality" (PC, p. 670). That seems to me to be often but not always true. In pluralist societies such as Greece and Rome there were in fact many ideas in the air, ready to be used for justificatory purposes by various social groups. In more monolithic societies, such as those described in the next chapter, not only do certain groups choose certain ideas, they also suppress competing ones, with the result that society ends up "having an ideology," at least in the sense that everyone is supposed to conform to it in public and even to some extent, by dissonance reduction, does so in private.

There is another objection to this first proposition. Defining ideology by means of the idea of justification seems to me too restrictive, because it rules out the "tendentious extrapolations" (PC, p. 663) arising not from a need to justify but from a distorted vision of reality provided by a specific standpoint. Ideologies may be cold as well as hot.[50] If Veyne stresses a narrow conception of ideology it is because he wants to avoid the excessively broad idea that sees it as "no longer the justificatory use to which the facts of the collective mentality can be put, but those facts themselves, when they are false, inconsistent and arbitrary" (PC, p. 672). But there is an idea between the two, in which ideology is not just any incorrect thinking about social life, but any one-sided vision of social structure arising from a certain position within that structure. The position defines not only interests but also perspective, whence the possibility of a cognitive distortion that is more like an optical illusion than the need to justify and be justified. Seen in this way, *ideology is the whole understood in terms of the logic of a part*, a definition which includes both the justificatory aspects mentioned by Veyne and the cognitive aspects. Central instances of the latter are the microeconomic and micro-political illusions mentioned earlier.

Second proposition: An unconscious ideology sometimes fails to achieve its objective, whereas a conscious one always does. I have already said enough about the second part of this prop-

50 Elster (1985a), ch. 8.

osition; the first, which is no less fundamental, is expressed as follows:

> Our vision of society is a much more ambiguous construction than an observation of reality and does not simply reflect our interests (as far as these are concerned, a society or class is often a victim of its own ideology). In short, ideologies are prejudices before they are pretexts; the logic of the passions involved in interests contributes to their falsity, but it abuses them in return. For interests have no sixth sense enabling them to cut through the obscure confusion of reality and spot their object immediately. (PC, p. 667)

Beliefs born of passion serve passion badly. To see why, consider Hume's observation that "reason is, and ought only to be the slave of the passions."[51] In affirming the primacy of the passions, Hume certainly did not mean that reason should obey their least whim, since, to be useful, a slave must enjoy some autonomy of action and thought. If the passions are to achieve their true aims, they must have at their disposal true facts and a correct perception of the relationship between means and end. Their role is to establish the goals for action and to motivate us to pursue them, not to interfere in cognitive processes.[52] The reason why justificatory ideologies are ambiguous is that although they arise from interests, they often deflect us from pursuing them effectively. In fact, the same holds for those that are cognitive in origin. Nations have been ruined by the mercantilist illusion that wars could never be lost as long as gold and silver remained in the country.[53]

Third proposition: "It is presenting an over-subtle picture of the world to imagine that ideology is rational behavior and to take into consideration the motives of the mystifier but never

---

51 Hume (1960), p. 415.
52 This ideal – having the motivation power of the passions without their distorting power – may not, unfortunately, be attainable. See Alloy and Abrahamson (1979), Levinson et al. (1980), as well as the comments on Tocqueville and Marx in the final note to Chapter 3.
53 Heckscher (1955), vol. 2, p. 203; Elster (1985a), pp. 655–6.

those of the justified. For the latter, ideology satisfies an irrepressible need to justify, and for the former a need for self-justification" (PC, p. 662). The point is not, as in "just-world theories," that oppressors, spectators, and victims conspire to blame the victims for their misfortune. Rather it is that the victims spontaneously tend to accept the legitimacy of the oppressive order. Manipulation is ineffective and in fact pointless, because the subjects invent their own mystification. The sovereign needs only to live as sovereign as the lion lives as a lion, and the narcissistic expression of his majesty is more impressive than any attempt to make an impression. According to Tocqueville: "Honor therefore is not strong because of being fantastic, but it is fantastic and strong for the same reason" (DA, p. 626). Veyne would add that it is legitimate, and hence more powerful, because it is fantastic. It is because of lack of majesty in this sense that the former Communist regimes had no legitimacy; their irrationality contributed to their weakness because it was a failed rationality. By contrast, the irrationality of Trajan's column could only strengthen the cult of the emperor: "Grandiloquent nonsense has always been the privilege and sign of gods, oracles and 'bosses' " (BC, p. 381). Veyne's realism is disconcerting and provocative, commanding our attention and often our assent. For example:

> An efficient cause – bourgeoisie or leaders – cannot endow
> matter with its form. It wrests from it a form that is already
> potentially present in it. Thus societies are at once unjust and
> relatively stable, and the underprivileged also make their
> contribution, if only to escape the anguish of being subject to
> no authority. The idea of depolitization moves from one
> contradiction to another. First it idealizes human beings,
> seeing political autonomy as part of their very essence; then it
> sees them as the lowest of the low, who need only the offer of
> circuses in order to be corrupted; and finally it reinstates
> them, ascribing their alienation to the tyrant's magic wand.
> (PC, p. 89)

This is not a matter of Gramscian hegemony of one class over another, or of the uneasy complicity of master and slave. On the one hand, uncontested submission can be explained in terms of the micropolitical illusion, for in society where everyone has a patron, the worst fate is not to have one. Thus Tacitus "despises 'the lowest classes' because, belonging to nobody, they are nothing" (BC, p. 393). On the other, it can be accounted for in terms of the involuntary stoicism of the sour grapes syndrome. What would I do without my boss? And in any case his pleasures are not mine. The inability to conceive of anything beyond local alternatives reduces the range of what is perceived as possible, while at the same time the pursuit of consonance reduces the range of what is desirable. I cannot say for sure that this will turn out to be the definitive analysis of submission, but I know of none more solidly based.

THE STRUGGLE FOR RECOGNITION

I conclude by some comments on a key sentence: "The other was not an *aliud*, a thing, but an alter ego" (PC, p. 406), an idea that operated downwards (BC, p. 259–60) as well as upwards (BC, p. 418–19). The oligarch or emperor experiences the desire "to rule also over the minds" (PC, p. 488) or "a desire for the other's desire" (BC, p. 398), whereas the subjects asked for the symbolic gestures that softened relations without modifying them (BC, p. 215). These are themes that are reminiscent of Sartre and Hegel, who are rarely quoted but constantly present. I have already commented on the contradictory beliefs that result when we view ourselves as at once thing and consciousness, hoping to survive as *pour-soi* to our transformation into *en-soi*. We shall see that the paradox is not less acute when we treat others with the same dual approach, wanting to rule over the other as an object and at the same time be recognized by the other as consciousness.[54]

The emperor commands, and wants to be loved, but he cannot command his subjects to love him. Such is the basic paradox

54 These are two varieties of psychological contradictions. Both differ from the social contradictions that arise when each person in a group sees himself as a consciousness and the others as things (Elster 1978, ch. 5).

of the Hegelian master–slave dialectic. The master cannot simultaneously enjoy his absolute power – which exists only insofar as he can abuse it (BC, p. 313–14) – *and* draw satisfaction from the recognition that the slave offers him. It would be like a nation seeking diplomatic recognition from one of its own colonies,[55] like the person checking the news in the paper by buying a second copy,[56] or the consumer feeling reassured by reading advertisements for a product he had already bought.[57] Only love freely given or information independently obtained give lasting satisfaction, whereas giving with our right hand and taking back with our left merely reinforces the needs they are supposed to satisfy. To "possess a freedom"[58] or avoid negative information[59] are intentions that cannot be fulfilled, which does not, however, rule out that one may build a life on the attempt to do so.[60]

Eugene Genovese's work had already used some of the same dialectic to cast light on American slavery, and Veyne's picture of the bad emperors – those who wanted to be loved on command – is strikingly similar. When Veyne refers to those "strange figures, those rulers of the early empire, tormented by their

---

55 For Veyne both domestic and foreign policy have to do with the struggle for recognition. "Thus the Acheans were unwilling to accept gifts from certain kings. Either, they said, we shall sacrifice our interests to the interests of those kings, or else we shall seem ungraceful if we oppose the wishes of our paymasters. To refuse a gift meant declining a friendship that could be domineering. Phocion refused the gifts of Alexander, who angrily informed him that he did not regard as true 'friends' those who were unwilling to accept anything from him. In fact, Phocion did not wish to be Alexander's unconditional friend, and accepting a gift and not obeying all the givers' commands would be equivalent to not keeping one's word" (BC, p. 103). In Chapter 2 I quote from an identical observation by Zinoviev.

56 Wittgenstein (1978), § 265.

57 Festinger (1964), p. 49.

58 Sartre (1968), p. 367; see also Proust (1957) or Fowles (1963).

59 Festinger (1964), p. 82, recognizes a difficulty that in his earlier work (Festinger 1957) had led him to confuse dissonance reduction and self-deception, namely that information about the existence of negative information concerning X, and hence to be avoided, is itself negative information, and hence unavoidable, about X.

60 Sartre (1968), passim.

contradictions to the threshold of madness (which some crossed), inclined to persecution mania, changeable, exhibitionistic, cultivated, moving from simple humanity to aestheticism or to a brutality which was in fact traditional in the ruling class" (BC, p. 413), one could almost be reading Genovese, whose slaveholders were "tough, proud and arrogant; liberal-spirited in all that did not touch their honor; gracious and courteous; generous and kind; quick to anger and extraordinarily cruel; attentive to duty and careless of any time and effort that did not control their direct interests."[61]

But there is more. In his relations with the people, the emperor was a prisoner of the master–slave dialectic, for what value can be ascribed to the recognition from someone whom one does not recognize oneself? By not recognizing the other, one is devaluing not only his person but also the recognition he can offer and, ultimately, the object of that recognition, by what could be called a contamination effect. The emperor's relations with the senate were just as paradoxical, although in a different way. Tocqueville expresses the source of the paradox very well: "to desire both that the head of state should be armed with great power and that he should be elected is, in my view, to express two contradictory wishes" (DA, p. 128). Or, in Veyne's words: "Caesarism was based on an absurdity. The Emperor, though sovereign by absolute right, had been made Emperor by his subjects. Could they give unconditional respect to their own creature?" (BC, p. 410).

For its part, the senate was reduced to passivity: "High politics was not allowed them, and occupying themselves with petty politics was just as dangerous, and more humiliating" (BC, p. 412). Even worse, it was exposed to abasement: The tyrant "will require from the grandees a mendacious flattery that deprives them of dignity" (BC, p. 406). Veyne quotes the thought-provoking observation by Tacitus on Tiberius, who "hated sycophancy as much as he feared candour" (PC, p. 720). When Tiberius

61 Genovese (1974), p. 96.

asked the advice of the senate, it very wisely refused to give it: Agreeing and disagreeing would have been equally disastrous. I came across the identical idea in an article by an author of detective stories: "I resent critics who suggest that I haven't written a masterpiece – and write off as a solid-gold idiot anyone who implies that I have."[62]

The phrase reminds me of Groucho Marx's unforgettable quip, that he wouldn't belong to a club that would accept him as a member. But, as we have seen, this does not mean that one cannot also be upset if turned down for membership. We want to be accepted, but the fact of being accepted makes the acceptance worthless.[63] What occurs here is a contamination effect in reverse, with the subject contaminating the person who is willing to accept him, and hence the acceptance itself. The only barrier to tyranny is tyranny itself, with the tyrant encountering his self-imposed limits at every turn in his path, asking for the spontaneous love of his people when he is not repressing them, and humiliating the senators whose flattery eventually becomes wearisome while punishing those who do not engage in it. Contaminating and contaminated, he loses all substance and all character.

At the end of this reading of *Le pain et le cirque*, let me pay homage to the temperament of the author, which makes the book an uninterrupted pleasure, an intellectual feast. He is a Provençal, and a Stendhalian, with a spare and vigorous style that enables him to say in eight hundred pages what for anyone else would have taken two thousand. I imagine the book as the fruit of twenty years of reflection, with each year that passed providing the opportunity for deeper thought and simpler expression, until it achieved that ultimate naturalness that lies beyond complexity.

62 Porter (1978), p. 82.
63 The Groucho Marx syndrome is due to incomplete information: Upon hearing that the club to which one has applied has accepted the application, one acquires new information about the club that, had one had it earlier, would have deterred one from applying. See Samuelson and Bazerman (1985) and Thaler (1992) for details about this "Winner's Curse."

2

INTERNAL AND EXTERNAL NEGATION: AN ESSAY IN IBANSKIAN SOCIOLOGY

A logician by profession and a novelist and sociologist by
vocation, Alexander Zinoviev has created a literary genre
of which his own work is the sole example. In order to have
an idea of the highly individual nature of his approach, one
would have to imagine someone with the ferocity of Swift, the
burlesque of Rabelais, the surrealism of *Catch 22*, the paradoxes
of Lewis Carroll (like Zinoviev, a logician) and the sociological
intuition of Simmel. But a description by juxtaposition is bound
to be inadequate. To summarize his work, I prefer to use a
comparison that might not be to his liking (but who knows?):
He does for contemporary communism what Marx did for the
capitalism of his time. Just as Marx strove to demonstrate the
workings of capitalist irrationality, Zinoviev takes us into a hal-
lucinatory world where even false teeth go bad (YH, p. 771)
and artificial flowers wither (YH, p. 780). But it is not a chaotic
world. It is governed by principles that are as irrational as they
are intelligible, and the task Zinoviev sets for himself is indeed
that of *understanding the irrational*. The irrational object is Soviet
society; the method adopted for understanding it derives largely

A first version of this chapter was read at the 12th World Congress of the
International Political Science Association, Moscow, 12–18 August 1978. It
was received by the Soviet delegates in a way that fully confirmed Zinoviev's
analysis, their main point being that as a guest of their country I should not
have criticized it. See in particular the discussion below of the relationships
between Ibanskians and foreigners.

from modal logic. We shall see that Zinoviev belongs not only to that tradition but also, and perhaps without realizing it, to the dialectical lineage of Hegel and Sartre.[1] In his analysis, social irrationality is not, as in capitalism, the product of a clash of uncoordinated and incompatible intentions, but rather something like a snake swallowing its own tail, a dog chasing its own shadow, or robbing Peter to pay Paul.

Analyzing Zinoviev's work is a delicate undertaking. It goes without saying that a society that is capable of putting a man on the moon cannot be as totally deprived of instrumental rationality as he makes it out to be. Soviet society as depicted by Zinoviev is to real Soviet society as a reflection in a distorting mirror is to the real person looking at himself in it.[2] In the image he presents, all the qualitative and topological features of its counterpart in reality are there, even if some are presented in atrophied form and others are hypertrophied for the sake of caricature.[3]

From the very first page of *Yawning Heights* we know where we are: "The aim of the experiment was to detect those who did not approve of its being carried out and to take appropriate

1 Dialectics is of course an integral part of the Soviet system, which is why it is often derided (YH, pp. 207–9, 214–17, 239–40, 267–9). Zinoviev's own writings, however, have nothing to do with this ossified version of dialectics ("diamat"). Although the autobiographical account in Zinoviev (1990), p. 132, refers approvingly to the dialectical method of Hegel and Marx, I believe his own practice is much closer to the Hegel–Sartre lineage than to the Hegel–Marx one.

2 The period he has in mind predates, of course, glasnost, perestroika, and the breakup of the Soviet Union. As is clear from Zinoviev (1990), he believes that even now nothing has changed. I am not sure he would be wrong. In his books, Zinoviev describes a state of equilibrium. To my mind, no one has the least (justified) idea of what the outcome of the present disequilibrium state will be – the creation of a new equilibrium or something more like the restoration of the old one. Dan Quayle's wonderfully absurd comment from May 1989 is apposite here: The movement towards democracy in China is irreversible – but that could change.

3 As in the previous chapter, I should disclaim any lack of substantive knowledge about the subject matter. Zinoviev's analyses, however grotesque, ring true, and they seem to be confirmed by casual impressions of the kind any newspaper reader could pick up, but more than that I cannot say.

steps" (YH, p. 14). On the one hand, the phrase suggests a political system devoid of any content, or in which the content *is* the form; on the other, it is representative of the paradoxes that have caused an upheaval in formal logic in this century and whose paradigmatic expression is the proposition, "This proposition is false."[4] Zinoviev suggests a practical version of the paradox: "This order is to be obeyed under penalty of death." Which order? The self-reference and infinite regression produce a sense of vertigo no doubt akin to the vague feelings of guilt and complicity that hover permanently over the citizens of Ibansk, the mythical setting of *Yawning Heights*.

There are other quotable paradoxes of the same kind. For instance, an Ibanskian delegation returning to Ibansk with a "pair of trousers with leather trimmage and the incomprehensible tag 'made abroad' " (YH, p. 81); or the slogan of Ibanskian democracy, that "everything obsolete and outmoded must be strangled in embryo" (YH, p. 161), or again the droll reference to Colleague, waiting for his pay "in the shortest queue, which was intended for people who had the right not to queue" (YH, p. 819); or this passage from *The Radiant Future*:

> In short, from whatever aspect we examine our life,
> everywhere we see the efforts of certain strata of our society to
> guarantee themselves the possibility, even if only in part, of
> evading the laws of communist existence and enjoying a more
> comfortable, free, happy and agreeable lifestyle. And a bitter
> struggle goes on within society to gain access to these strata. It
> is one more paradox of our life: one of the fundamental
> tendencies of the communist way of life is the attempt to
> escape from the rules of that very way of life. (RF, p. 237)

However, the essence of Zinoviev is not there. The organizing principle of his analysis is the logical distinction between what I shall call *internal and external negation*, a distinction that goes back to Kant and more recently has assumed crucial importance in modern logic and psychology. The core thesis of Zinoviev's work is, I believe, that the basic irrationality of the regime lies

4 For amusing and instructive discussions, see Smullyan (1978).

in the pervasive confusion or conflation of internal and external negation. This confusion could perhaps be described as typical of the *primitive mentality*, provided that we rigorously eschew all the other connotations that now-discredited term has had in the past.[5] In exploring the vicissitudes of this mentality I begin with logical analysis, go on to the history of ideas, and then finish up with Zinoviev.

THE LOGIC OF NEGATION[6]

Using "A" to refer to a person and "p" to a proposition, let us consider the following propositions:

Example 1

I   A believes p.
II Not (A believes p)
III A believes not-p.

I shall say that II is the external negation of I, whereas III is its internal negation. Another and, as we shall see, formally identical example is the following:

Example 2

I'   Necessarily p
II' Not necessarily p
III' Necessarily not-p

Using "P" to refer to a predicate and "S" to refer to a subject, the same distinction applies to the following:

5 Along with Zinoviev's work, Thomas (1973) should be consulted. The practices catalogued in this magisterial work – astrology, witchcraft, augury, etc. – are accounted for by the lack of "that ability to tolerate ignorance which has been defined as an essential characteristic of the scientific attitude" (Thomas 1973, p. 790).
6 Horn (1989) offers a full account of the role of negation in logic and in natural language.

Example 3

I″   All S are P
II″   Not (all S are P)
III″   All S are not-P

The first two examples involve modal logic. The third example involves quantified nonmodal logic. More complex examples can be generated from quantified modal logic, which allows us to distinguish between *three* forms of negation:

Example 4

I‴   A believes that necessarily p
II‴   Not (A believes that necessarily p)
III‴   A believes that not necessarily p
IV‴   A believes that necessarily not-p.

With one exception[7] I shall ignore such nested cases in the following, and focus on the two simpler ones. For a preliminary explanation of why these distinctions matter, consider the two classical laws of logic: the Principle of Contradiction and the Principle of the Excluded Middle. In terms of the first example, the Principle of Contradiction asserts: "Not (I and II)." Someone imbued by the primitive mentality might, however, extend the principle to internal negation as well: "Not (I and III)." This would amount to asserting that two contradictory opinions, or more generally a set of opinions from which a contradiction can be deduced, is an impossibility. A. MacIntyre makes a claim of this kind in his analysis of Weber's *Protestant ethic*:

> Calvin was committed to the following propositions. 1. God commands good works; 2. It is of the highest importance possible to do what God commands; 3. Good works are irrelevant to what is of most importance to you, your salvation. It is a requirement of logic, not of psychological

7 See note 43 below.

pressure, that one of these propositions be modified; the alternative is contradiction.[8]

For the sake of argument, let us accept that these three propositions do in fact constitute a contradiction. But why should we not have contradictory beliefs? For centuries there were people who believed it possible to trisect the angle using only ruler and compass, a belief we know today to have been contradictory. We have seen other examples in Chapter 1 above. Although the Principle of Contradiction can be extended to internal negation in cases like Examples 2 and 3, it makes no sense to do so in Example 1.[9]

The Principle of the Excluded Middle cannot be extended to internal negation in any of the three examples. By doing so, one would obliterate, for example, the distinction between atheism (the internal negation of God) and agnosticism (the external negation). In certain religions, no differentiation is made between apostates and heretics (this is one aspect of the Rushdie affair).[10] The primitive mentality abhors indifference, ignorance, and suspended judgment, and imposes a dreadful transitivity in personal relations, as in everyday Manicheanism: "He who is not for me in everything is against me in everything"[11], "The enemy of my enemy is my friend" or "The friend of my enemy is my enemy."

8 MacIntyre (1962), p. 55.
9 Let us observe in passing the existence of the following, related fallacy. Instead of affirming the Principle of Contradiction for internal negation in cases like Example 1, one could deny it for external negation. A frequently made argument to this effect goes as follows. When an individual holds contradictory beliefs, they may be justified and indeed required by the fact that reality is itself contradictory. How could Freud, for instance, avoid contradicting himself when he was concerned with that outstandingly contradictory phenomenon, the human mind? (Laplanche 1970, p. 6) In Chapter 3 I discuss how a similar problem arises in trying to understand the contradictions in Tocqueville's reasoning.
10 However, in this case what is confused with heterodox belief is not mere disbelief, but discarded belief. Hence the confusion is a little bit less confused, as those who leave a religion tend either to adopt another or to become militant atheists.
11 Or, as Janos Kadar said to justify the regime he set up in Hungary in 1956: "He who is not against me is for me." Similarly, losing political parties claim

The examples I have given belong to a particular application of modal logic.[12] In *alethic logic*, the classical paradigm of modal logic, "Np" indicates the necessity and "Mp" the possibility of the truth of proposition p. The external negation of "Np" is thus "Not(Np)," which is equivalent to "M(not-p)," while the internal negation is "N(not-p)." But the operators "N" and "M" can also be understood in different ways. In *deontic logic*, "Np" is taken to mean that p is obligatory and "Mp" that it is permissible. We shall see later that the distinction between internal and external negation becomes important in this case. Then there are several versions of *epistemic logic*. In the *logic of knowledge* "Np" is read as "A knows p to be the case," and in the *logic of beliefs* as "A believes p to be the case." Usually, the logic of belief is presented as an axiomatic statement of *rational* belief,[13] which implies that the Principle of Contradiction is valid even for internal negation. It does not however, even in that case, imply the Principle of the Excluded Middle. One cannot rationally believe both p and not-p, but one can rationally refuse to believe both.

Among modal systems we can also note the *logic of desire*, which divides up into that of *wish* and *intention*. Whereas the object of a wish is a state, that of an intention is the act leading to a desired state. Thus, to use an example from Chapter 1, further discussed below, there is nothing contradictory about the wish to be spontaneous, whereas an intention of being spontaneous is self-defeating. The crucial contradiction within the logic of wishes lies elsewhere, in the idea that the absence of a wish for x implies a wish for the absence of x (see below).

Two other related points are worth making here. The first concerns the distinction between the negation of a conjunction and the conjunction of negations. The primitive mentality[14] views

---

the support of those who did not vote to show that the winner is in a minority in the nation.

12 For an elementary introduction, see Snyder (1971) or, for an even more elementary one, ch. 1 of Elster (1978).
13 See for instance Hintikka (1961).
14 Inhelder and Piaget (1959).

the denial of the conjunction of propositions p, q, r. . . ., as equivalent to denying each of them, so that a system of thought or a political platform has to be taken or left in its entirety. This state of thinking can be seen in its pure form in a Norwegian fairy tale.[15] Two girls, one angelic and the other wicked, have to go through a series of obstacles arranged in sequence, so that they have to cope with each one successfully if they are to win through in the end. The good girl, of course, surmounts all the obstacles, *and the other none*, even though a single failure would have been enough to deprive her of victory. In traditional societies (Chapter 1), it is hard to imagine that excellence can be divided up or that there can be many dimensions of superiority. Recourse to stereotypes means a simpler life and greater peace of mind, while status inconsistency makes for cognitive dissonance. This is not to deny that the elements of a negated combination are sometimes causally linked in a way that justifies treating them as a single whole; however, the characteristic feature of the primitive mentality is to go beyond experience and lapse into prejudice. Wealth and money tend to create each other and to reinforce each other, but nothing authorizes us to believe that the wealthy and the powerful are necessarily also intelligent and beautiful.

A second distinction belongs to a classical logical conundrum: how to analyse definite descriptions, that is, those beginning with the definite article, "the." In a famous article Bertrand Russell argued that such descriptions can only be understood within the context of a sentence.[16] Thus, "The King of France is bald" states (i) that there is an object x such that it possesses the property of being king of France; (ii) that for any y with that property, $y = x$; and (3) that x is bald. But how are we to spell out its negation, "The King of France is not bald"? The external negation is the true proposition that denies the combination of (i), (ii), and (iii). The internal negation is the false proposition which asserts (i) and (ii) but denies (iii). Faced with

15 Asbjørnsen and Moe (1957).
16 Russell (1905).

the question, "Is the King of France bald?", we feel that both "yes" and "no" are equally inappropriate answers, because each inadmissibly presupposes the existence of a King of France whose baldness alone is in question. We are reminded of the catch question, "Have you stopped beating your wife?"[17] Ibansk as well as the world of *Catch 22* are now on the map of places where all questions are traps. And the primitive mentality is not only characterized by its tendency to fall into traps; it knows how to set them too. We could even say that the primitive mentality excels at setting them, because deliberate manipulation is generally less effective than complicity in the absurd (Chapter 1).

SOME HISTORICAL ANCESTORS

The distinction between internal and external negation was introduced by Kant in his short precritical treatise, *Versuch den Begriff der negativen Grössen in die Weltweisheit einzuführen*. The text is obscure, and forms part of a physico-philosophical controversy that no longer concerns us.[18] It is useful nevertheless to consider the examples Kant uses to explain the distinction. (1) The external negation of movement is rest, its internal negation movement in the opposite direction. (2) The external negation of wealth is poverty, its internal negation indebtedness. (3) The external negation of pleasure is either indifference or equilibrium, corresponding respectively to the absence of causes of pleasure and to the presence of causes of pleasure and displeasure that cancel each other out; the internal negation is displeasure. (4) The external negation of virtue is not (as one might think) sins of omission, which no less than sins of commission are its internal negation; only the default of the saint and the fault of the noble are its external negation. (5) The external negation of attention is indifference, its internal negation is disregard. Or, in the language I shall use here: Absence of awareness of x differs from the

17 Watzlawick et al. (1974).
18 Elster (1975), pp. 224 ff.

awareness of the absence of *x*. (6) The external negation of obligation is nonobligation, its internal negation is prohibition. (7) The external negation of desire is, once again, indifference; its internal negation is repugnance. In other words, the absence of a desire for *x* differs from the desire for the absence of *x*.

These examples fall in two categories. The first, which includes cases (5), (6), and (7), embodies the modal distinction between "Not(Np)" and "N(not-p)." The second, which includes cases (1)–(4), stands for a very different idea. It can be stated in terms of a mathematical group containing a neutral element and, for each element, another which is its inverse, the neutral element being its own inverse. Thus the external negation of a given element is the neutral element, and the internal negation is its inverse. These two structures have little in common with each other. My concern here is mainly with the first.[19]

The desire for the absence of *x* is not the absence of desire. Kant made this observation more or less in passing. In Hegel it is the object of a systematic development, notably in Chapter 4 of *The Phenomenology of Mind*, which presents consciousness primary as desire (*Begierde*). The fundamental project of consciousness is to dominate the external world, and affirm itself by consuming it. The satisfaction it obtains in doing so, however, turns out to be far from durable:

> In this satisfaction, however, experience makes it aware that the object has its own independence. Desire and the self-certainty obtained in its gratification, are conditioned by the object, for self-certainty comes from superseding this other: *in order that this supersession can take place, there must be this other.* Thus self-consciousness, by its negative relation to the object,

19 We shall see, nevertheless, that Zinoviev also has recourse to both these ways of understanding the distinction between external and internal negation, in fact, linking them to each other. He distinguishes between positive personalities (with positive qualities), mediocre personalities, and negative personalities (with negative qualities). Unlike mediocre personalities, who are quite simply unaware of the good, negative personalities recognize it and fight against it. At the same time, they are the inverse of positive personalities, whereas mediocrities form a neutral element on the scale of qualities.

is unable to supersede it; it is really because of that relation
that it produces the object again, and the desire as well.[20]

In the sentence I have italicized, Hegel explains with exemplary
clarity one of the paradoxes of internal negation: A person whose
independence requires the destruction of an external object,
depends on that object in his very being and hence cannot
without contradiction desire its destruction. Two hundred years
earlier John Donne had the same insight, in "The Prohibition":

> Take heed of hating me,
> Or too much triumph in the victory
> Not that I shall be mine own officer,
> And hate with hate again retaliate;
> But thou wilt lose the style of conqueror,
> if I, thy conquest, perish by thy hate.
> Then, lest my being nothing lessen thee,
> If thou hate me, take heed of hating me

Once we start thinking about it, the phenomenon is ubiquitous.
It explains why militant atheism cannot do without believers,
just as a certain kind of communism lives symbiotically with
private property.[21] Similarly, an anticommunist's world would
be ruined if one day he managed to destroy "the God that
failed." After the fall of the Soviet Union and the Soviet empire,
not only do many Westerners see their career threatened, they
see their lives without focus. Their nostalgia for the Cold War
is not simply (as usually asserted) due to the stability and pre-
dictability it offered, but also to the meaning it provided.

Atheism, considered more closely, actually raises two distinct
paradoxes. On the one hand, there is the difficulty we have
already observed of getting zealots to see the distinction between
atheism and agnosticism. On the other, there is the difficulty of
making the atheist understand that he cannot wipe out the
religious mentality as long as he is attached to religion as to an
enemy. He may even hate it enough to ensure its survival when

20 Hegel (1977), p. 109.
21 Kolakowski (1978), vol. I, p. 140.

no one really believes in it any more. Both paradoxes are interlinked, with persecution turning the agnostic into an atheist, and his atheism keeping alive the faith of his persecutors even when they have stopped believing.

I shall not dwell on the further development of these ideas in the early Sartre, through the mediation of Koyré and Kojève. Instead I conclude this historical digression with a note on their importance in contemporary psychology. According to the so-called Palo Alto school in psychiatry,[22] one significant element in the etiology of certain family pathologies is the so-called contradictory injunction, a command such that its overt content contradicts its pragmatic presuppositions. Thus the order "Don't be so obedient" (corresponding to Sartre's idea of love) places the person in an impossible position, since to obey he has to disobey.[23] Similarly, the exhortation to be spontaneous demands a conscious and deliberate attempt to induce a state of non-deliberation.[24] Likewise, the injunction "Forget it" calls for an effort that can only engrave what we are supposed to forget more firmly in our memory. Imagine, for example, a mother telling her daughter to remember that she must not even think about some forbidden thing; saying, in fact, that she must think about it, constantly even, in order never to think about it. It is easy to imagine the pervasive guilt induced by such injunctions if taken seriously.[25] As Emily Dickinson wrote (*Complete Poems*, no. 1560):

22 Watzlawick et al. (1974).
23 Elster (1983b), ch. II.4.
24 To show that such commands are in fact contradictory in a strict sense, we may rely on an extension of the ideas in Hintikka (1961). In his analysis of beliefs, Hintikka shows that the criterion for a noncontradictory belief cannot simply be that there exists a possible world in which the belief in question is true. We have to demonstrate the existence of a possible world in which the belief would be true *and believed*. Similarly, for an order to be noncontradictory, there must be a possible world in which it is satisfied *and the recipient tries to satisfy it*.
25 For a large-scale example, see the study in Levy (1973) of the impact of the Christian idea of sinful thoughts on the Tahitians.

The Heart cannot forget
Unless it contemplate
What it declines

The will to forget is a case of what I called "willing what cannot be willed" (Chapter 1), an impossible undertaking because it depends on the confusion of internal and external negation. Forgetting or indifference is an external negation, a mere lack of awareness of x, whereas the desire to forget presupposes a representation of the absence of x and hence of x itself. Trying to forget is like using a flashlight to create darkness.

FUNDAMENTALS OF IBANSKIAN SOCIOLOGY

Returning now to Zinoviev, I shall examine his analysis of the basic structure of Ibanskian life; the relation between the regime and the opposition; and how the basic rules of society turn power into impotence.

The simultaneous tragic and farcical aspects of *The Yawning Heights* is a consequence of the fact that Zinoviev is analyzing phenomena, such as denunciation or opportunism, which are individually farcical and collectively tragic. Marx said that history repeats itself, the first time as tragedy, the second time as farce. Zinoviev turns him around: "a farce which constantly repeats itself is actually a tragedy" (YH, p. 468), since "one triviality just gives place to another . . . but the system of trivia remains" (YH, p. 374). In a more direct play on Marx, he also asserts that "History repeats itself, the first time as a tragedy, and the second time as a catastrophe" (YH, p. 710).

Informing, a constituent phenomenon of every social group in Ibansk, tends to take the place of information. "Where [information] is public and official, it is false, and, where it is secret, it rapidly tends towards denunciation." (YH, p. 107) We might naively think that even in a totalitarian regime there would be some office in the Ministry of the Interior with complete and accurate information, if only to make oppression more efficient. For Zinoviev, however, this is not so, since it would be in no one's interest to tell the truth.[26] Tsarist rule has been variously described as despotism tempered by incompetence, or autocracy tempered by assassination. Zinoviev would probably say that the inefficiency of the Ibanskian regime makes its despotism even more terrible, because lack of information about someone is taken to mean that there is information against him. Similarly, I expect he might say that assassination, were it to occur, would matter only because it would provide the authorities with reliable information about the resistance to the regime.

Zinoviev must be counted among the founders of the sociology of opportunism, that fundamental and universal feature of Ibanskian society. In *The Radiant Future* the ambiguous protagonist explains how the phenomenon works. In its most intelligible form it is characterized by cynicism, lack of conscience and skill in personal relationships. But that is only a beginning:

> Afganov has confused all my ideas about Soviet careerism. He is a handsome enough lad, although not exactly a film star. You can't say that he is particularly bright, but neither is he stupid. He won't say no to a drink. He's not malicious. He is good natured. Idle. A bit sleepy. And he has no family connections. No one to protect him in the way Karaneikin has protected me. He's published a couple of down-market pamphlets on philosophy (philosophy for housewives and mental deficients, as they were described by such outstanding degenerates as Karaneikin and Petin). And yet he took off like a rocket for no particular reason. He was suddenly included in the editorial board of a leading journal, given a professorship, appointed editor and elected a corresponding member all before my very eyes. (RF, p. 143)

Just as incomprehensible is the award of a literary prize to an author who is not only totally lacking in talent (that goes without saying), but has never even served state or party

---

26 Two well-known mechanisms are the following. Because nobody wants to be the bearer of bad tidings, there is a systematic tendency to overstate positive achievements. Because nobody wants to raise the expectations of the authorities, there is a systematic tendency to understate positive achievements.

(RF, p. 235 ff.). It is in the *Yawning Heights* that we find the key to this higher form of opportunism, in the observation that Stalin was not a talented careerist, but just a total mediocrity (YH, p. 398). A talented careerist needs remarkable negative qualities, whereas to be an extraordinary mediocrity a remarkable lack of qualities is required. In Ibanskian society, the greatest success comes to the latter kind of person, since "the most able careerist is the one with the least talent as a careerist" (YH, p. 398). Or again:

> The most successful method of making a career in Ibanskian conditions, and this is certainly the method chosen by that undoubtedly talented careerist Claimant, gives enormous advantages to the *un*talented careerist. Even the Boss himself [i.e., Stalin] seized power and established his own system of power not because he was a genius at his own filthy business, but exclusively because even in that very business he was a total nonentity. He was completely fitted to that business as a person. The leader of rats cannot be a lion. (YH, p. 214)

Hence the impression of "being up against an extraordinarily insignificant force which, by virtue of this very fact, is invincible" (YH, p. 399). It is impossible to struggle against an absence that offers no purchase to those opposing it; better to be faced with the presence of a negative that can be criticized and resisted.[27] This is the theme of the banality of evil. According to Yeats, the situation most to be dreaded is that in which "The best lack all conviction, while the worst are full of passionate intensity"; to Tocqueville, the crisis of religion is due to the fact that it has "tepid friends and ardent adversaries" (DA, p. 300); for the young Marx, the threat to freedom of the press in Germany was

---

27 Many readers will recognize a similar predicament from the experience of marking examination papers. A paper that makes identifiable errors is much easier to assess than one that sins mainly by vagueness and triviality. To explain to the author of the latter kind of paper why he got a bad grade can be literally impossible: "Gegen die Dummheit kämpfen selbst die Götter vergebens." Zinoviev's point, of course, is that in Ibansk bland stupidity is an asset rather than a liability.

that of having platonic friends and passionate enemies.[28] In Zinoviev's view they are wrong, because there are worse things than persecution. To exist as an object of passionate negation is still preferable to being totally absent from the consciousness of men. The triumph of evil is incomplete as long as it remains an internal negation of the good.

To account for the triumph of mediocrity we can appeal to the principle discussed at some length in Chapter 1: Certain kinds of conduct are efficacious only when efficacy is not the aim. Think, for instance, of the problems encountered by a talented writer setting out to write a best-seller in order to make a living. The end result almost invariably is either too good or too bad. To hit the right note of mediocrity, he would have to share, rather than exploit, the blinkered vision and the prejudices of a mass readership. As Zinoviev remarks, "the better you do your work, the worse for you. And if you do it badly, you'll only be crushed the more thoroughly, since shoddy work is something They're really good at" (RF, p. 100).

That view of Ibanskian man seems, however, to contradict the picture that emerges from the following passage:

> An outstanding intelligence is regarded here as an abnormality, and outstanding stupidity as outstanding intelligence. Highly moral people are regarded as amoral villains, and the most abject nonentities as models of virtue. What is in question here is not the absence of one quality, but the presence of another. As a result a strangely negative type of personality is formed which reacts to the positive in the same way as the electron to the positron (or vice versa). Just as the presence of a negative charge is not the absence of a positive, and of a positive charge is not the absence of a negative, so in the given case, I repeat, a negative type of personality is a personality which has certain specific attributes. (YH, p. 102)

Is the citizen of Ibansk the internal negation of the moral and rational individual, as this passage seems to suggest, or the

28 Marx (1842).

external negation of the Afganov type? We have to assume that external negation is the most highly developed form of the Ibanskian personality, even if the internal negation is the most striking one precisely because of its specific attributes. This interpretation is supported in particular by Zinoviev's insistence on the *normality* of the world he describes. That world cannot be cured, since it is perfectly normal and healthy (RF, p. 194). Nor is it inhabited by evil and immoral people; at most we can speak of amorality. It may be true that "moral consciousness has withered away, just like the classical types predicted" (RF, p. 133; translation slightly modified), but the result has been to create its external rather than internal negation.

Contradiction dominates every aspect of Ibanskian life, be it economic planning, education, or the fight against crime. The general principle is that instead of looking for effective solutions to real problems, the authorities look for a problem that will match desired or possible solutions. For instance, in order to reduce the percentage of unpunished crimes, the number of fictitious crimes is increased (RF, p. 77).[29] An alternative would be to "destroy the criminals before they manage to commit their crime" (YH, p. 819).[30] The only snag is that those who fight crime "need to reconcile objectives that are in dialectical contradiction: there should be no crimes committed in any unit; it has to be demonstrated to higher authorities that any crimes committed are successfully uncovered" (YH, p. 72). Ibanskian society aims at two contradictory goals, the external negation of crime (its disappearance) and its internal negation (efficacious punishment).

29 Using n for the number of real crimes, m for the number of real crimes that are punished, and a for the number of fictitious crimes attributed to innocent people and immediately punished, it is in the interest of the authorities to make a as large as possible, because for $m < n$ the percentage $(m + a)/(n + a)$ is an increasing function of a.

30 This ludicrous idea recurs in the fight against speculators and swindlers who try to reestablish the monetary system. To block them, all one needs is to stop the "production of goods which are the object of speculation" (YH, p. 804).

With regard to education, let me quote the fine passage in which Zinoviev explains how ordinary hypocrisy is preferable to the "hypocrisy squared" that is practised in Ibansk:

> I become more and more convinced that the critical literature of the recent past has done a great deal of harm by attacking worldly hypocrisy. It's been based on a very banal principle, that a man who behaves very decently towards others (smiles, says he's pleased to see you, sympathises when things go wrong, and so on) thinks something else privately (that he looks down on you, envies you, is pleased with your failures, upset by your successes, and so on). This was seen as hypocrisy. It was considered that people who were of little worth were passing themselves off as decent and good. But that isn't only (or always) hypocrisy. It can also be the result of good education, which is one of the social means of self-defence that people can use against their own selves. It's the ability to control oneself, without which no normal relationships are possible. Without this good education, life becomes a nightmare. Without it, it's virtually impossible to meet anyone. We cannot talk of man as if he possessed something secret and genuine which developed as mask to suit any given situation. A man's character includes what he is at home and what he is at work, and what he is among friends and acquaintances, and what he thinks and what he says. "Yes, but there's more than a lack of worldly education here", said Chatterer. "You'd have to talk more about anti-worldly education. To ignore and trample underfoot everything that is outstanding and to hold up mediocrity for praise is a particular kind of education, not a void. Hypocrisy that takes the form of a negation of hypocrisy is hypocrisy squared." (YH, pp. 350–1.)

This means that the citizens of Ibansk are both the external negation of rational and moral man, and the product of an education which is the internal negation of a rational and moral education. Anti-education does not create anti-man. The conclusion may be surprising at first sight, but becomes more convincing on reflection. The systematic absence of either positive or negative outstanding features could never be achieved in the absence of a systematic education. A mere lack of education would produce all sorts of men, which would be incompatible with the Ibanskian norm of mediocrity. Although one cannot produce a state of external negation in oneself by means of an internal negation, there is nothing to stop us managing to do so in others. We may not, for instance, be able to compel ourselves to forget, but we may induce a state of no-knowing in others. This being said, however, we should not read Zinoviev as saying that the Ibanskian authorities are consciously manipulating their subjects since, as we shall see later, in their world deliberate planning is doomed to failure. What we observe in the citizens of Ibansk is the result of education, not the realization of its aim.

OPPOSITION AT HOME AND ABROAD

We can approach the relationship between the regime and the opposition by first examining Ibanskian law. By now, the reader will not be surprised to learn that its fundamental feature is the confusion of nonobligation and prohibition. In a rational society, "a distinction must be drawn between the absence of a standard and the existence of a negation-standard" (YH, p. 618), but in Ibansk the absence of an obligation normally entails the presence of a prohibition, unless the contrary is clearly stated. "And there are cases, too, when it is not enough to have no ban on an action, but official permission has to be sought as well. Sometimes even that is not enough, and a rule is needed to prevent the obstruction of acts which are permitted or at any rate not prohibited" (YH, p. 78–9).[31]

We shall see later that this confusion haunts even the attempts to dispel it. First, however, we may note two further contrasts between Ibanskian and rational law. The right to emigrate is a fundamental human right, as is the absence of any right of

31 The tendency is apparently even stronger in the People's Republic of China. At one point, for instance, wall newspapers were expressly authorized by law; when the authorization was withdrawn – but not replaced by a prohibition – everyone understood that henceforth anyone putting them up might be punished (Hungdad 1987). Compared to the Chinese legal system, Soviet law appears as a model of rationality (Hungdad 1987).

government to exile its subjects.[32] In the upside-down world of Ibansk, however, the government reserves itself the right to exile; considers the desire to emigrate a crime so serious in itself that it might warrant expulsion; and yet refuses requests to emigrate. It is worth reflecting on the dreadful sentence in which Zinoviev captures the characteristic irrationality of Ibansk:

> And I was forced to leave of my own free will at the will of a free people, with only one difference – that at the end I myself wanted to leave and so for two years I was prevented from doing so since my voluntary desire to fulfil the wishes and the will of the people was self-will. And a free people cannot allow that. *They even want to fulfil their own will as regards me despite my own will.* (YH, p. 541: my italics)[33]

We are immediately reminded of the world of *Catch 22*. In Joseph Heller's novel, the paradox in the title is as follows. Anyone willing to fly combat missions is by definition insane and hence has the right to be exempted from them on psychiatric grounds. He has only to ask. But the very fact of asking, the very wish to fly no combat missions, shows that he is sane and prevents him from being exempted.[34] In Zinoviev, military life obeys other but equally paradoxical laws. In the world of *Catch 22*, both expressing and not expressing the wish to avoid a dangerous mission provide equally valid reasons for the authorities to make it compulsory. In Ibansk, saying that you want to carry out such a mission is enough to stop you:

32 In Hodfeld's terminology, the citizens have, with regard to leaving the territory, both a *power* and a *counterimmunity* against the state.

33 This kind of pathological behavior, then, takes the form: "I want you to do as I wish, but only on the condition that you do not want to do so." It can be contrasted with a commoner and more innocent one: "I want you to do as I wish, but I want you to do so freely and not because I wish it" (see Elster 1983, ch. II.4).

34 An American colleague once told me a symmetrical anecdote. During the Vietnam war, leaders of a revolutionary Maoist organization asked their members to volunteer for the army so as to be able to "turn their guns the other way," that is, against the Americans. The military authorities declared them unfit for service, probably in the belief that volunteering was a sure sign of incapacitating mental instability.

[The Patriot] . . . had been sentenced to ten days for
requesting to be sent to the front, but . . . he could see no
logic in this, since fifty cadets were being despatched to the
front without the slightest desire to go. Deviationist observed
that this merely demonstrated the iron logic of the social laws
since, according to these laws, Patriot's destiny was not under
his own control, and by putting in a request for transfer to the
front, he had offended the social laws by evincing a wish to
control his own fate by his own will – so he had got
everything he deserved. (YH, p. 64)[35]

Another major difference concerns the relationship between
the letter and the spirit of the law. We know that the Chinese
have always been keen to avoid an elaborate code of law, fearing
that those with enough cunning might try to invoke the letter
of the law against the spirit.[36] By contrast, the Western notion
of law allows the possibility or indeed the inevitability of unintended consequences of legislation, and asserts that in such
cases one should change the letter of the law rather than appeal
to its spirit. In the West, one is not indicted for libel for saying,
"If I said what I think about him, I would be indicted for libel."
In Ibansk, one ignores the letter and homes in on the spirit:

What matters above all is not whether a law is bad or good.
What matters is whether or not the law exists. A bad law is
nevertheless a law. Good illegality is nevertheless illegal. I
shall take it upon myself to prove the mathematical theorem

35 As is made clear in Zinoviev (1990), p. 281, this story builds on an episode
from Zinoviev's army service in the Second World War.
36 Needham (1956), p. 522. According to Hungdad (1987), the idea has survived
up to the present. In contemporary China, for instance, the principle of
analogy is applied not only in civil law, where it is indispensable, but also
in criminal law. First one decides that somebody ought to be punished, and
then one seeks for a legal statute that, by analogical reasoning, will enable
one to do so. Once again, I have the impression that the tendencies Zinoviev
found in Soviet society are even more pronounced in China. The following
Catch 22 story from the Cultural Revolution is instructive. At that time
workers no longer got a bonus according to productivity or seniority; only
ideological purity was supposed to count. However, the only practical way
of demonstrating such purity was to refuse the bonuses to which it made
one entitled (Walder 1986, pp. 173–4).

that any society with a rule of law, no matter how bad that
law may be, allows the existence of an opposition. The very
existence of an opposition is a sign that society lives by the
law. And the absence of an opposition is an indication that a
society is lawless. But let us look more closely at this question.
Let us take a certain text A. Let there be a legal system B,
according to which this text is assessed to be "hostile" to the
given society (as an "anti" text). Consequently, the author of
A is prosecuted. And if, for example, I say "N asserts that A",
I am not asserting A, I am asserting that N asserts A. What
then, from the point of view of B, is the nature of a text of the
type "N asserts that A"? Is that an "anti" text? Fine, but how
will the prosecutor look, when in court he accuses me of
asserting the text "N asserts that A"? Will he be seen as a man
pronouncing an "anti" text? No? But why? Where is the
formal criterion which lets us make this distinction?
Admittedly, I have used the word "asserts" once, and the
prosecutor has used it twice. But if such a law is adopted, all
I have to do is to pronounce in advance the following text:
"M asserts that N asserts that A". I have only cited one logical
progression. But there are many more, Construct for me a
code B of laws which permits texts to be assessed as "anti",
and I will undertake, for any text which is so assessed, to
construct a text which cannot be assessed according to code B,
but which all the same will be understood as an opposition
text. Every rigorous law is *a priori* a possibility of opposition.
(YH, p. 306–7)[37]

37 Compare a classical text by Tocqueville: "If someone showed me an intermediate position I could hope to hold between complete independence and
entire servitude of thought, perhaps I would adopt that position; but who
can discover any such position? Starting from license of the press and wishing
to move to something more orderly, what do you do? First you bring writers
before juries; but the juries acquit, and what had been the opinion of only
an isolated man becomes that of the country. You have therefore done both
too much and too little and must try again. You hand the authors over to
permanent magistrates, but judges have to listen before they can condemn,
and things which men fear to avow in a book can be proclaimed with
impunity in pleadings; and what would have been obscurely said in one
written work is then repeated in a thousand others. Its expression is the
external form and, if I may put it so, the body of the thought, but it is not
the thought itself. Your courts may arrest the body, but the soul escapes
and subtly slips between their fingers." (DA, pp. 180–1)

The relation of the regime to the opposition can be one of either internal or external negation, condemnation or silence. Its dilemma is stated as follows: "It was time, it was necessary to make a high-level response to that individual. But on the other hand, that would attract attention to his filthy little books. However, if we keep silent, people will think that they are right." (RF, p. 230) Condemnation, in fact, is also a form of recognition and diffusion, even if it is also to make a threat. For the opposition, therefore, the move from silence to condemnation is a step forward. If modernist painters are to be criticized, for example, their works have to be reproduced and hence made known (RF, p. 134), which provides the opposition with a weapon: "Condemn me."[38]

In fact, if the regime chooses silence, the mere fact that it *chooses* to do so shows that it is not really an external negation in the full sense of the term. It is a willed silence that is not the same as genuine indifference; an intended internal negation that hides behind an apparent external negation. However, a willed indifference and a true one can easily be told from another, because of the systematic character of the former.[39] Once again

38 Conversely, Zinoviev (1990, p. 321) notes that the authorities were careful not to criticize his work, because doing so would have drawn attention to them.

39 Similarly, "going back to normal" after a political crisis tends to mean going back beyond the normal, and in fact to the opposite extreme. The following item from Beijing in the *International Herald Tribune* of July 25, 1989 illustrates the point:

A Chinese official beamed with a mixture of pride and relief as he treated a foreign guest to a car ride around central Tiananmen Square the other day.

"See how normal the square looks now," he asked, turning to his guest for a sign of approval.

The guest, an American woman living in Hong Kong, glanced around the empty square, now guarded by armed soldiers.

"Where are all the people," she asked. "It's empty. I'm afraid I don't think that is very normal."

Almost reluctantly, the official admitted that the square, a busy tourist spot that was transformed into a democracy campsite in May, was actually closed to the public.

(Chapter 1), intentions are difficult to hide.[40] By never speaking of someone whose existence one cannot plausibly claim to ignore, one can say as much as by talking about him constantly, as any husband whose wife is having an affair will know.

In Ibansk, too, the opposition is aware of the implications of silence:

> It is not the attacks that are frightening, said Chatterer. Persecution amounts to official recognition. It's the deliberate indifference to everything you do. And the more important your work is, and the better its results, the greater the indifference becomes. I'm not talking about indifference as a mere lack of interest, but an active indifference. That's something positive. (YH, p. 745)

Active indifference is internal negation masking itself as external negation. One can easily imagine an endless series of such masks, each more sophisticated than the last and capable of deceiving a greater number of people, but ultimately unable to blot out their origin in an internal negation.

There is opposition not only at home, but also abroad. The West is always there. In Zinoviev's work, there are frequent references to trips abroad, particularly to attend scientific conferences. Foreigners exercise a powerful attraction on the Ibanskians, but only as long as they reject their advances:

> Ibanskians adore foreigners and are prepared to give them their last shirt. If the foreigner doesn't take the shirt, he's called a swine. And quite rightly. Take what you're given, without wanting to get yourself thumped. So take it, damn you, if you don't want a thick ear. There's no need to play hard-to-get. They're being good-hearted, showing good

---

40 Of course, the suspicious mind, or the mind in search of meaning, will sometimes see intentions where none exist. During the Second World War, Londoners were persuaded that the Germans systematically concentrated their bombing in certain parts of their city, because the bombs fell in clusters (Feller 1968, p. 161). This inference reflected a lack of understanding of the statistical principle that random processes tend to generate clustering. If the German bombs had been evenly spaced, it would have been evidence for nonrandom distribution.

feelings. So go on, make the most of it, they're not like this every day, and if you don't . . . . But if the foreigner accepts the shirt and goes on behaving as he feels like doing, he's still called a swine. And that's only right. He could've refused it. But if he accepts, he ought to abide by the rules. We've acted with the best intentions, with open generosity. But as for him . . . . It's no use looking for gratitude. They're swine, and that's all there is to it. But if the foreigner takes the shirt and behaves like a proper Ibanskian, then he's an even bigger swine, because then he's clearly one of our own people, and with our own people there's no need to stand on ceremony. (YH, p. 460)

This is the idea of *Timeo Danaos* already encountered above.[41] There is also a contamination effect: If the foreigner is really stupid enough to recognize *us*, we should also be very stupid to recognize *him*.

Krushchev occupies a special place in the Ibanskian world, symbolizing the inability of the regime to bring about change or to change itself: "Even if they were suddenly to wish to stop being oppressors they could not desist from oppression, since their lack of will to oppress could only be realised in the form of oppression, which could entail nothing more than a change in the aspect and sphere of application of oppression" (YH, p. 582).

Earlier I mentioned the deceptively liberating injunction to be less obedient. Krushchev's failure to de-Stalinize was due to a similar entrapment. During a very short period (between 1953 and 1956) it was permissible not to quote Stalin, but very soon it was recommended not to do so (RF, p. 58), as if the first state of merely external negation was too fragile to last.[42] Stalin triumphed even in his defeat, since the method used to reject him was based on the very same confusion he had fostered.

The distinction between external and internal negation also explains why Krushchev was never able to bring his project to fruition:

41 See note 55 to Chapter 1.
42 Zinoviev (1990), pp. 372–3.

Half-measures in such situations always end in defeat. You say that he wouldn't have been allowed to? That he would have been toppled? They would have had no chance! Before they could have got themselves together, he would have done so much that it would have been far too late to have taken any steps against him. The further he had gone, the stronger his position. It is true that he could not deal a really heavy blow. But not because he understood the objective impossibility of a heavy blow, but because he subjectively did not understand the possibilities before him. (YH, p. 188).[43]

This analysis of Krushchev's impotence ("he could not") may be contrasted with the following passage, which states two other ways of being powerless:

"How do you know what's senseless and what's not?", asked Panicker. "Maybe they have no option". "What do you mean by that?" asked Humorist. "Do you mean that they acted the best way they could in conditions over which they had no control? Or that they acted as they did because it was in their nature? That's very far from being the same thing. The former presupposes intelligence and a rational approach. The latter, not." (YH, p. 417)

Any action may be seen as the outcome of two successive filters, the first being made up of the structural constraints of the situation and the second of the mechanism by which one action is selected among those that satisfy all the constraints.[44] Lack of power may then be seen either as the effect of constraints that are so strong that even rational choice within them can do little to affect the outcome; or as the effect of a selection mechanism which owes more to, say, social norms or private obsessions than to rational choice. That is roughly the distinction that Zinoviev makes in the passage just cited. But Krushchev's dilemma was different. It was not that he had no objective room for maneuver

43 The final sentence of this passage embodies an exceptional use of mixed modalities of both the alethic and the epistemic types. Using N for the necessity operator and B for the epistemic operator, Zinoviev here makes a distinction between $B(N(not\text{-}p))$ and $Not(B(Not(N(not\text{-}p))))$.

44 Elster (1984), p. 113ff.

or was incapable of rational action, but rather that he did not see that he had the means of implementing his policy.

That blindness, in turn, may have been due to insufficient liberation from the mental habits of the system he wanted to abolish. In this regime, even the opposition is impregnated with the confusion between the two types of negation. Thus a dissident

> said previously that he didn't want to submit himself to the ballot [to the elections to the Academy of Sciences], but he was proposed, and he signed the papers. And he was accused of inconsistency. Now was he inconsistent? When I came here today, I didn't want a drink. You offered me one, and I took it. Inconsistent? No. We merely have to distinguish between the absence of a desire to do something, and the presence of a positive disinclination to do it. (YH, p. 105)[45]

If the other dissidents fall into this now familiar trap, it is because they bear the stamp of the society within which – and not only against which – they are struggling. "It is impossible to live in a society and remain free from it." (YH, p. 561). Or again,

> As a man overcomes these resistances he gradually assumes an ever closer resemblance to that society's Mr. Average. If he fails to do so, he will not be able to penetrate the fissures in the obstacles he faces. It may seem to him that he has preserved his creative individuality and is bringing his ideas to fruition; but in fact he is increasingly conforming to the standard. (YH, p. 761)

This remark is particularly applicable to the sculptor Dauber, a central and ambiguous character in *The Yawning Heights* who before the reader's eye is transformed from a natural dissident into an unwitting opportunist. When he says that the gravestone he has carved for Krushchev is an uncompromising work, one

---

45 Raymond Aron once told me that he followed three principles when offered decorations or honorary doctorates: Never solicit them, never refuse them, never wear them. Even better, perhaps, to do as Sartre: to be offered the Nobel prize and let it be known that you refuse it. The desire to be well known as an anonymous donor to charity would satisfy a similar ambition.

of his friends replies, "That's true, if the lack of any search for compromise can be regarded as an absence of compromise" (YH, p. 467). It is possible to reach a compromise without searching one; the distinction made earlier between two kinds of careerist even suggests that the most compromising adaptations arrive spontaneously and without any deliberate effort.

POWER AND IMPOTENCE

"Ibanskian power is both omnipotent and impotent . . . . It has a huge destructive force, and a wholly insignificant power of creation." (YH, p. 483) To explore these propositions, let us first note that the idea of power is doubly counterfactual. Power is the ability to realize one's goals, *whatever they may be*, and *whatever obstacles others may put in one's way*. In Ibansk, it is certainly true that resistance to the efforts by the authorities to achieve their aim makes no difference to the outcome. It is also true, however, that these authorities are severely limited in the positive aims they can achieve. Tocqueville noted that a centralized power (what we would call today an authoritarian regime) "excels at preventing, not at doing" (DA, p. 91); "it seldom enjoins, but often inhibits action; it does not destroy anything, but prevents much being born" (DA, p. 692). Zinoviev makes a related but different contrast, when he endows the totalitarian regime with enormous destructive powers and no creative potential.

This asymmetry between doing and undoing does not come about simply because "it is easier to destroy than to construct" (YH, p. 484). Above and beyond any obstacle that the second law of thermodynamics may put in the way of creative effort, there are certain specifically Ibanskian hurdles. First, there is the tendency, noted above, for information to degenerate into informing. Second, there is the tendency to assess solutions in terms of their ideological rather than their technical efficacy, to seek "a correct social solution for an insoluble economic problem" (YH, p. 683). Third, there is the omnipresent influence of contradictory plans, such as the attitude toward crime (see above)

97

or the directive "to enhance the leadership role of the leadership cadres and to activate an initiative from below" (YH, p. 179). Fourth, there is a systematic production of mediocre personalities, capable at most of hindering the plans of others. Fifth, "the effect of social relationships is such that any important problem is regarded as a difficult one" (YH, p. 672).[46] Finally, "an amoral society wastes a huge amount of energy because of its very lack of a high enough level of morality" (YH, p. 800), because people "expect the worst" (TF, p. 187) and take their precautions accordingly, thus contributing to the realization of their fears.

We can now state the *first law of Ibanskian life*: it is "the well-known rule whereby people who want to make a change never change anything, while changes are only effected by people who had no intention of doing so" (YH, p. 198). In other words, the set of political possibilities is empty.[47] In Ibansk, all effects are essentially by-products (Chapter 1). It is not that there cannot be changes and even profound transformations, but simply that they can never be brought about intentionally and deliberately. On the one hand, "any decisions taken by the leadership about a particular problem have one and the same result" (YH, p. 154); on the other, "directives are a result, not a cause" (YH, p. 338). A distinction has to be made between a solution and the result of a search for a solution (YH, p. 749), just as it is necessary "to make a distinction between what is the product of time and what is the product of the new social system" (YH, p. 530). In Ibansk, it is known in advance that any attempt to take action will trigger off a counteraction that will nullify it:

> I was in no way surprised to learn that two diametrically
> opposed meetings had been held virtually simultaneously, and
> that each had adopted measures which paralysed measures
> adopted by the other. That's the normal run of things, and I
> have been used to that for a long time. For example, Stupak's
> father in one and the same day received the Order of Lenin

46 Zinoviev (1990), pp. 100, 292, recounts several episodes from his own life
   that illustrate this mechanism.
47 Elster (1978), ch. 3, especially pp. 49, 56.

and was expelled from the party (he was arrested later that night). (RF, p. 58)

In Ibansk, guilt takes the place of causality. The *second fundamental law* states, in effect, that "success achieved under any leadership must be success achieved by that leadership" (YH, p. 156) or, alternatively, that "the leadership attributes for itself everything positive and calculates its actions so as never to be held responsible for failures and any negative phenomenon" (YH, p. 410). Or again,

> from the scientific point of view . . . one must talk of the causes of certain manifestations. But from the official point of view, such a statement of the problem is unacceptable. In any situation, the official consciousness always poses the question: "Where does the fault lie?" And as for the official consciousness, guilt must be personified, since only human beings can be accused, and not inanimate nature or dumb beasts, the problem is posed even more sharply: "Who is responsible for this?" From the official point of view, even natural disasters like earthquakes, drought and floods, must be the responsibility of specific individuals. (YH, p. 99–100)

Thus we arrive at the *third fundamental law*: For every disaster, a guilty person outside the leadership can be found. In one sense, this attitude can be found in every age. As Veyne notes, the ruler is the source of the good but not responsible for the bad, even if he is sometimes deposed if it rains too much during his reign. In Ibansk, however, nobody really believes in these attributions. The second and third laws do not reflect the spontaneous attitude of the people, but are simply the principles on which bureaucratic promotion is based or denied. The regime takes credit for all the good it is incapable of doing, and washes its hands of the evil which is all it can achieve.

A literal reading of Zinoviev's work will only engender frustration and irritation in the reader. To appreciate him, one has to enter into his spirit, take him on his own terms and suspend disbelief. One may then find, as I did, that the exuberantly grotesque details add up to a coherent pattern, which I have tried to spell out in this chapter. Whether the more lasting value of his work will be found in the vision of totalitarian regimes or in the insights into irrational processes that can be observed in any society, I have tried to show that it is richly rewarding in both respects.

3

TOCQUEVILLE'S PSYCHOLOGY I

A generation ago it would have seemed absurd to see Tocqueville as the greatest political thinker of the nineteenth century. Nowadays, there is nothing unusual in this view. Nevertheless, not all who agree on this judgment will necessarily accept my reasons for holding it. To my way of thinking, it is not possible to extract general and wide-ranging theories from his work; or perhaps I should say that whatever such theories we can find are not very interesting. In his writings, the details are of greater interest than the whole, the reasoning is more compelling than the conclusions, and the partial mechanisms more robust than the general theories. In arguing for this evaluation, I shall proceed to a close reading of the texts with a view to singling out the *topoi*, *Gestalten* or patterns of his thought – causal mechanisms or mechanism-generating frameworks that remain remarkably fertile and novel, one hundred and fifty years after they were first formulated. I shall focus on his analysis of psychological mechanisms, leaving the analysis of more aggregate processes for another occasion.[1]

Tocqueville mastered three different levels of analysis with a success that has never been equalled. In *Democracy in America*, the framework is that of equilibrium analysis. Here, Tocqueville aims at depicting democratic institutions and the psychology of democratic citizens as they can be observed when "democratic society is finally firmly established (*assise*)" (DA, p. 628). In *The*

This chapter and the following are heavily indebted to collaborative work with Stephen Holmes over the last ten years or so, which will, we hope, one day emerge as a book.
1 Elster (1991a) offers a preliminary analysis of this aspect of Tocqueville's thought.

Old Regime the subject is long-term change, the process of transition that leads from one equilibrium to another. In the *Recollections*, finally, he deals with short-term "histoire événementielle." At all three levels the building blocks of the explanations are the same, viz. psychological mechanisms that revolve around desires, beliefs and actions. In the short term, motivations and attitudes are treated as given and so to speak fixed for the purposes of analysis.[2] The desires and beliefs offer an explanation of human action without being explained themselves. In the long term, and in equilibrium, they require explanation, and they do in fact receive one. I shall focus on the equilibrium analyses of *Democracy in America*. Democratic institutions are shown to generate beliefs and aspirations that, in turn, support those same institutions. Although Tocqueville points to some possible sources of instability in democratic societies, his central assumption is very clearly that the America he had observed around 1830 was in stable equilibrium.

It might appear anachronistic to impute the concept of an equilibrium state of society to Tocqueville. Yet I believe this is what he has in mind when he uses the word *assiette* (or the corresponding verb "assis") in contexts such as "assiette tranquille et définitive" (DA, p. 216) or "assiette naturelle et permanente."[3] In one passage (DA, p. 226) he uses the phrase "état naturel" to express the same idea. I shall not try to provide an adequate discussion of what is involved in an equilibrium state of society, as Tocqueville's views on the topic are complex and somewhat confused. In particular, as we shall see, he did not fully understand the notion of circular causality. A brief definition could be that a society is in equilibrium when the attitudes – beliefs and aspirations – generated by its institutions support both the latter and each other.

---

2 I am simplifying. In his *Recollections*, Tocqueville shows that the beliefs and aspirations of political actors are constantly modified by events. But those modifications are ephemeral changes, not to be confused with the slow and lasting transformation of popular mentality.

3 Tocqueville (1968), p. 166.

This chapter and the following will deal with Tocqueville's "psychology," a term that will be understood, however, in two very different ways. In this chapter I discuss Tocqueville's own psychology – his emotional and intellectual makeup. I shall focus on the qualities that come across in his writings rather than on the details of his biography. One may perhaps argue, following André Jardin, that Tocqueville was basically a spoilt child who failed as a politician because he was overambitious.[4] From that point of view, his self-portraits in the *Recollections* are doubly revealing, since he is both the artist and the subject. But my concern is to paint a picture of the writer rather than of the politician or the private man, and the details of that portrait emerge most clearly when he is writing about something other than himself. More specifically, I want to present the psychology of the author of *Democracy in America*, for it is in that book that his prejudices and contradictions are most clearly visible. It is a young man's book, written with a young man's pride and irrepressible exuberance. Later he managed to discipline himself, even in the *Recollections*, which he offered to the reader as a spontaneous and artless work.

In the next chapter I shall examine the psychological theories that Tocqueville proposed and used, or rather the repertory of psychological *mechanisms* he established. For a general discussion of the idea of a mechanism the reader is referred to the Introduction; specific Tocquevillian mechanisms are examined in Chapter 4. Here I want to point out that the discussion later in this chapter of Tocqueville's tendency to contradict himself on a number of major points is also part of the groundwork for my claim that he is worth studying for his partial insights rather than for his general theories.

A SPECIMEN OF TOCQUEVILLE'S REASONING

Any portrait of Tocqueville as a writer must begin with his exceptional intellectual brilliance. I hope that for readers not

4 Jardin (1984), pp. 43, 289.

already acquainted with his writings, the cumulative impact of the analyses discussed in the next chapter will be enough to convince them of this fact. However, before I proceed to the somewhat negative evaluations that form the core of the present chapter, I want to offer a specimen of Tocqueville at (what I think is) his very best, viz. the virtuoso performance in *Democracy in America* where he considers the apparent failure of marriages for love. I am under no illusion that these passages will create in the reader's mind the almost unbearable excitement that I felt on reading them for the first time; intellectual chemistry is too idiosyncratic for any such effect to be reproduced in the same form. Nevertheless, I hope the reader will agree that it is only in the very greatest authors that we find individual analyses with such a potential for general application. Anyone can spend his life constructing a comprehensive general theory, which will soon be refuted or outdated. The gift of setting out, in a few lines, a precise, novel and fertile causal analysis is far rarer.

Tocqueville starts with the following observation:

> Our ancestors conceived a singular opinion with regard to
> marriage. As they had noticed that the few love matches
> which took place in their days almost always ended in
> tragedy, they came to the firm conclusion that in such matters
> it was very dangerous to rely on one's own heart. They
> thought that chance saw clearer than choice. (DA, p. 597)

He then proceeds to give a number of arguments to question the logic of this inference. First he observes that in this case as in many others, the ills of democracy can be cured by more democracy. "A democratic education is necessary to protect women against the dangers with which the institutions and mores of democracy surround them" (DA, p. 592). If women in democracies were uneducated, love marriages would be disastrous – as they are in effect when they occur in aristocracies. Since, however, the education of women is itself an endogenous effect of democracy, this danger does not arise. The tendency for democracy to compensate or neutralize its own excesses is a constant *topos* in *Democracy in America*; further examples are provided in the next chapter.[5] There is also another constant motif that takes the opposite tack. To correct the excesses of democracy one must impose constraints that are essentially foreign to its nature – such as bicameral government, indirect elections, the protection of individual rights, the respect for forms, an independent judiciary, and the like. Because they indicate possibilities rather than necessities, the two *topoi* do not contradict each other; Tocqueville offers a repertory of democracy-stabilizing mechanisms, not a theory of democracy.

Also, in democracies women have the "time to know" (DA, p. 597) their future husbands, whereas in aristocracies women are kept so cloistered that they have no occasion to form an opinion about them. The fact that marrying for love is disastrous in societies that allow women neither the ability nor the opportunity to judge does not entitle us to infer that the same effect will be produced in democracies.

Tocqueville shows that the inference rests on a further fallacy. Suppose that in an aristocratic society two young, well-educated and well-acquainted people make a love match. By going against the current they will tend to encounter the hostility of their friends and relatives, a situation that "soon wears down their courage and embitters their heart." (DA, p. 597). In a society in which this practice was general, this effect would not arise.

Finally, he points to another mechanism that explains why we cannot generalize from exceptional cases to the general case. For a man to marry for love in societies in which this practice is uncommon he must have "something of violence and adventure in his character, and people of this type, whatever direction they take, seldom achieve happiness or virtue" (DA, p. 596). And one might add that a marriage of *two* people of this disposition is even less likely to be happy.

The last two arguments are quite remarkable. Each of them amounts to a refutation of the fallacy of composition, that is, the belief that whatever is true at the margin will remain true

5 See also Elster (1991a).

when generalized to all cases.[6] The first rests on a causal aftereffect: The fact of going against the current generates a causal process that ultimately changes the individuals and makes them unhappy. The second, by contrast, rests on a sampling effect: Only those individuals who are destined to become unhappy in any case are likely to go against the current in the first place. The distinction is of fundamental importance for the interpretation of social processes.[7] Tocqueville, characteristically, does not make much of it. It is embedded in the flow of the discussion, and it is left to the reader to appreciate its explanatory potential.

In each of the arguments, individual psychology is invoked both as the cause and the effect of aggregate social phenomena. The first states that the impact of democracy on women tends to stabilize democratic marriages, the second that the impact of democracy on the relations between unmarried men and women have the same effect, the third that an aristocratic environment tends to destabilize marriages, and the fourth that in an aristocratic environment only unstable persons will be attracted by this form of marriage. This is the general pattern of Tocqueville's analyses: to understand aggregate patterns by individual psychology and vice versa.

Tocqueville's various observations of this kind tend to be made in passing. Rather than stressing their potential for general applicability, he leaves the reader to reflect on them for himself. That is the main reason why reading him is so intellectually

6 For an analysis of this fallacy see Elster (1978), pp. 97ff.
7 For the general distinction between aftereffects and sampling effects see Feller (1968), pp. 199ff. For an application, consider the problem of unemployment. One knows that the longer the time an individual has already been without work, the smaller the chances that he will find work again. This fact can be explained by invoking an aftereffect: Being out of work changes the individual (or the employer's perception of him) so as to make him less employable. One may also appeal to a sampling effect: Those who are naturally less employable tend for that reason both to be unemployed for longer periods and to have greater difficulties in finding work. (For details, see Elster 1988.) Rates of social mobility (Boudon 1973) or length of stay in mental hospitals (Gullestad and Tschudi 1982) can also be understood according to both models.

exciting. He offers us a succession – there must be literally hundreds of them in *Democracy in America* – of short, quasidescriptive arguments that are so lucid, profound, and surprising in their logical structure that any other author would have trumpeted them from the rooftops. One is tempted to think that he knew very well what he was doing, but that the historian's or the aristocrat's arrogance led him to hide the scaffolding that supports the narrative.

TOCQUEVILLE'S PREJUDICES

In the remainder of this chapter I shall consider the two main defects in Tocqueville's thinking. On the one hand, *Democracy in America* and to a lesser extent his other writings abound with prejudices and moral clichés that sometimes hinder the progression of his thinking. On the other hand, that book (and much less the other writings) is chock-full of the most glaring contradictions, often on points of crucial importance. The prejudices are glaringly obvious, but ultimately they turn out to be fairly unimportant. The opposite is true of the flaws in his reasoning. Tracing the swarm of inconsistencies is painstaking work, but once they have been discovered they determine the whole way in which we then read him.

In Tocqueville's mental universe there are three things for which he feels spontaneous respect and affection: aristocracy, monarchy, and masculinity. His attitude is most unambiguously positive in the last case. Although his admiration for kings and nobles can sometimes lead him into absurd pieties, he is also capable of taking an uncompromisingly realistic view of their behavior. By contrast, his innumerable references to the "male and virile" virtues are not counterbalanced in his writings by any criticism of male domination or questioning of female submission.

Let us begin by juxtaposing two passages from *Democracy in America*. "When kings feel their people's heart drawn toward them, they are merciful because they know they are strong; and they cultivate their subjects' love, for that is the bulwark of the throne" (DA, p. 313). This is clearly an idyllicizing and romanticizing text. Although it does not go as far as to say that kings act out of love for their subjects, it does suggest the idea of a mutually beneficial social contract. Elsewhere, however, Tocqueville makes a more realistic and brutal observation:

> It is vain to object that the people's interest properly
> understood should lead it to be careful with the fortunes of
> the wealthy, because it is bound at no long delay to feel the
> effects of the trouble it has caused. Is it not also the interest of
> kings to make their subjects happy and of nobles to know
> when to open their ranks? If remote advantages could prevail
> over the passions and needs of the moment, there would have
> been no tyrannical sovereigns or exclusive aristocracies.
> (DA, p. 210)[8]

His attitude toward the nobility is similarly ambiguous. In his considered moments, he asserts that the good of the greatest number is more important than the excellence of the few: "It is natural to suppose that not the particular prosperity of the few, but the greater well-being of all, is most pleasing in the sight of the Creator and Preserver of men. . . . Equality may be less elevated, but it is more just" (DA, p. 704). The manners of the aristocracy may embellish virtue and even appear as a substitute for virtue, but this appearance is an illusion (DA, p. 608). But when Tocqueville is following his natural bent, he expresses himself in a different way:

> Nothing in the world is so fixed as an aristocracy. The mass of
> the people may be seduced by its ignorance or its passions; a
> king may be taken off his guard and induced to vacillate in
> his plans; and moreover, a king is not immortal. But an

---

8 Or again, "If from the beginning of the world nations and kings had kept nothing but their real advantage in view, we should hardly know what war between men was" (DA, p. 383). This is an exaggeration. Open conflict – wars or strikes – often have their origin in the "blind" and "unreflecting" passions that Tocqueville opposes to rational self-interest. But even perfect rationality on both sides may give rise to conflict, mainly for reasons related to the presence of asymmetric information.

aristocratic body is too numerous to be caught, and yet so
small that it does not easily yield to the intoxication of
thoughtless passion. An aristocratic body is a firm and
enlightened man who never dies. (DA, p. 230)

One would think he had never heard of a body of divided
aristocrats. And are aristocracies really enlightened? Do they
not rather follow blindly unreflecting prejudices and codes of
honor? It is probably true that aristocracies have enduring opinions
that change very slowly, but that does not imply that they behave
with an eye to the distant future. Rather, any calculating attitude
is viewed as dishonorable.

Another sentimental text on the nobility is the following: "The
nobles, placed so high above the people, could take the calm
and benevolent interest in their welfare which a shepherd takes
in his flock" (DA, p. 13). But he is also capable of a sharp realism
about the class to which he belonged:

When the chroniclers of the Middle Ages, who were all by
birth or assimilation aristocrats, relate the tragic end of a
noble, there is no end to their grief; but they mention all in a
breath and without wincing massacres and tortures of the
common people. That is not because these writers entertained
a habitual hatred or systematic contempt for the common
people. War between the different classes in the state had not
yet been declared. They obeyed an instinct rather than a
passion; as they did not form a clear idea of the sufferings
of the poor, they took but a feeble interest in their fate.
(DA, p. 562)

The above are scattered dicta on kings and nobles, without
any common theme except for the tension between Tocqueville's
class prejudices and the more reflective views he expresses as a
democrat and an historian. A more systematic tension arises in
his variations on a theme that plays an important part in his
thinking, that of *voluntary servitude*. His attitude toward the phenomenon is ambiguous, for while he detests any kind of servitude,
he respects any kind of voluntary commitment. Because of his
inborn prejudices, the ambiguity is resolved differently in the

four cases I shall consider: slavery, political associations, monarchy, and marriage.

I begin with two examples where his evaluation clearly is negative. In his analysis of slavery in the United States, he notes that "the Negro . . . admires his tyrants even more than he hates them and finds his joy and pride in a servile imitation of his oppressors" (DA, p. 317), and asks whether he should "call it a blessing of God, or a last malediction of His anger, this disposition of the soul that makes men insensible to extreme misery and often even gives them a sort of depraved taste for the cause of their afflictions" (DA, p. 317). There is no doubt that he is offering the second answer.

Elsewhere he speaks of the life of political associations in Europe:

> Members of these associations answer to a word of command like soldiers on active service; they profess the dogma of passive obedience, or rather, by the single act of uniting, have made a complete sacrifice of their judgment and free will; hence within associations there often prevails a tyranny more intolerant than that exercised over society in the name of the government they attack. This greatly diminishes their moral strength. They lose the sacred character belonging to the struggle of the oppressed against the oppressor. For how can a man claim that he wants to be free when in certain cases he consents servilely to obey some of his fellow men, yielding up his will and submitting his very thoughts to them?
> (DA, p. 195)

In two other cases Tocqueville refers to voluntary servitude in positive terms. One refers to the relationship between kings and their subjects: "Some nations have taken a kind of pleasure and pride in sacrificing their wills to that of the prince, and by this means introducing a sort of independence of mind into the very heart of obedience" (DA, p. 257). Or again, "There was a time under the old monarchy when the French experienced a sort of joy in surrendering themselves irrevocably to the arbitrary will of their monarch" (DA, p. 235).[9]

9 See, however, the passage in Tocqueville (1953), p. 331, cited in note 36 to Chapter 1.

A similar kind of reasoning is used to glorify and justify women's submission to men in marriage: "One may say that it is the very enjoyment of freedom that has given [the American woman] the courage to sacrifice it without struggle or complaint when the time has come for that" (DA, p. 593). Or again, "I have never found American women regarding conjugal authority as a blessed usurpation of their rights or feeling that they degraded themselves by submitting to it. On the contrary, they seem to take pride in the free relinquishment of their will, and it is their boast to bear the yoke themselves rather than to escape from it" (DA, p. 602).

It is hard to escape the conclusion that some ideological or affective bias is at work in these passages. With different political inclinations, he might have praised the abdication of personal will on the part of revolutionaries in a Jacobinist party, or denounced the idea that the king's subject or married women take pride in sacrificing theirs. Or he might have taken a more analytical approach, distinguishing between adaptive preferences and character planning (see the Introduction); or between (conscious or unconscious) adaptation to unavoidable submission and a rational decision to accept an avoidable submission[10]; or, in the case of political parties or religious sects, between rational submission and submission caused by the need to fill a social void or to reduce a painful state of doubt and uncertainty. These are exactly the kinds of distinction and nuance at which Tocqueville usually excels. If, in the cases I have cited, his usual perspicacity is blunted, an explanation in terms of bias and prejudice seems at least plausible.

Prejudice must be distinguished from self-deception. In his *Recollections*, Tocqueville claims that, unlike other politicians, he is incapable of deceiving himself:

> They are often accused of acting without conviction; but my experience goes to show that this is much less frequent than is supposed. It is just that they have a faculty, which is precious and indeed sometimes necessary in politics, of creating

10 For the latter idea, see Elster (1985a), ch. 7.1.4.

ephemeral convictions in accordance with the feelings and interests of the moment; and in this way they can with a tolerably good conscience do things that are far from honest. Unluckily I have never been able to illuminate my mind with such peculiar and contrived lights, or to persuade myself so easily that my advantage and the general weal conformed.[11]

But adopting passing convictions for one's own ends is not the only kind of bad faith. Another is to allow one's interpretation of events to be based on biased preconceptions. As a noble, Tocqueville was too prejudiced to see the prejudices of the nobles. This fact is entirely natural and unremarkable. What *is* remarkable, is that most of the time he managed to rid himself of clichés, stereotypes and prejudices, and to adopt realistic, even brutally realistic views about his own class. The only case in which he seems to be completely and consistently the prisoner of prejudice is when he refers to women. Writing of George Sand, he says that he detests women writers,[12] probably because he found them "noisily proclaiming the rights of women while stamping the most hallowed duties under foot" (DA, p. 602). Apart from this one exception, however, his instinctive and emotional reactions are usually well under control. They serve as raw material for his analyses without dominating them.

TOCQUEVILLE'S CONTRADICTIONS

This most striking aspect of *Democracy in America* is, as I said, the intoxicating energy of its ideas. Once the effect of that first shock has worn off, however, there is another to come, viz. the realization of just how many ambiguities and even flagrant contradictions the book contains. There is no point beating about the bush: There is no other great thinker who contradicts himself so often and on such central questions. With a somewhat artificial precision that ought not to be taken too seriously, I shall list *six varieties of contradictions* occurring in Tocqueville. Some are easily

11 Tocqueville (1970), p. 84.
12 Ibid., p. 134.

excused, and others at least explicable, but there remain a fair number of brute contradictions that merely seem to reflect a lack of concern for consistency. Each individual paragraph or chapter is polished in the extreme, but he took no similar care in ensuring the coherence of the work as a whole.

The most interesting of these contradictions may be seen as a result of the tendency of going to the extremes discussed in Chapter 1 above. Whenever Tocqueville observes an interesting causal pattern or mechanism, he tends to blow it up into a lawlike proposition. From an ingenious and powerful observation that some A are B, he concludes for instance that all A are B. Some pages or chapters later, an equally fruitful observation that some A are C is turned into the proposition that all A are C. But if B and C are mutually exclusive, these general propositions are inconsistent with each other. In such cases we should adopt the hermeneutic guideline of offering a decoding principle that will allow us to retain what is valuable in his analyses, while discarding what is excessive and exaggerated.

(1) The first category of contradictions are those that obtain between the two volumes of *Democracy in America*. In the second volume, published five years after the first, Tocqueville often returns to a thesis he has propounded in the first, to restate it, complete it – or contradict it. He provides, for instance, two distinct accounts of the attitude toward bankruptcies in the United States. In the first volume, he observes that "There is no American legislation against fraudulent bankruptcies. Is that because there are no bankrupts? No, on the contrary, it is because there are many. In the mind of the majority the fear of being prosecuted as a bankrupt is greater than the apprehension of being ruined by other bankrupts" (DA, p. 224). In the second, "the reason for the altogether singular indulgence shown in the United States toward a trader who goes bankrupt" is said to be that boldness, with the concomitant risk of failure, is essential for the "rapid progress, power and greatness" of the Americans (DA, p. 622). The first analysis suggests the idea of rational choice behind the veil of ignorance. The second implies rather a functionalist ex-

planation (see Chapter 4): any society will adopt the norms and attitudes that encourage its prosperity. Although not exactly contradictory, the two arguments are of very different character.

A second example is closer to outright contradiction. In the first volume, Tocqueville offers an account of the lack of educated Americans that is more striking than convincing: "In America most rich men began by being poor; almost all men of leisure were busy in their youth; as a result, at the age when one might have a taste for study, one has not the time; and when time is available, the taste of gone" (DA, p. 55). The structure of this argument will concern us in Ch. 4 below. Here I simply want to point out the contrast with a more sober passage from the second volume: "Free democratic societies will . . . always include a number of people who are rich or comfortably off. . . . These persons will not be strictly tied to the drudgery of practical life, and they will be able, in different degrees of course, to devote themselves to the labors and pleasures of the mind" (DA, p. 457). And he goes on to say that they will in fact indulge in these pleasures.

An even more outright contradiction between the two volumes occurs in his discussions of the great number of newspapers in the United States. In the first volume, the following explanation is offered: "In the United States printers need no licenses, and newspapers no stamps or registration; moreover, the system of giving securities is unknown. For these reasons it is a simple and easy matter to start a newspaper; a few subscribers are enough to cover expenses, so the number of periodical or semi-periodical productions in the United States surpasses all belief" (DA, p. 184). In the second, this explanation is explicitly rejected: "It is generally believed in France and in England that to abolish the taxes weighing down the press would be enough to increase the number of newspapers indefinitely. That greatly exaggerates the effect of such a reform. Newspapers do not multiply simply because they are cheap, but according to the more or less frequent need felt by a great number of people to communicate with one another and to act together." (DA, p. 519)

Now, it is quite normal for a writer to contradict himself on relatively minor issues when he returns to them after a lapse of five years. What is more surprising is that Tocqueville seems to be unaware that he is doing so. Perhaps his pride prevented him from pointing out to his readers that he had changed his mind. However, a more parsimonious explanation – that he simply did not notice – is supported by the fact that he also, and abundantly, managed to contradict himself within one and the same volume.

(2) A second class of contradictions are those that stem from his tendency to confuse what is specifically American and what is specifically democratic. I am not claiming that he was unaware of this distinction. On the contrary, it rivals in importance the distinction between the social phenomena that are the effect of the state of equality and those that are the effect of the process of equalization.[13] He notes, for instance, that "In America conscription is unknown; men are induced to enlist for pay. Compulsory recruitment is so contrary to the conceptions and alien to the habits of the people of the United States that I doubt whether anyone would ever dare to bring in such a law" (DA, p. 222). Elsewhere (DA, p. 651) he argues that "democratic societies are . . . soon led to give up voluntary recruitment and fall back on conscription." The explanation is simple: America is one of the few countries that can afford a relatively small army, since its geographical situation means that it has no enemies. There is not a shadow of a contradiction there. The statement about democratic societies holds only *ceteris paribus*. The exceptional situation of the United States ensures that other things are not equal.

Other passages are more ambiguous. In the second volume, the reader often has the impression that Tocqueville shifts imperceptibly from observations about America to general statements hardly relevant to the United States and apparently more applicable to France, a country which is seldom named but always

13 See Elster (1991a).

present. In the second volume Tocqueville often implies that in France we can observe democracy in its pure state (or on its way toward that state) – a society dominated by the obsessive quest for equality that can only be satisfied in shared subjection. American democracy is exceptional in that it is based on local government and a multitude of intermediate bodies which work against the leveling process and encourage freedom and participation. The second volume should, therefore, simply have been called *On Democracy*, which would have left him free to start from other conditions than those peculiar to the United States. Instead, although it clearly hampered his thinking, he kept the conceptual framework of the first volume.

We can see the confusion at work in the chapter "Why there are so many men of ambitions in the United States but so few men of lofty ambition." His answer is that democratic men are impatient and shortsighted: "Another impediment making it far from easy for men of democratic ages to launch on great ambitions is the length of time that must elapse before they are in a position to undertake any such matter." (DA, p. 629) Or again, "They see a multitude of little intermediate obstacles, all of which have to be negotiated slowly between them and the great object of their ultimate desires. The very anticipation of this prospect tires ambition and discourages it" (DA, p. 630–1). Given the title of the chapter, these observations are evidently offered as valid for *Americans*, not just for citizens in democratic societies. However, in the earlier chapters on enlightened self-interest he claims that by virtue of this motivation, the Americans are less subject to myopia than other peoples: Although it "does not inspire great sacrifices . . . every day it prompts some small ones" (DA, p. 527). An individual thus motivated "habitually and effortlessly sacrifices the pleasure of the moment for the lasting interest of his whole life" (DA, p. 529). To disentangle the mess we only have to read "democratic society" for "America" when he refers to myopia as if it were especially characteristic of the Americans, and understand the reference to America more literally in the earlier chapters where he explicitly exempts them from this flaw.

116

A similar decoding principle can be used to make sense of another, doubly confused passage from the chapter on ambitions:

> From hatred of privilege and embarrassment in choosing, all men, whatever their capacities, are finally forced through the same sieve, and all without discrimination are made to pass a host of petty preliminary tests, wasting their youth and suffocating their imagination. So they come to despair of ever fully enjoying the good things proffered, and when at last they reach a position in which they could do something out of the ordinary, the taste for it has left them. In China, where equality has for a very long time been carried to great lengths, no man graduates from one public office to another without passing an examination. He has to face this test at every stage of his career, and the idea is now so deeply rooted in the manners of the people that I remember reading a Chinese novel in which the hero, after many ups and downs, succeeds at last in touching his mistress' heart by passing an examination well. Lofty ambitions can hardly breathe in such an atmosphere. (DA, p. 630)

Let us disregard Tocqueville's absurd views on Chinese equality, which do not really affect his argument, and focus on the no less laughable idea that Americans are exhausted by the need to take a mass of competitive examinations and tests. In the first place, this text contradicts the passages (DA, p. 91n., p. 464) that draw a sharp contrast between China and the United States. In the second place, however, we need not worry too much about the confusion, which can be eliminated by the simple decoding principle of reading "French" for "democratic" and sometimes even for "American." Tocqueville's real target in this passage is the French civil service and its mandarins, although the general framework of the book forced him to couch his criticism in this inappropriate language.

(3) From a methodological point of view, a third type of contradiction is more interesting. It takes the form of asserting that A causes both B and C, which are mutually incompatible. In the three examples I shall discuss he asserts that democracy gives rise to independence *and* conformism, to pride *and* submission, to belief *and* doubt.

117

The second volume of *Democracy in America* opens with the statement that "in most mental operations each American relies on individual effort and judgment. So, of all countries in the world, America is the one where the precepts of Descartes are least studied and best followed" (DA, p. 429). And he goes on to explain how this methodical independence of mind is a direct consequence of equality. In the next chapter, however, Tocqueville takes a very different tack: "The nearer men are to a common level of uniformity, the less inclined they are to believe blindly in any man or any class. But they are readier to trust the mass, and public opinion becomes more and more mistress of the world. Not only is public opinion the only guide left to aid private judgment, but its power is infinitely greater in democracies than elsewhere" (DA, p. 435).

Later, he uses a similar argument to explain how equality leads man in two opposite directions. On the one hand, "he is full of confidence and pride in his independence among his equals," but on the other "he ends by regarding [the state] as the sole and necessary support of his individual weakness" (DA, p. 672). The passage obviously refers to France rather than to America, with the state now substituting for public opinion as the crutches that support the individual.

In much the same way, democracy is said to create religion and doubt at the same time. On the one hand, "men who live in times of equality find it hard to place the intellectual authority to which they submit, beyond and outside humanity. . . . One can anticipate that democratic peoples will not easily believe in divine missions, that they will be quick to laugh at new prophets, and that they will wish to find the chief arbiter of their beliefs within, and not beyond, the limits of their kind" (DA, p. 435). On the other hand we may quote the striking passage, further discussed in the next chapter, where he says that "For my part, I doubt whether man can support complete religious independence and entire political liberty at the same time. I am led to think that if he has no faith he must obey, and if he is free he must believe" (DA, p. 444).

There are several ways of reading these passages. On the one hand, we may see them as expressing tendencies or, in my language, mechanisms. Tocqueville himself asserts, in the context of the second passage cited above, that the conditions of equality "give the citizen of a democracy extremely contradictory instincts" (DA, p. 672). Similarly, anticipating on the next chapter, one might conjecture that the spillover effect would create a tendency for democratic citizens to be irreligious, whereas the compensation effect would lead them in the opposite direction. On the other hand, it is sometimes hard to resist a less charitable interpretation. In the opening chapters of the second volume, Tocqueville really seems to be saying that democratic men are independent to the core *and* conformist to the core, and *not* that some are independent and others conformist; or that they are sometimes independent and sometimes conformist; or that they are torn between their tendency to think for themselves and their tendency to lean on others. Similarly, he seems to say both that there are more believers and that there are fewer believers in democracies than elsewhere.[14]

But it should be evident from what I have said so far that this question really does not matter. We read Tocqueville (or at least I read him) for his acute insight into psychological patterns, such as the spillover effect, the compensation effect and other mechanisms identified in the next chapter. I believe that sometimes his joy of identifying the mechanism at work misled him into thinking that it had a more universal application than it really has. In such cases, we must simply use one of the decoding principles suggested above. When he says that all A are B and that all A are C, we should take him to say that some A are B and some A are C, or that A's are sometimes B and sometimes C, or that A's are torn between B and C as opposite, conflicting tendencies. As was argued in Chapter 2, there is nothing con-

---

14 I should add that Tocqueville's views on religion are very complex and that I do not claim to have done them justice here. However, I defy any reader of *Democracy in America* to come up with a clear answer to the question of whether or not democracy turns men into believers.

tradictory in asserting the presence in one individual of two contradictory tendencies (e.g., desires). What is contradictory, is to say that both can be realized.

(4) A further type of contradiction is the following. In a given passage, Tocqueville will tell us that A is *the* cause of C, not, that is, simply *a* cause, but the main one. In another he states just as categorically that B is the cause of C. Sometimes, he also says that A and B are themselves the effects of a common cause D, such as democracy or equality.

Here is an example. In his analysis of the effects of the freedom of the press Tocqueville offers two different explanations of the tenacity with which the citizens of democratic societies stick to their opinion. The first goes as follows:

> Once the American people have got an idea into their head, be it correct or unreasonable, nothing is harder than to get it out again. The same can be noticed in England, which for a century has been the European country with the greatest freedom of thought and with the most invincible prejudices. I think this is due to that very fact that at first glance one would have thought bound to prevent it, namely the freedom of the press. People enjoying that freedom become attached to their opinions as much from pride as from conviction. They love them because they think them correct, but also because they have chosen them; and they stick to them, not only as something true but also as something of their own. (DA, p. 186)

A page further on he comes up with a different story:

> It has been noted that in ages of religious fervor men sometimes changed their beliefs, whereas in skeptical centuries each man held obstinately to his own faith. In politics the same thing happens under the reign of a free press. All social theories having been contested and opposed in turn, people who fixed on one of them stick to it, not because they are sure it is good but because they are not sure there is a better one. (DA, p. 187)[15]

---

15 An explanation of the same kind is offered in the second volume: "[D]emocratic nations have neither leisure nor taste to think out new opinions. Even when

In these passages Tocqueville suggests first a "hot" and then a "cold" mechanism. In the first case, opinions are held out of pride, in the second out of inertia, for want of anything better. Firmness of belief (C) is seen as having its cause both in an invincible prejudice (A) and in a Cartesian rule of prudence (B). But once again we can propose a decoding principle. Instead of taking A as *the* cause of C we can take it as *a* cause of B or as *sometimes* causing B. In the example just given, the second reading is preferable. Although Tocqueville is not, as we shall see in Chapter 4, averse to multifactorial explanations, he uses them only when he can show the precise mechanism that dovetails the causes at work.

(5) I shall now consider the type of contradiction that arises from the conjunction of two propositions: "A is the cause of B. B is also the cause of A."[16] The most important (and most complex) example concerns the relationship between the social state of equality, laws, and mores. In the title of one chapter, mores are explicitly said to be more important than the laws: "The laws contribute more to the maintenance of the democratic republic in the United States than do the physical circumstances of the country, and mores do more than the laws" (DA, p. 305). Toward the end of the chapter he asserts that mores are supremely important (and not just more important than laws): "The importance of mores is a universal truth to which study and experience continually bring us back. I find it occupies the central position in my thought; all my ideas come back to it in the end" (DA, p. 308). Now, saying that A is more important than B could mean several things. On the one hand it could mean that A offers an explanation of B, typically through being a cause of B. On the other hand it could mean that A explains more phenomena or more important phenomena than B, or contributes

they are doubtful about accepted ideas they still stick to them because it would take too much time to examine and change them" (DA, p. 643).

16 In the next chapter I also consider cases in which Tocqueville asserts both that "A tends to produce B" and "B tends to undermine A." Although infrequent in *Democracy in America*, such destabilizing mechanisms have pride of place in *The Old Regime*.

more powerfully to the explanation of the phenomena jointly caused by A and B. Whichever of these ways we choose to understand it, the idea that mores are more important than laws is incompatible with a number of other passages that I shall now cite.

Tocqueville mentions that "More than once in this work I have tried to point out the prodigious influence which, I believe, the social state exercises over laws and mores" (DA, p. 328). Or consider the opening sentence of the second volume: "The Americans have a democratic social order which naturally suggested to them certain laws and certain political mores."[17] But if laws and mores are both the effects of a common cause, one can hardly claim that mores are fundamental. One may still claim, perhaps, that they are more important than laws. That claim, however, is hard to reconcile with passages in which laws are said to shape the mores. Such is the case with the legal institution of slavery, which "explains the mores and the social state of the South" (DA, p. 35: translation slightly modified).[18] By giving priority to the social state over the laws, this passage also goes against the two passages cited at the beginning of this paragraph. Another assertion of this priority comes in the important discussion of the effect of inheritance laws: "I am surprised that ancient and modern writers have not attributed greater importance to the laws of inheritance and their effect on the progress of human affairs. They are, it is true, civil laws, but they should head the list of all political institutions, for they have an unbelievable influence on the social state of peoples" (DA, p. 51).

17 "Les Américains ont un état social démocratique qui leur a naturellement suggéré de certaines lois et de certaines moeurs politiques." In the translation that I have been using, this sentence is mistranslated in a way that reverses the direction of the causal chain: "The democratic social order in America springs naturally from some of their laws and conceptions of public morality" (DA, p. 417).
18 See Chapter 4 below for a fuller discussion of the ways in which the institution of slavery shapes the mores of the South.

In these passages, then, we have seen Tocqueville asserting (1) the priority of mores over all other causes, (2) the priority of mores over laws, (3) the priority of the social state over laws and mores, (4) the priority of laws over mores, and (5) the priority of laws over the social state. Although some of the passages assert a general priority and others simply the priority in special cases, the overall impression they leave (at least on me) is one of sheer muddle. However, we can dispel the confusion by a simple decoding principle, replacing two or more statements that stipulate causal chains working in different directions by a single statement about mutual causality. In equilibrium, social conditions, legal institutions, and customs support each other mutually. However, it then becomes pointless to discuss which is the more important.

Let me now consider some more specific examples. One glaring case can be found in the discussion of slavery. On the one hand, Tocqueville asserts, in a passage already quoted, that the slave "finds his joy and pride in a servile imitation of his oppressors" (DA, p. 317). Slavery, in other words, causes servility. On the other hand, we find him comparing the two oppressed races in America in the following terms: "The Negro would like to mingle with the European and he cannot. The Indian might to some extent succeed in that, but he scorns to attempt it. The servility of the former delivers him into slavery; the pride of the latter leads him to death" (DA, p. 320). Servility, in other words, causes slavery. Charitably interpreted, the two passages need not contradict each other. We can read them simply as saying that slavery generates mental attitudes in the slaves that tend to stabilize the institution. (A more literal and less charitable interpretation might, however, read the second passage as saying that servility *creates* slavery rather than stabilizing it once it has arisen from other causes.)

A more complex set of examples arise from Tocqueville's anatomy of social life. Roughly speaking, he saw society as comprising four distinct spheres: family life, economic life, political life, and religion. Like Hegel and Marx, he tried to analyze the causal connections among these spheres. Unlike them, however, he insisted on psychological links rather than functional ones. His full repertory of psychological mechanisms will be discussed in the next chapter. Here I shall restrict myself to a mechanism that I have briefly mentioned above, the *spillover effect*. When a particular mental habit has been established in one of the four spheres, it sometimes spills over into one of the others.

We often find Tocqueville arguing for spillover effects in both directions. Consider first the relationship between family life and political life. On the one hand, he tells us that "Whereas the European tries to escape his sorrows at home by troubling society, the American derives from his home that love of order which he carries over into affairs of state" (DA, p. 291–2). On the other hand, we read that "in Europe, we often carry the ideas and habits of private life into public life. . . . But the Americans almost always carry the habits of public life over into their private lives" (DA, p. 305). A similar bi-directional relationship obtains between economics and politics. On the one hand, "The passions that stir the Americans most deeply are commercial and not political ones, or rather they carry a trader's habits over into the business of politics" (DA, p. 285). On the other hand, "politics spread a general habit and taste for association" (DA, p. 521) that spills over into civil life and helps people to associate for economic purposes.

A more complex relationship obtains between religion and civil life. First, Tocqueville states that "Religions instill a general habit of behaving with the future in view. In this respect they work as much in favor of happiness in this world as of felicity in the next" (DA, p. 547). Second, he stipulates the opposite relationship:

> I do not see . . . any plain reason why the doctrine of self-interest properly understood should drive men away from religious beliefs, but rather do I see how to unravel the ways in which it brings them close thereto. Let us start from the assumption that in order to gain happiness in this world a

man resists all his instinctive impulses and deliberately calculates every action of his life, that instead of yielding blindly to the first onrush of his passions he has learned the art of fighting them, and that he habitually and effortlessly sacrifices the pleasure of the moment for the lasting interests of his whole life. If such a man believes in the religion that he professes, it will hardly cost him anything to submit to such restrictions as it imposes. Reason itself advises him to do so, and habits already formed make it easy. (DA, p. 529)

Thirdly, Tocqueville tells us a little story that would show us how to combine the two mechanisms. If religion loses its grip on the minds of men, we will see them "wholly renouncing whatever cannot be acquired without protracted effort" (DA, p. 548). If, however, the leading men in democracies govern wisely, striving in particular "to banish chance, as much as possible, from the world of politics" (DA, p. 549), they can "give men back that interest in the future which neither religion nor social conditions any longer inspire" (DA, p. 549), a love from which religion may again arise in the fullness of time: "Once men have become accustomed to foresee from afar what is likely to befall them in this world and to feed upon hopes, they can hardly keep their thoughts always confined within the precise limits of this life and will always be ready to break out through these limits and consider what is beyond" (DA, p. 549).

The passages that I have contrasted with each other are not so much contradictory as confused and confusing. The reason, it seems to me, is that Tocqueville almost but not fully grasped the idea of reciprocal causality. When two phenomena are linked by bi-directional causal links, he usually focuses on one link at a time, giving the impression that he is dealing with the impact of an independent variable on a dependent one. The reader is then easily thrown off track when in some other passage the role of the variables is reversed. However, once we see what is going on we can simply take the final step that Tocqueville did not take for himself. The only statements that cannot be salvaged in this way are those imputing greater causal significance to some phenomena than to others. It is possible for A to cause B and for B to cause A; but not for A to be more important than B and for B to be more important than A.

(6) I conclude with some examples of what one may call *brute contradictions*, taken rather randomly from *Democracy in America*. Others are cited in the next chapter. Some of them are relatively trivial, whereas others have a central place in the argument. However, the most important fact is their overall impact on our understanding of Tocqueville. They reinforce the need for a disaggregated reading of the texts and, by the same token, tend to undermine any interpretation that seeks to present Tocqueville as a coherent theorist of democracy.

Were the first immigrants rich or poor?

On the one hand, Tocqueville tells us that "all [the] new colonies contained the germ, if not the full growth, of a complete democracy. There were two reasons for this; one may say, speaking generally, that when the immigrants left their motherlands they had no idea of any superiority of some over others. It is not the happy and powerful who go into exile; and poverty with misfortune is the best-known guarantee of equality among men" (DA, p. 33). A few pages later, however, we read that "all the immigrants who came to settle on the shores of New England belonged to the well-to-do classes at home" (DA, p. 35).

Is the grip of religion on Americans strong or weak?

On the one hand, we read that "One may suppose that a certain number of Americans, in the worship they offer to God, are following their habits rather than their convictions. Besides, in the United States the sovereign authority is religious, and consequently hypocrisy should be common. Nonetheless, America is still the place where the Christian religion has kept the greatest power over men's souls" (DA, p. 291). On the other hand, he also says that "The majority in the United States takes over the business of supplying the individual with a quantity of ready-made opinions and so relieves him of the necessity of forming his own. So there are many theories of philosophy, morality, and politics which everyone adopts unexamined on the faith of public opinion. And if one looks very closely into the matter, one finds that religion is strong less as a revealed doctrine than as a part of common opinion" (DA, p. 435–6). Now, these two passages may not yield an outright contradiction. It is possible that habitual belief is even more common in other countries than in the United States. I find it hard to believe, however, that this is what Tocqueville had in mind.

Do Americans understand the link between
national wealth and individual prosperity?

On the one hand, we read that "The common man in the United States has understood the influence of the general prosperity on his own happiness, an idea so simple but nevertheless so little understood by the people. Moreover, he is accustomed to regard that prosperity as his own work. So he sees the public fortune as his own, and he works for the good of the state, not only from duty or from pride, but, I dare almost say, from greed" (DA, p. 237). Elsewhere, however, he explicitly denies that the American identifies his fate with that of the country: "It is difficult to force a man out of himself and get him to take an interest in the affairs of the whole state, for he has little understanding of the way in which the fate of the state can influence his own lot" (DA, p. 511).

Can the central government execute its own laws?

On the one hand, Tocqueville asserts that the feature that dis-tinguishes the American federation from all earlier ones is that "The Americans . . . agreed not only that the federal government should dictate the laws but that it should itself see to their execution" (DA, p. 156). On the other hand, we read that the

127

commands of "the central government have to be carried out by agents who often do not depend on it" (DA, p. 262–3).

Does patriotism extend only to the states or to the whole country?

On the one hand we read that "it is that same republican spirit, those same mores and habits of liberty, which, having come to birth and grown in the various states, are then applied without any trouble in the nation as a whole. . . . Every citizen in the United States may be said to transfer the concern inspired in him by his little republic into his love of the common motherland" (DA, p. 162). Or again, for a slightly different argument to the same conclusion: "The inhabitants of democracies love their country after the same fashion as they love themselves, and what is habitual in their private vanity is carried over into national pride" (DA, p. 613). On the other hand, we read that American patriotism stops at the state border. American legislators "give the Union money and soldiers, but the states retained the love and the prejudices of the peoples "(DA, p. 166). Or again, "Patriotism, which is most often nothing but an extension of individual egoism, . . . remains attached to the state and has not yet, so to say, been passed on to the Union" (DA, p. 367). Note that three of these four passages invoke the spillover effect.[19] Tocqueville first tells us that love of the state spills over into love of the Union; then that self-interest or vanity spills over into love of the Union; and finally that self-interest spills over into love of the state, but not into love of the Union as a whole.

Is instinctive or reflective patriotism to be preferred?

On the one hand, Tocqueville is skeptical towards the kind of patriotism that is grounded in reason: "I confess that I have no

19 The first two passages use the verb "transporter," which is usually employed to denote this effect.

great confidence in that calculated patriotism which is founded on interest and which a change of interest may destroy" (DA, p. 373). But he also draws a contrast between "instinctive patriotism" and "another sort of patriotism more rational than that; less generous, perhaps less ardent, but more creative and more lasting, it is engendered by enlightenment, grows by the aid of laws and the exercise of rights, and in the end becomes, in a sense, mingled with personal interest" (DA, p. 235).

Does democracy predispose for or against Catholicism?

On the one hand, Tocqueville asserts that "Our contemporaries are naturally little disposed to belief, but once they accept religion at all, there is a hidden instinct within them which unconsciously urges them toward Catholicism" (DA, p. 450). On the other hand, he claims that "even when equality does not bring religions crashing down, it simplifies them and turns attention away from secondary beings to concentrate it chiefly on the Supreme Being" (DA, p. 483). But isn't Catholicism precisely the religion in which secondary beings such as angels and saints proliferate? In arguments such as these we recognize the spirit of Marx, who stressed some aspects of mercantilism to bring out its natural affinity with Catholicism and others to argue for its special links with Protestantism.[20] There may be some truth in Tocqueville's principle, that "The spirit of man, left to follow its own bent, will regulate political society and the City of God in uniform fashion; it will, if I dare put it so, seek to *harmonize* earth with heaven" (DA, p. 287). There are, however, so many different ways of harmonizing heaven and earth and, in choosing a religion, so many more important reasons than the desire for harmony, that it is more plausible to think that the harmony comes after the event, to consolidate a choice that has already been made or imposed on other grounds (Chapter 1).

20 See Elster (1985a), pp. 504–10.

129

Are the citizens of democratic societies selfish or altruistic?

On the one hand, Tocqueville asserts that there is no altruism in democratic societies, in which the individual turns to the state for the "outside help which he cannot expect from any of his fellows, for they are both impotent and cold" (DA, p. 672). On the other hand, however, he argues that democracy promotes altruism and mutual assistance. Having first observed that in Europe one often finds members of the same profession helping each other in times of need, he adds that there exists "between all the citizens of a democracy an understanding analogous to that which I have described. They all know themselves weak and subject to like dangers, and interest as well as sympathy prompts a code of lending each other mutual assistance at need" (DA, p. 572). In Chapter 4 below the idea of self-interested altruism is further discussed. Here, however, we should note the assertion that the mutual help also springs from "sympathy," in clear contradiction to the statement that democratic citizens are "cold."

Are there classes in the United States?

First, we read that in America "poor men have few means of escaping from their condition and becoming rich, but the rich are constantly becoming poor or retiring from business when they have realized their profits. Hence the elements forming the poor class are more or less fixed, but that is not true of those forming the rich class. To be exact, although there are rich men, a class of the rich does not exist at all, for these rich men have neither corporate spirit nor objects in common, neither common traditions nor hopes" (DA, p. 557). Next, "one may almost say there are no more classes, and such as do still exist are composed of such changing elements that they can never, as a body, exercise real power over their members" (DA, p. 430). Finally, "As one must be very rich to embark on the great industrial undertakings of which I speak, the number of those engaged in them is very small. Being very few, they can easily league together and fix the rate of wages that pleases them" (DA, p. 583). Do American industrialists have class consciousness? The first two passages give a negative answer; the third a positive one. Can social classes have a high turnover rate? The first passage gives a negative answer; the following offers a positive one: "When conditions are almost equal, men are continually changing places. There is still a class of valets and a class of masters, but they are not forever composed of the same individuals, and more especially, not of the same families" (DA, p. 576).

Is industry or agriculture most congenital with risk taking?

In one set of passages Tocqueville opposes agriculture to industry as risk aversion to risk taking. "To cultivate the ground promises an almost certain reward for his efforts, but a slow one. In that way you only grow rich little by little and with toil. Agriculture only suits the wealthy, who already have a great superfluity, or the poor, who only want to live" (DA, p. 552). The typical American being neither very rich nor very poor (DA, p. 635), "His choice is made; he sells his field, moves from his house and takes up some risky but lucrative profession" (DA, p. 552). Hence democracy gives men "a distaste for agriculture and directs them into trade and industry" (ibid.). In fact, for the Americans "industry appears as a vast lottery" (DA, p. 622). In another set of passages, the contrast is reversed. The Americans "like order, without which affairs do not prosper" (DA, p. 285). More to the point, industry "cannot prosper without exceedingly regular habits and the performance of a long succession of small uniform motions" (DA, p. 615). Moreover, the love of risk is now said to characterize the agricultural settlers rather than the industrial entrepreneur: "To start with, emigration was a necessity for them; now it is a sort of gamble, and they enjoy the sensations as much as the profit" (DA, p. 283).

Do Americans talk poetry or prose?

Tocqueville draws two very different portraits of the American national character. On the one hand, there are many passages that suggest an emotionally limited and almost subhuman people without any generous passions or grand longings. The American nation "is, most assuredly, the coldest, most calculating, the least militaristic; and if one may put it so, the most prosaic in all the world" (DA, p. 278). Or again, "There is nothing more petty, insipid, crowded with paltry interests – in one word an- tipoetic – than the daily life of an American" (DA, p. 485). And finally, "The ever-increasing number of men of property devoted to peace, the growth of personal property which war so rapidly devours, mildness of mores, gentleness of heart, that inclination to pity which equality inspires, that cold and calculating spirit which leaves little room for sensitivity to the poetic and violent emotions of wartime – all these causes act together to damp down warlike fervor" (DA, p. 646).

On the other hand, there are passages that suggest a recklessness and restlessness that is at the opposite end of the emotional spectrum. For the American settlers, the "desire for well-being has become a restless, burning passion which increases with satisfaction" (DA, p. 283). In even stronger terms:

> The universal movement prevailing in the United States, the frequent reversals of fortune, and the unexpected shifts in public and private wealth all unite to keep the mind in a sort of feverish agitation which wonderfully disposes it towards every type of exertion and keeps it, so to say, above the common level of humanity. For an American the whole of life is treated like a game of chance, a time of revolution, or the day of a battle. (DA, p. 404)

In fact, "it is hard to give an impression of the avidity with which the American throws himself on the vast prey offered him by fortune. To pursue it he fearlessly braves the arrows of the Indian and the diseases of the wilderness; he goes prepared to face the silence of the forest and is not afraid of the presence of wild beasts. A passion stronger than love of life goads him on" (DA, p. 283). And finally, "Chance is an element always present to the mind of those who live in the unstable conditions of a democracy, and in the end they come to love enterprises in which chance plays a part. This draws them to trade not only for the sake of promised gain, but also because they love the emotions it provides" (DA, p. 553).

It will probably be objected that the contradiction is intentional, and that Tocqueville is deliberately painting a picture of a paradoxical creature who can be hot and cold at the same time. Referring to the Americans on the right bank of the Ohio, he does in fact say that there is "a sort of heroism in his greed for gain" (DA, p. 347) and, talking about the Americans more generally, that they "put something heroic into their way of trading" (DA, p. 403). Energetically spoken prose, it would seem, amounts to a kind of poetry. The contradiction, if there is one, lies in the object under consideration – the racked and tormented citizen of democracy – and not in the analysis itself. In fact, if anyone is guilty of a fallacy it is myself rather than Tocqueville: by reading into him the contradictions of his subject matter I am committing a kind of converse of the pathetic fallacy.

To counter this objection, let me first repeat that I am not at all averse to admitting the idea of contradictory mental attitudes, which I have discussed at length in Chapters 1 and 2 above and elsewhere.[21] But *even contradictions must have a structure* to be intelligible. To juxtapose the statements "Americans are passionate" and "Americans lack all passion" is not to offer a profound analysis of the paradoxes of democracy, but to talk nonsense. At least, such statements are nonsensical if taken literally. I have tried at various places in this chapter to suggest decoding principles that may help us make good – even if more modest – sense out of such apparently inconsistent assertions. In the present case, it seems clear that Tocqueville is not in fact describing *the* national

21 See notably ch. 4 of Elster (1978).

character of the Americans or of democratic citizens, but simply two different types of personality – the one coldly and patiently calculating, the other recklessly and restlessly flamboyant – who may, albeit for different reasons, have strong affinities with the institutions of an industrial democracy.

This being said, I do not claim that all the inconsistencies I have identified in Tocqueville will survive further scrutiny. Of the thirty or so contradictions cited above, others to be quoted in the next chapter, and yet more omitted to avoid boring the reader, some will no doubt turn out to be factitious. It is quite possible that my fascination with the Tocquevillian contradictions has led me, in some cases, to forget the principle of charity that should, as a rule, govern textual interpretation. Others may find vagueness or ambiguity where I have discerned outright contradiction. However, even charity has its limits. In cases where only a very heavy exegetical superstructure can render the texts consistent with each other, I have preferred parsimony over charity. My hope is that even the readers who disagree with my interpretation of this or that passage, will be converted, by the cumulative impact of the analyses, to my central claim: no other thinker of Tocqueville's status comes anywhere near him as far as the number and centrality of internal contradictions are concerned.

Suppose that my claim is granted. What can we conclude about Tocqueville's psychology as a writer? It is hard to avoid seeing him as irresponsible, undisciplined, perhaps, indeed, as a kind of spoilt child. The universe he creates is to some extent a dream world in which reality barely offers any resistance to thought and almost any connection among phenomena can be defended because everything is a little bit like everything else. His search for dramatic, epigrammatic and striking expressions led him to generalizations that are often absurd or hyperbolic taken individually and inconsistent taken collectively. For anyone hoping to find in Tocqueville the theorist of modern democracy, this is obviously bad news.

The news is less discouraging for someone who, like myself, does not believe in the possibility of creating a general theory of modern democracy or of democratic citizens. As I argued in the Introduction, our psychological and sociological knowledge does not enable us to do more than to draw up a list of *mechanisms*, that is, of causal patterns that are sufficiently precise and general to allow us to subsume apparently different events under the same heading. Properly read, Tocqueville can be immensely helpful in this task. The substantive argument for that statement is offered in the next chapter. Here I only want to conclude on a Tocquevillian note, by suggesting that his achievements might have been fewer had he set himself more modest aims. Without the ambition to create a general theory of democracy, he would perhaps have been unable to muster the will power and energy that enabled him to produce so many passages of genius. If he failed in politics through excessive ambition, it was quite possibly the same excess that ensured his success as a writer.[22]

22 This conclusion can be supported by the reasoning in note 52 to Chapter 1. Schematically, let us suppose that real achievements are a function of the time and energy spent on them, which are in turn a function of expected achievements. If achievements are measured on a scale from 0 to 10, an individual with a level of aspiration of 8 might then score 6, whereas another with equal ability hoping to score 6 might only manage 4. Only the modest and realistic person hoping to score 2 would actually achieve his aim. Elsewhere (Elster 1985b), I have referred to this dilemma between realism and achievement as "the Karl Marx problem" because I believe it captures an important aspect of his mind. But I might equally well have named it after Tocqueville.

4

TOCQUEVILLE'S PSYCHOLOGY II

IN the last chapter I said that the basic building blocks of Tocqueville's analyses are the mechanisms of individual psychology. He was, in other words, a practitioner of methodological individualism. Of the great nineteenth-century thinkers, only John Stuart Mill and Tocqueville managed to avoid the pitfalls of an organicist and teleological position, by insisting resolutely on the need for microfoundations in the analysis of institutions and social processes.[1] Needless to say, Tocqueville did not limit himself to the study of individual psychology. In saying that the psychological mechanisms are the basic building blocks I clearly implied that they serve to construct and explain something else. The explananda in the three major works are, as I remarked in Chapter 3, social equilibrium, long-term social mutations, and short-term social change.

In outline, the difference between the three works can be summarized as follows. In *Democracy in America*, Tocqueville offers an analysis of the social state of democracy, comparing it both to the aristocratic regime which preceded it and to the process of transition between one regime and the other. In that equilibrium, everything – mental attitudes no less than institutions – is endogenous and, moreover, interlinked and mutually reinforcing. In *The Old Regime* he also insists on the endogeneity of mental facts, but no longer assumes that they tend to perpetuate and maintain the institutions that produce them. Instead, he

1 This assertion may surprise the reader of the introduction to the first volume of *Democracy in America*. I believe, however, that a careful reading of the work as a whole will show that Tocqueville's main claim is that there can be no stable halfway house between hierarchy and equality, neither in the political nor in the social realm. For this argument see also Elster (1991a).

tries to exhibit the "perverse effects" by which institutions change mentalities in a way that ultimately undermines their own authority and efficacy.[2] In the *Recollections* he is also concerned with the unintended and destabilizing consequences of action, but in a quite different register. He demonstrates wonderfully the political dynamics by which overbidding and demagoguery induce false polarization or false consensus, as well as the ways in which myopia and lack of strategic thinking induce failures of rationality.[3]

Generally speaking, explanation in the social sciences proceeds at three levels.[4] At the level of "sub-intentional causality" we try to account for beliefs and desires in terms of reactions to the social environment as well as to other mental facts. At the intentional level, the goal is to explain behavior by means of given beliefs and desires, an important special case being that of rational-choice explanations. At the level of "supra-intentional causality," finally, we try to account for social institutions and social change as the aggregate outcome of many individual actions. Tocqueville offers a masterly performance at the first level: this is the object of the present chapter. He is equally and superlatively insightful at the third level, a specimen of which was offered in the previous chapter.[5] He has, however, comparatively little of interest to say at the second level. Compared with theories of rational action,[6] in particular, his views are both wider and more restricted. His

---

2 There are, however, two different readings of the work and notably of the "Tocqueville effect," which asserts that social frustration increases as conditions improve. The standard interpretation assumes, as I said in the text, that desires and aspirations grow faster than the means of satisfying them when people are liberated from their adaptive preferences. An alternative interpretation (Boudon 1982, ch. 7) is that even when desires remain constant, improved conditions may cause frustration because the number of those who rationally decide to invest in upward mobility grows faster than the number of positions they can aspire to.

3 See Holmes (1989).

4 See Elster (1983a) for a fuller account.

5 See Elster (1991a) for other examples.

6 For representative examples, see the essays by Becker and Harsanyi in Elster (1968).

approach is wider in that, unlike the vast majority of neoclassical economists, he claims to explain the formation of desires and not simply action on the basis of given desires. It is also more restricted in that he ignores the nuts and bolts of the transmission machinery that mediates between desire and action.

Let me show briefly why the explanation of action in terms of motivations is a nontrivial task. In the first place, we often have many reasons for doing things. Far from being homogeneous and simple, our motives have a complex internal structure. We can often see conflicts of interest between short-term and long-term gains: should we choose A or B when A offers an immediate return of 5 and a long-term reward of 3, and the corresponding numbers for B are 2 and 8? There may also be a conflict between maximizing average reward and minimizing the spread around the average: Should we choose A or B when A offers a 50 percent chance of getting 5 and a 50 percent chance of getting 3, while the corresponding numbers for B are 2 and 8? Conflicts may also arise in trading off personal reward against the reward of others, or, within the former, in choosing among wealth, power and prestige. In the second place, rational action often requires the ability to anticipate the rational behavior of others who are simultaneously trying to anticipate ours. We can even engage in such strategic actions with regard to ourselves, in anticipating and frustrating likely future choices that we might make. The complexity and interplay of these intrapersonal and interpersonal conflicts create severe problems for the theory of rational action, sometimes to the point of indeterminacy.[7]

Yet such calibrations of interest, whether within the actor or across actors, are of little interest to Tocqueville. On the one hand he tends to see the individual as dominated and even consumed by a single desire. Below I note some exceptions to this statement, but I believe it to be at least roughly valid. On the other hand, he tends to see individuals as incapable of strategic action and anticipation. In the *Recollections*, politicians are con-

7 Elster (1989d), ch. I.

stantly being caught in the traps they have set for their rivals because it did not occur to them that these others might not accept events passively. Tocqueville alone, among the actors on the political stage, is seen as capable of making strategic use of the vanity of others, as when he offers symbolic concessions in return for substantial gains.[8] Now, I do not think Tocqueville was entirely wrong on this point. Theorists of rational choice certainly exaggerate, and sometimes *ad absurdum*, when they present us with a picture of *homo economicus* or *politicus* who remains optimizing and calculating even in his most intimate and passionate activities, such as marriage, suicide, drug taking or church going.[9] However, Tocqueville goes too far in the opposite direction when he implicitly denies the ability for deliberation, anticipation and decision. It *is* hard to keep the two images of man in one's mind at the same time – as a rational creature capable of reflection and choice and as the passive plaything of causal forces that operate "behind his back" – but it is precisely the need to juggle these two visions that give the social sciences their specific nature.

TOCQUEVILLE'S ANATOMY OF THE MIND

In this chapter I shall try to achieve three aims. The first is to offer a *catalogue raisonné* of the motivations that Tocqueville finds underlying human behavior. Although the aim is largely typological, I also try to make some substantive points. The second is to discuss Tocqueville's pathbreaking analyses of the interaction among desires and opportunities in the explanation of human behavior.[10] The final goal is to spell out his analyses of intrapsychic

8 Tocqueville (1970), p. 215.
9 Becker (1976) is the outstanding exponent of this approach. The role of Becker and his school in the social sciences is best summarized in one of William Blake's *Proverbs of Hell*: "You never know what is enough unless you know what is more than enough."
10 To my knowledge, the only study of this fundamental mechanism (or mechanism-generating framework) is that of White (1987), chs. 9–10. However, even White's analysis disregards the relations of correlation or causation that can obtain between desires and opportunities.

causality, with special emphasis on the three mechanisms that I call the spillover, compensation and crowding-out effects. It probably goes without saying that most of the claims I shall make are the product of a reconstruction, as Tocqueville himself certainly does not present these mechanisms in anything like a systematic way. For readers whose primary interest lies in the interpretation of Tocqueville my reading may be a bit too much on the reconstructive side. For other readers, however, and even for the historian of thought, the intrinsic interest of the arguments I impute to Tocqueville may, or at least so I hope, offset any exegetical deficit or surplus in my analysis.

Tocqueville offers a social psychology which, however, goes much beyond what is usually referred to by that name today. It is more akin to what in Chapter 1 above I called philosophical anthropology, a study of psychological universals that can suggest precise explanatory mechanisms in a variety of historical situations. Now, for Tocqueville psychological universals are not a matter of immutable desires and beliefs present at all times and places. Rather, as we shall see, they consist of *permanent possibilities*, of mechanism that can be activated anytime or anywhere by triggers that are much less well understood than those mechanisms themselves.

We may begin by noting, however, that Tocqueville was not totally averse to unconditionally general statements. He asserts, for instance, that "Alone among all created beings, man shows a natural disgust for existence and an immense longing to exist; he scorns life and fears annihilation. These different instincts constantly drive his soul toward contemplation of the next world, and it is religion that leads him thither" (DA, p. 296). But that rather insipid observation, reminiscent of Pascal but without his vigour, is infinitely less interesting than the analyses of specific forms of religion (and irreligion). In another would-be universal proposition we are told that "With lawyers, as with all men, it is particular interest, especially the interest of the moment, which prevails" (DA, p. 264). Disregarding the fact (Chapter 3) that two of these allegedly universal tendencies – religion and myopia – actually work against each other, I simply want to observe that it is more interesting to read what Tocqueville has to say about altruism in democratic societies or about "self-interest rightly understood" than about the universal tendency for short-term self-interest to dominate. More generally, we learn less from what he has to say about man's "natural bent" than from his discussion of the causes that work against that bent – or reinforce it.

Nor should we look for psychological universals in the aphorisms scattered throughout his work. Here are a few typical examples of the latter:

> For apart from hating one's enemies, what is more natural to man than flattering them? (DA, p. 179)

> It has been noticed that a man in imminent danger hardly ever remains at his normal level; he rises above or falls below it. (DA, p. 199)

> Such deviations . . . attest the inferiority of our nature, which, unable to hold firmly to what is true and just, is generally reduced to choosing between two excesses. (DA, p. 43)

> A great man has said that *ignorance lies at both ends of knowledge*. Perhaps it would have been truer to say that deep convictions lie at the two ends, with doubt in the middle. (DA, pp. 186–7)

Even if striking, such aphorisms do not amount to a psychological theory. They suggest plausible mechanisms without any connotation of determinism or inevitability. However, even as mechanisms they are at a low level of generality. In the later subsections of this chapter I discuss a number of mechanisms capable of much wider application because they fall into what I have called *mechanism-generating frameworks*. Before proceeding to physiology (to say nothing about pathology), however, I shall say a few words about Tocqueville's anatomy of the mind.

Tocqueville's vocabulary in describing human motivations is very rich and varied. The terms "interest" and "passion" are used constantly, as they were by the eighteenth-century môr-alists.[11] Their meaning in his writings is further discussed below. More specifically Tocquevillian is the use of the word "taste," sometimes as synonymous with "desire," sometimes in the sense of habit, instinct, or inclination. An example of his terminology can be found in a lapidary summary of his theory of the coun-terweights to individualism: "At first it is of necessity that men attend to the public interest, afterward by choice. What had been calculation becomes instinct. By dint of working for the good of his fellow citizens, he in the end acquires a habit and taste for serving them" (DA, p. 512–13). Most of these nouns are used to denote such varied things that it is hard to see any systematic purpose behind the terminology. I certainly have not found one.

What we need to grasp, behind the fluctuations of language, is that in addition to passions and interests there are *propensities*, relatively weak and sometimes barely conscious motivations which direct behavior except when opposed by one of the two stronger motives.[12] I shall adduce three examples to show that in Tocqueville's view such propensities generally have a non-decisive effect on behavior. He observes that "It is not that peoples with a democratic social state naturally scorn freedom; on the contrary they have an instinctive taste for it. But freedom is not the chief and continual object of their desires; it is equality for which they feel an eternal love" (DA, p. 57). In the long term, a taste for liberty cannot overcome the passion for equality.[13] Also, he notes that "If their tastes naturally draw lawyers toward the aristocracy and the prince, their interest as naturally pulls them toward the people" (DA, p. 266). The shared interest is seen as more powerful than the "natural affinity" (DA, p. 265) of tastes: "I have no intention of saying that these natural in-

11 Hirschman (1977); Holmes (1989).
12 These propensities may be related to what Bourdieu (1979) calls "habitus," except for their relatively subordinate place among the motivations.
13 In *The Old Regime*, the taste for liberty is elevated into a "passion" (Tocqueville 1955, pp. 209–10), but is still said to be "superficial and short-lived" compared with the "obstinate and blind" passion for equality.

clinations of lawyers are strong enough to bind them in any irresistible fashion. With lawyers, as with all men, it is particular interest, especially the interest of the moment, which prevails" (DA, p. 264). Finally, "the excessive taste for general political theories which is prompted by equality" (DA, p. 442) is overridden by material interests: "Merchants eagerly grasp all philosophic generalizations presented to them without looking closely into them, and the same is true about politics, science, and the arts. But only after examination will they accept those concerning trade, and even then they do so with reserve" (ibid.).

It seems reasonable, therefore, to identify interests and passions as the most important elements among the motivations mentioned so far, not necessarily because they influence more, or more important, actions but because they are the more decisive whenever they come into conflict with the propensities and habits of everyday life.[14] I shall soon discuss the all-important question of what happens when an interest and a passion are in conflict. Later, I shall also consider a third type of motivation just as important as passions and interests, namely *social norms*. Although Tocqueville does not refer to them by that name, he discusses them at some length in two chapters of *Democracy of America* to which I shall return. First, however, I shall take a closer look at the concept of self-interest in Tocqueville.

Tocqueville observes that in the transition period between the old regime and the new democracy "The poor have kept most of the prejudices of their fathers without their beliefs, their ignorance without their virtues; they accept the doctrine of self-interest as motive for action without understanding that doctrine; and their egotism is now as unenlightened as their devotion was formerly" (DA, p. 15–16). The Americans, by contrast, have adopted the doctrine of self-interest properly understood, which enables them to see, for instance, that "sacrifice [for one's fellows] is as necessary for the man who makes it as for the

14 Compare also the remark by Veyne quoted in Chapter 1: People do only what they have no interest in not doing.

beneficiaries" (DA, p. 525). One ought to "work for the good of all" (ibid.), through cooperation, mutual help and small sacrifices, because in the long run one ends up as beneficiary, an observation already made by Montaigne (cited by Tocqueville) and by Descartes (not cited).[15] Tocqueville does not even try to explain, however, *why* enlightened self-interest requires us to work for the good of others. Although he speaks of a "convention" (translated as "understanding" in DA, p. 572) of mutual help, it cannot be in the sense in which there is a convention to drive on the right side of the road. Conventions of the latter sort are self-sustaining, whereas a rule of mutual help would be vulnerable to free riding. Although Tocqueville in other passages shows himself to be aware of the fact that collective benefits are insufficient to generate (and explain) individual cooperation,[16] his analysis of why individuals would find it in their long-term interest to help each other seems to rest on this fallacious inference.[17]

A sacrifice for the sake of others means to give up some short-term interest. The converse implication does not hold, however. Even if a person were quite alone, like Robinson Crusoe on his

15 Descartes (1875–90), vol. IV, p. 34.
16 "When an individual is actually positively harmed by an administrative offense, it is assumed that personal interest will be sure to make him lodge a complaint. But it is easy to foresee that in the case of some legal regulation that, although useful to society, has not the sort of usefulness an individual can actually feel, each man will hesitate to stand up as the accuser" (DA, pp. 79–80). Or again, "Democratic ages are times of experiment, innovation, and adventure. There are always a lot of men engaged in some difficult or new undertaking which they pursue apart, unencumbered by assistants. Such men will freely admit the general principle that the power of the state should not interfere in private affairs, but as an exception, each one of them wants the state to help in the special matter with which he is preoccupied, and he wants to lead the government on to take action in his domain, though he would like to restrict it in every other direction" (DA, p. 672 n.). By contrast, he did not understand that the utility of religion for the maintenance of public order (DA, p. 530) hardly constitutes a reason for individual adherence to religion.
17 Descartes's argument is that those who help others are likely to receive help in return. For elaborations of this idea, see Axelrod (1984) and Taylor (1987).

island, there would still be a conflict between the demands of immediate advantage and those of delayed gratification. Is Robinson to spend his life catching fish by hand or go without food for a few days while he weaves a net? The logic of "one step backwards, two steps foward" – to consume less today in order to consume more tomorrow – is universally applicable.[18] It is, I believe, the essence of "self-interest properly understood." As is clear from Tocqueville's discussion, the concept has both a motivational and a cognitive component. One has to be motivated by long-term reward and not simply by immediate gain. And one has to understand that the path to long-term gains often requires indirect strategies of considerable subtlety.

Why might people act against their self-interest? There is a large repertoire of answers that I shall canvass in the following: ignorance, excess of will, myopia, inconstancy, lack of means, weakness of will, blindness, and self-deception. Of these, Tocqueville tends to rely mainly on blindness (or deafness) induced by passion, consistently with what I said earlier about his view of human motivations. But the other answers also seem worth while discussing, partly because they, too, are sometimes invoked by Tocqueville and partly because the fact that he does *not* give them can tell us something about the way his mind worked.

Sheer ignorance provides a deep-seated reason why the citizens of democratic societies will always tend to act against their self-interest. One aspect of the contrast between equality and liberty is that the material benefits derived from the latter, although more important than those derived from the former, are also later to make their appearance and thus harder to identify. "The good things that freedom brings are seen only as time passes, and it is always easy to mistake the cause that brought them about. The advantages of equality are felt immediately, and it is daily apparent where they come from" (DA, p. 505). Or again: "People passionately bent on physical pleasures usually observe how agitation in favor of liberty threatens prosperity before they appreciate how liberty helps to procure the same" (DA, p. 540). Although liberty, objectively speaking, is favored by enlightened self-interest, the insight needed for liberty to become part of *perceived* self-interest is difficult to achieve.

But there is more. Even if liberty was correctly identified as a vehicle for enlightened self-interest, it could never serve that end if that was all it was supposed to do. There is a brief and somewhat unfocused remark to this effect in *Democracy in America*, in the chapter on "How excessive love of prosperity can do harm to it" (DA, pp. 546–7). A more powerful and direct statement is found in *The Old Regime*:

> Nor do I think that a genuine love of freedom is ever quickened by the prospect of material rewards; indeed, that prospect is often dubious anyhow as regards the immediate future. True, in the long run freedom always brings to those who know how to retain it comfort and well-being, and often great prosperity. Nevertheless, for the moment it sometimes tells against amenities of this nature, and there are times, indeed, when despotism can best ensure a brief enjoyment of them. In fact, those who prize freedom only for the material benefits it offers have never kept it long.[19]

Because the benefits of freedom are essentially by-products of the love of freedom for its own sake, they are not within the scope of self-interest however enlightened. As with other cases of excess of will (Chapter 1), the attempt to promote self-interest works against that interest.

Brute myopia – the sheer preference for present pleasures over future ones – also provides a reason why people act against their self-interest. According to Tocqueville, democratic equality tends to reinforce the natural myopia of humankind: "One of the characteristics of democratic times is that all men have a taste for easy successes and immediate pleasures" (DA, p. 440). And he refers to the "secret means [by which] equality makes the passion for physical pleasures and an exclusive interest in

19 Tocqueville (1955), p. 168.

immediate delights predominate in the human heart" (DA, p. 631).[20] However, his more detailed analyses suggest a different and, to my mind, more profound view. His fundamental idea is not that democratic citizens are myopic, but that their desires are constantly changing:

> When everyone is constantly striving to change his position, when an immense field of competition is open to all, when wealth is amassed or dissipated in the shortest possible space of time in the turmoil of democracy, men think in terms of sudden and easy fortunes, of great possessions easily won and lost, and chance in every shape and form. Social instability favors the natural instability of desires. Amid all these perpetual fluctuations of fate the present looms large and hides the future, so that men do not want to think beyond tomorrow. (DA, p. 548)

Or again, "Add to this taste for prosperity a social state in which neither law nor custom holds anyone in one place, and that is a great further stimulus to this restlessness of temper. One will then find people continually changing path for fear of missing the shortest cut leading to happiness" (DA, p. 537). This vision of democratic life does not exclude that each successive desire can have a distant temporal horizon, with the citizens pursuing distant and constantly changing aims at each particular moment. This idea would be an application to desires of an argument that Tocqueville uses elsewhere in connection with beliefs: "for a long time [freedom of the press] does not disturb [the] habit of firm belief without reflection, but it does daily change the object of their implicit belief. The human mind con-

20 Elsewhere (DA, p. 537), Tocqueville attempts to derive the second effect of equality from the first: "It is . . . easy to understand that although those whose passions are bent on physical pleasures are eager in their desires, they are also easily discouraged. For as their ultimate object is enjoyment, the means to it must be prompt and easy, for otherwise the trouble of getting the pleasure would be greater than the pleasure when won." The argument is unpersuasive, as it neglects that the passage of time may increase the number of objects one can enjoy or the enjoyment derived from a given object. Even – in fact, especially – ardent wine lovers are willing to wait a long time before opening a vintage bottle.

tinues to discern only one point at a time on the whole intellectual horizon, but that point is constantly changing" (DA, p. 187).

We might wonder, however, whether this paradoxical state of affairs could continue to operate in a state of equilibrium. Would people not eventually come to recognize the fluctuations in their beliefs and desires? According to Tocqueville, this is indeed what happens in the cognitive sphere: "soon almost the whole range of new ideas has been canvassed. Experience plunges mankind into universal doubt and distrust" (DA, p. 187). In an important passage devoted to the shorter term of lease in democratic societies he states that a similar learning experience is observed with respect to desires:

> In the Middle Ages almost all land was leased in perpetuity, or at least for very long terms. When one studies the domestic economy of those times, one finds that leases of ninety-nine years were more common then than are leases of twelve years now. At that time people thought of families as immortal, conditions seemed fixed forever, and the whole of society appeared so stable that no one imagined that anything could ever stir within it. In times of equality thoughts take quite a different turn. It is easy to suppose that nothing stays still. The sense of instability is in the air. In such a mental climate landlord and tenant too feel a sort of instinctive terror of long-term obligations; they are afraid that one day they will be hampered by the agreement which at the moment profits them. They are vaguely conscious of a sudden and unexpected change in their condition. They are afraid of themselves, dreading that, their taste having changed, they will come to regret not being able to drop what once had formed the object of their lust. And they are right to feel this fear, for in ages of democracy all things are unstable, but the most unstable of all is the human heart. (DA, p. 582)

Even though one should not confound myopic desires and short-lived desires, the *anticipated* instability of desires might give rise to myopic behaviors. Why work for future benefits when experience teaches us that we may well no longer want them when we eventually have them? Similarly, why create something lasting when we know that it will soon be obsolete?

"I once met an American sailor and asked him why his country's ships are made so that they will not last long. He answered offhand that the art of navigation was making such quick progress that even the best of boats would be almost useless if it lasted more than a few years" (DA, p. 453).

Are such patterns of behavior contrary to self-interest? Wouldn't they rather seem to embody a prudent technique for minimizing frustration and regret? The fallacy behind this suggestion lies in the implicit assumption that change of desire is something that simply *happens* to one.[21] One can, however, plan one's behavior so as to make changes less likely and durable satisfaction within reach. Suppose that at the moment I am passionately interested in playing the violin. Should I start to learn it when it is quite possible that next year I might prefer the piano? Wouldn't it be better to buy some records of violin music that I could easily exchange for piano records later on? However, playing the piano and listening to piano records are very different activities. The former is an act of self-realization, the latter one of consumption.[22] The former tends to generate desires that stabilize it, the latter to give rise to destabilizing feelings of boredom and jadedness. Planning all one's activities as if they were a form of consumption would not, therefore, be in accordance with self-interest properly understood.[23]

Tocqueville also observes that "There is another reason which is bound to make the efforts of a democratic government less enduring than those of an aristocracy. The people not only see less clearly than the upper classes what can be hoped or feared for the future, but they also suffer the ills of the present in quite another way" (DA, p. 223). The idea is easily generalized. If the poor do not adopt indirect strategies – one step backward and two steps forward – it is not necessarily because they cannot

21 Some of the arguments in Parfit (1984) also seem to rest on this assumption.
22 Elster (1986b).
23 Needless to say, this paragraph is a reflection on Tocqueville, not an interpretation. It embodies a notion of character planning that is quite foreign to Tocqueville's rather mechanical psychology.

foresee the future or do not care about it. The reason may simply be that they cannot afford to take the one step backward that might put them at unacceptable risk. If Robinson Crusoe is so close to starvation that he cannot take time off to make a net, he is condemned to starve forever.

It is also possible to act against one's interest by weakness of will (see below for a definition and further discussion). This case, however, is not one that is given much prominence in Tocqueville. The only passage, to my knowledge, that invokes lack of will-power is the following:

> The majority, when it has had time to examine itself and to prove its standing, is the common source of every power. But even then the majority is not all-powerful. Humanity, justice, and reason stand above it in the moral order; and in the world of politics, acquired rights take precedence over it. The majority recognizes these limits, and if it does break through them, that is because, like any man, it has its passions and, like him, may do evil knowing what is good. (DA, p. 395–6)

But even here it is a matter of a conflict between passion and morality, not between short- and long-term interest. The reason why Tocqueville neglects this phenomenon has to do with his view of the role of the passions in human life, a topic to which I shall now turn.

First we need to clear up a verbal ambiguity. When referring to the passions, Tocqueville seems to use the word in two senses. Sometimes, it seems to indicate any very powerful desire, including those which constitute interests in the meaning of the term described above. Thus he often speaks of the *passion* for well-being and material enjoyment that characterizes the Americans (DA, pp. 283, 531, 537, 541, 663), notwithstanding his tendency to characterize the desire for well-being as their primary interest (DA, pp. 237, 527–8). In what follows I shall avoid this general sense of the term, and use only the more restricted one in which a passion is a desire that is not oriented towards any kind of advantage (personal or general) and can indeed divert men from the pursuit of their own interest.[24] To illustrate the idea, I shall consider the passion for equality in democratic societies.

In the previous chapter I quoted Tocqueville's observation that "If remote advantages could prevail over the passions and needs of the moment, there would have been no tyrannical sovereigns or exclusive aristocracies" (DA, p. 210). A more complete statement to the same effect is the following:

> One should not fancy that the states which are losing power
> are also losing population or fading away; there is no halt to
> their prosperity; they are even growing faster than any
> kingdom in Europe. But they feel that they are getting poor
> because they are not getting rich as quickly as their neighbors,
> and they think they are losing their power because they have
> suddenly come in contact with a power greater than theirs.
> So it is their feelings and passions that are wounded rather
> than their interests. But is not that enough to keep the
> confederation in danger? If from the beginning of the world
> nations and kings had kept nothing but their real advantage in
> view, we should hardly know what war between men was.
> (DA, pp. 382–3)

The theme of democratic *envy* that is struck up here is central to Tocqueville's analyses. Usually, of course, this passion is attributed to individuals rather than to states. The "democratic sentiment of envy" (DA, p. 310) incites people to act against their interest, and to "a debased taste for equality, which leads the weak to want to drag the strong down to their level and which induces men to prefer equality in servitude to inequality in freedom" (DA, p. 57). In a discussion of compulsory military service he observes that "it is the inequality of a burden, not its weight, which usually provokes resistance" (DA, p. 652). The consequences of the democratic passion for equality are described as follows:

> Democratic people always like equality, but there are times
> when their passion for it turns to delirium. This happens when

24 This sentence reflects the distinction between interest (the pursuit of personal advantage), reason (the pursuit of general advantage), and passion made in the Introduction.

the old social hierarchy, long menaced, finally collapses after a severe internal struggle and the barriers of rank are at length thrown down. At such times men pounce on equality as their booty and cling to it as a precious treasure they fear to have snatched away. The passion for equality seeps into every corner of the human heart, expands, and fills the whole. It is no use telling them that by this blind surrender to an exclusive passion they are compromising their dearest interests; they are deaf. It is no use pointing out that freedom is slipping from their grasp while they look the other way; they are blind, or rather they can see but one thing to covet in the whole world. (DA, p. 505)

Some of these passages suggest only weak envy: If I can't have it, nobody shall. Others suggest strong envy, cutting off one's nose to spite one's face.[25] It is only in the latter form that envy leads one to act against one's own interest. In particular, the democratic passion for equal well-being[26] can induce people to give up freedom, even though, as we have seen, freedom in the long run increases well-being. True, one reason people are willing to make this sacrifice may be that they do not understand the causal connection between freedom and well-being. The last-quoted passage, however, suggests that it is not merely a matter of intellectual deficit. The lack of insight has motivational roots in the "deafness" or "blindness" induced by equality.

As to the causes of envy, the central paradox is that "Men's hatred of privilege increases as privileges become rarer and less important, the flame of democratic passion apparently blazing the brighter the less fuel there is to feed it. . . . When conditions are unequal, no inequality, however great, offends the eye. But amid general uniformity, the slightest dissimilarity seems shocking, and the completer the uniformity, the more unbearable it seems"

---

25 For a discussion and further examples, see Elster (1991d).

26 It might seem tendentious and contentious to identify envy and the passion for equality. However, I have in mind the desire for equality per se, not the indirect desire for equality that follows from the primary desire to improve the condition of the worst off. Nor do I identify envy and the desire not to be taken advantage of (see Hirshleifer 1987 for this distinction).

(DA, pp. 672–3). This view – that envy increases with equality – can be understood in several ways. Is Tocqueville asserting that envy is negatively correlated with the income gap or that, for a given income gap, envy is negatively correlated to the overall amount of inequality in society? (Or does he hold both views, which are perfectly consistent with each other?) The second view can in turn be taken in two ways, as asserting that overall equality is either a cause of the envy function or an argument in it.[27]

It is clear, and not only from this example, that passions and interest can be in conflict. It is in my interest to tolerate religion because of its social utility, but my hatred for superstitious beliefs dictates a very different attitude (DA, p. 294). Refusing to fight a duel is dishonorable (DA, p. 585), although it is in my interest. In such cases, there are four elements – a desire for x that involves an interest, a desire for y that involves a passion and that is incompatible with x, the actor's judgment that one of the two desires is the stronger and ought to win out, and the fact that one of the desires is translated into action. We can then distinguish between four cases. (1) A judgment that interest should prevail over passion followed by an action based on interest. (2) A judgment that passion should prevail over interest followed by an action based on passion. (3) A judgment that interest should prevail over passion followed by an action based on passion. (4) A judgment that passion should prevail over interest followed by an action based on interest.

The first case needs no comments. Accepting a challenge to a duel may (depending on the case) be an instance of the second. The third and fourth cases involve weakness of will, in the sense of acting contrary to what, all things considered, one believes one ought to do.[28] Of these, the fourth might seem paradoxical, but on reflection there is nothing strange in the idea of akrasia

27 The distinction is analogous to that between conformism and altruism. In conformism, other people's behavior changes my preferences. In altruism, it affects the extent to which they are satisfied.
28 For analyses, see Davidson (1980), ch. 2, and Ainslie (1992).

as an obstacle to passion. Tocqueville provides a wonderful example in his 1835 sketch of French history before 1789:

> Not only were the nobles precluded from increasing or repairing their own fortunes by commerce and industry, but custom forbade them even to appropriate by marriage, wealth so acquired. A nobleman would have deemed himself degraded by an alliance with the daughter of a rich *roturier*. Nevertheless such unions were not uncommon among them; for their fortunes decreased more rapidly than their desires. These plebeian alliances, while they enriched certain members of the *noblesse*, put the finishing stroke to the ruin of that influence over opinion, which was the only power the body, as a body, retained.
>
> We must consider what are men's motives, before we applaud them for having elevated themselves above common prejudices. To judge of their conduct, we must place ourselves at their own point of view, and not at the point of view of abstract truth. To run counter to a common opinion because we believe it to be false, is noble and virtuous; but to despise a prejudice merely because it is inconvenient to ourselves, is nearly as dangerous to morality as to abandon a true principle for the same reason. The nobles were wrong in the first place, when they believed themselves degraded by marrying the daughters of *roturiers*. They were still more wrong in the second place, by marrying them under that persuasion.[29]

By contrast, one finds no example in Tocqueville of the more familiar third case. In his discussions of conflicts in which passion prevails over interest, the mechanism invoked is not that of weakness of will. As defined above, the latter phenomenon involves seeing the good but doing what is wrong. According to Tocqueville, however, what happens is simply that passion makes us forget or lose sight of interest. There is no judgment that one desire is more worthy on being acted upon than the other, nor even an awareness of the other desire. He constantly refers to the passions as "deaf," "blind," and "unreflective"; they are obsessions that blot out everything else. As I have said, this is an excessively mechanical view of human motivation. It rules

29 Tocqueville (1836), p. 42.

out not only the sort of conflict found in cases (1) to (4) above, but also cases in which passions and interest stand to each other as vectors in a parallelogram of forces, with the final action taken owing something to each.

To subvert interest the passions can also use another means, namely self-deception. Under their influence we are easily persuaded that what they urge us to do is not only compatible with but actually called for by our interest.[30] Perhaps a little bit of adultery is actually good for my marriage. My envious passion for equality may mask itself behind the idea that the more wealthy might use their fortune to oppress me.[31] To my knowledge, Tocqueville never refers to this kind of mechanism. By contrast, he offers vivid analyses of the converse pattern, in which passion adjusts to interest. In political arguments, nothing works better than genuine enthusiasm, hence a good politician must be able to enthuse about what also accords with his interest. In Chapter 3 I quoted the reference to "a faculty, which is precious and indeed sometimes necessary in politics, of creating ephemeral convictions in accordance with the feelings and interests of the moment." A more general analysis is the following:

> What I call great political parties are those more attached to principles than to consequences, to generalities rather than to particulars, to ideas rather than to personalities. Such parties generally have nobler features, more generous passions, more real convictions, and a bolder and more open look than others. Private interest, which always plays the greatest part in political passions, is there more skillfully concealed beneath the veil of public interest; sometimes it even passes unobserved by those whom it prompts and stirs to action. On the other hand, small parties are generally without political faith. As they are not elevated and sustained to lofty purposes, the selfishness of their character is openly displayed in all their actions. They glow with a factitious zeal (*Ils s'échauffent*

30 Pears (1984) has subtle analyses of this kind of mechanism.
31 Thus the German chancellor, Helmut Kohl, suggested that other nations' fear of a united Germany may really be "economic jealousy" (*International Herald Tribune*, February 5, 1990).

toujours à froid); their language is violent, but their progress is timid and uncertain. (DA, p. 175)

To summarize, the passions can both subvert and promote our real interest. They subvert it because they may induce wrong beliefs about what serves our interest, and also because they make us unmindful about our advantage. But the passions can also promote our interest, either because they boost our self-confidence or because passionate convictions inspire greater trust in our fellows than to those that smack of calculation. Of these various mechanisms Tocqueville neglects, as far as I can see, the one that relies on "motivated irrationality," or self-deception about where our interest really lies. I find this neglect puzzling, given the massive importance of this phenomenon in private and public life and Tocqueville's otherwise keen insight into what makes us tick. Perhaps I've just missed the relevant passages in his writings.

It is time to clear up an ambiguity in the idea of passions, by distinguishing between impulsive emotions and the social ones. By the latter I mean those lasting emotional propensities that are supported by the social norms in a given society; by the former the fleeting passions that arise spontaneously without any such normative basis. To illustrate the distinction we may look at a passage in which both kinds of passions are asserted: "As soon as landowners are deprived of their *strong sentimental attachment* to the land, based on memories and pride, it is certain that sooner or later they will sell it, for they have a powerful pecuniary interest in so doing, since other forms of investment earn a higher rate of interest and liquid assets are more easily used to satisfy the *passions of the moment*" (DA, p. 53: italics mine).

In traditional societies based on primogeniture, landed estates are frequently the object of a deep and constant passion, since they are an "imperishable witness to the past and a precious earnest of the future" (DA, p. 52). Selling land, in such societies, was sanctioned by strong social norms.[32] For the sake of this passion people are willing to renounce interest in both senses of that term, advantage and return on capital. Egalitarian systems of inheritance undermine that passion and replace it with naked self-interest and the passions of the moment. We may note the two characteristics of floating capital cited by Tocqueville: it attracts a higher rate of interest and it is more liquid. It is easy to understand why it is to my advantage that my capital should give a high return, and why liquid capital makes it easier to satisfy the passions of the moment, but harder to follow Tocqueville's suggestion that it is to my advantage to have my capital in a form that makes it easy to dissipate it quickly. The opposite, in fact, would seem to be true. It is clearly in my interest — properly understood — to keep my capital more or less tied up so that I am protected against the passions of the moment.[33]

Tocqueville often refers very critically to the impulsive passions of the people in democratic societies. As election time draws near, the President becomes the prisoner of the people: He "no longer rules in the interest of the state, but in that of his own reelection; he prostrates himself before the majority, and often, instead of resisting their passions as duty requires, he hastens to anticipate their caprices" (DA, p. 135). Writing of lawyers, he says that their "habit of directing the blind passions of the litigants towards the objective gives them a certain scorn for the judgment of the crowd" (DA, p. 264).

---

32 Stone (1972), p. 73.
33 Compare the analysis of Christmas saving accounts in Thaler and Shefrin (1981), where it is shown that many individuals are willing to accept a lower rate of interest in exchange for heavy penalties against frequent withdrawals. Because they know they are incapable of controlling themselves, they buy self-control from the banks. However, this technique for mastering one's irrationality is itself irrational, for why shouldn't the banks pay for the privilege of being able to use the deposits in a more predictable manner? I do my own forced saving by putting some of my income into a high-interest account with a penalty for frequent withdrawal.

The same effect is also obtained in a different manner: "Men who have made a special study of the laws and have derived therefrom habits of order . . . are naturally strongly opposed to the revolutionary spirit and to the ill-considered passions of democracy" (ibid.). Or again, "When the American people let themselves get intoxicated by their passions or carried away by their ideas, the lawyers apply an almost invisible brake which slows them down" (DA, p. 268).

Elsewhere, he recognized that these popular passions have more positive, if limited, aspect:

> It is incontestable that in times of danger a free people generally displays infinitely more energy than one which is not so, but I am inclined to believe that this is especially true of a free people in which the aristocratic element is dominant. Democracy seems to me much better suited to directing a peaceful society, or if necessary, to making some sudden and violent effort rather than to braving over a long period the great storms that beset a nation's political existence. The reason for this is simple: enthusiasm leads men to face dangers and privations, but only reflection will induce them to continue to brave them over a long period. Even in what is called instinctive courage there is more of calculation than is usually supposed; and though it is generally passions alone which cause the first efforts to be made, it is with a view to the outcome that they are continued. (DA, p. 223)

It seems to me that Tocqueville here gets his own thinking wrong. He stresses the contrast between the short-lived passions of the crowd and that calculated self-interest which alone is capable of maintaining an ongoing effort in view of a distant goal. But, as I remarked in Chapter 3, isn't the distinguishing feature of an aristocracy rather the fact that it has *durable passions*, as distinct both from more passing ones and from long-term self-interest? He reserves his respect for those who are "more attached to principles than to consequences" (DA, p. 175). When he praises the nobility, it is usually for their character rather than for their foresight. "That is why aristocrats often show a haughty contempt for the physical comforts they are actually enjoying and show singular powers of endurance when ultimately deprived of them" (DA, p. 531). Or again, "While the nobility enjoyed its power, and for a long time, too, after it had lost it, aristocratic honor gave extraordinary strength to individual resistance. Then here were men who, in spite of their impotence, still held a high idea of their individual worth and dared in isolation to resist the pressure of public authority" (DA, p. 313). The reference to the foresight and prudence of the nobles is an exception in a work that tends rather to stress their sometimes absurd attachment to principles and their scorn for petty, consequentialist calculation.

These remarks suggest the need to introduce a third type of motivation, *social norms*, which are maintained both by internalization and by external sanctions.[34] There is quite frequent reference to such norms in *Democracy in America*, and two chapters are specially devoted to them.

In the chapter on American manners, a basic paradox of social norms is very precisely identified: "Nothing, at first sight, seems less important than the external formalities of human behavior, yet there is nothing to which men attach more importance" (DA, p. 605). We need only read Proust's *Du côté de chez Guermantes* or Bourdieu's *La distinction* to realize just how subjectively important the rules of social etiquette can be, and how wretched those who break them can feel, and yet nothing could be intrinsically less serious. Although Tocqueville describes them as "conventions' (DA, p. 606), this cannot be in the same sense in which there are conventions of mutual help, since unlike the latter the rules of etiquette have no individual or social utility.[35]

In the chapter on honor in America and in democracy, this phenomenon is defined as a "particular rule, based on a particular state of society, by means of which a people distributes praise or blame" (DA, p. 617). That definition would also cover manners and in fact offer a general characterization of social norms, of

---

34 See also chs. 3, 5, and 6 in Elster (1989b).
35 This is obviously a controversial and contestable proposition. It is defended in Elster (1989b), pp. 101–2, 140–1.

Political Psychology

which manners and honor are but two special cases. Tocqueville deals first with feudal honor, emphasizing two features. First:

> In the feudal world actions were by no means always praised or blamed with reference to their intrinsic value, but were sometimes appreciated exclusively with reference to the person who did them or suffered from them, which is repugnant to the universal conscience of mankind. Some actions could thus have no importance if done by a commoner but would dishonor a noble. (DA, p. 617)

Second, the actions commanded by honor often had a bizarre and capricious aspect:

> In some cases feudal honor enjoined revenge and stigmatized forgiveness of insults; in others it imperiously commanded men to master their own passions and forget themselves. Humanity and gentleness were no part of its law, but it praised generosity; it set more store by liberality than benevolence; it allowed men to enrich themselves by gambling or by war, but not by work. It preferred great crimes to small earnings. Greed struck it as less revolting than avarice. It often sanctioned violence but invariably reprobated cunning and treachery as contemptible. (DA, p. 618)

The essential elements of the feudal code of honor are explicable by the fact that "the feudal aristocracy was born of war and for war" (DA, p. 618) Feudal honor, far from being arbitrary, is explained by "the special habits and interests of the community" (DA, p. 620). The same applies to honor in America, which can be reduced to two principles: chastity in private life and boldness in public life. About the former, he says that "American public opinion . . . is particularly hard on bad morals, which distract attention from the search for well-being and disturb that domestic harmony which is so essential to business success" (DA, p. 622). Here is what he has to say about the latter:

> In the United States martial valor is little esteemed; the type of courage best known and best appreciated is that which makes a man brave the fury of the ocean to reach port more quickly, and face without complaint the privations of life in the wilds

160

and that solitude which is harder to bear than any privations, the courage which makes a man almost insensible to the loss of a fortune laboriously acquired and prompts him instantly to fresh exertions to gain another. It is chiefly courage of this sort which is needed to maintain the American community and make it prosper, and it is held by them in particular esteem and honor. (DA, pp. 622–3)

These are essential functionalist explanations: A social group provides itself with the norms and codes of honor it needs to support its fundamental principle, be it prowess in war or the pursuit of well-being. As I argued in Chapter 1, such explanations are largely arbitrary. In the absence of some kind of micro-foundation, why should we believe that the American indulgence toward bankruptcies (Chapter 3) and the austerity of American morals can be accounted for in terms of the commercial needs of American society? The analyses of feudal society may seem more plausible, yet to my knowledge other societies with aristocratic warring classes, such as Japan or Sparta, did not exhibit the bizarre and extravagant characteristics of European feudalism.

According to Tocqueville, social norms are stronger in aristocratic societies than in democracies, mainly because the latter have a higher degree of mobility.[36] "There is too much mobility in the population of a democracy for any definite group to be able to establish a code of behavior and see that it is observed" (DA, p. 606). Or again, "In democracies . . . where all are jumbled together in the same constantly fluctuating crowd, there is nothing for public opinion to catch hold of; its subject matter is ever vanishing from sight and escaping. In such circumstances honor must always be less binding and less urgently pressing" (DA, p. 626). It is hard, however, to see how this statement can be reconciled with what Tocqueville says about the importance of public opinion in democracies (see below).

Let me end this subsection on a note of caution, to make up for what some readers may have perceived as an air of pseudoprecision in the previous discussions. The full range of human

36 For a similar argument, see Tumin (1957).

motivations constitute a terrain that can be divided up in any number of ways, none of which is canonical. Unlike the anatomy of the body, the anatomy of the mind does not lend itself to objective determination. This being said, I do believe that the Tocquevillian distinction between interest, passions and social norms provides a classification that is as good as any and better than most. It is often a fertile research strategy to ask, for a given piece of behavior, which of the three are most likely to provide an explanation. Consider, as an example, acts of revenge.[37] I take revenge to make another suffer because he has made me suffer, even if in doing so I impose further suffering on myself. Such actions have a strong appearance of irrationality: why run a risk in order to obtain a result that will not benefit me in any way? As I said in the Introduction, rational actors let bygones be bygones rather than add new losses to the old ones. One possible explanation is that I take revenge out of spontaneous anger, a reaction seen in its purest form when I kick a stone that I've stumbled over. Another is that I take revenge because there is a social norm that tells me that my honor will be tainted unless I do so. And thirdly, revenge may be undertaken quite rationally out of self-interest, to create a reputation for vengefulness that may prove useful on later occasions. I am not saying that any action could plausibly be understood in each of the three perspectives, but that does not detract from the value of the distinction for hypothesis-generating purposes.

DESIRES AND OPPORTUNITIES

The remainder of this chapter will be devoted to what I take to be Tocqueville's most original contributions to the study of human motivation and behavior. The first is his theory of the relations between desires to act and opportunities for action; the other his theory of intrapsychic mechanisms in preference formation.

37 The following draws on Elster (1990b).

To understand the originality of Tocqueville's view of the relation between desires and opportunities, we may begin by setting out the standard economic model of human action, which rests on a similar but much impoverished view of the same relation.[38] According to this model, agents face *choices under constraints*. The constraints jointly determine the *opportunities* of the agents, or their feasible set. If the agents are rational, they will choose the element in the feasible set that best satisfies their desires, that is, the element that is top-ranked in their preference order.

Consider the simple case of a consumer with a given income, which he has to spend on bread and milk, available to him at given prices. In Figure 4.1, the triangle OAB contains all the combinations of milk and bread that the consumer can buy with his income. Assuming that he intends to spend his entire income on these commodities, the feasible set shrinks to the line AB. The slope of this line expresses the relative prices of the two commodities. I_1, I_2 and I_3 are indifference curves, which can be derived from his preferences. As the name indicates, the consumer is indifferent among all milk-bread combinations that lie on the same indifference curve. Given the choice between two combinations on different curves, he always prefers the one that lies on the indifference furthest away from the origin. He will, therefore, choose a point on *AB* that is tangential to an indifference curve. In Figure 4.1 this is point *C*, corresponding to quantities *m* and *b* of milk and bread.

Although simple, this example captures all the features of the standard economic model that are relevant for our purposes. On the one hand, the agent faces certain opportunities, defined by his income and commodity prices. On the other hand, he has certain desires or preferences, expressed in the family of indifference curves. Opportunities and desires jointly determine

---

38 The discussion below draws heavily on my "Desires and opportunities: Alexis de Tocqueville's political psychology," delivered and printed as the Duijker Lecture, Amsterdam University, 1990.

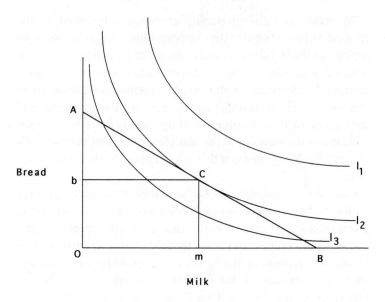

Figure 4.1.

what he will do. These two determinants of actions are standardly assumed to be independent of each other, in the sense that each is allowed to change freely while the other remains the same. In the simple case I have discussed, this assumption seems clearly justified. Two consumers with different preferences might face the same feasible set. One consumer with unchanging preferences might face different opportunities when prices or his income change. In broader social contexts, however, this independence assumption[39] may not hold. Desires and opportunities may be causally related to one another, in one of two ways. First, one of these determinants of action may causally influence the other,

---

39 The idea that preferences should not vary with the feasible set is often referred to as the "independence of irrelevant alternatives." Assume that in the set {a, b} I prefer a to b. It should not then be the case that in the set {a, b, c} I prefer b to a. There is no similar standard expression of the idea that the feasible set should not vary with the preferences.

positively or negatively. There may be a causally efficacious desire to increase one's opportunities (case F) or to reduce them (case H). Similarly, the opportunity to act in a certain way may stimulate the desire to act in the way (case E) or inhibit it (case G).[40] Secondly, the two determinants may have a common cause that causally influences both of them. These are the cases A, B, C, and D in Figure 4.2.

Elsewhere I have discussed cases E and H, an example of E being the fox who found the grapes too sour because he could not get them[41] and an example of H being Ulysses who had his men bind him to the mast.[42] Tocqueville refers frequently to the former, only exceptionally (and ironically) to the latter. I would like to begin, however, with the other cases, which in my opinion represent his most original contribution.

The central idea is very simple. A priori there is no reason to think that all logically possible combinations of desires and opportunities could actually be realized. On the contrary, sociology shows that desires and opportunities co-vary, so that certain combinations are impossible or at least unstable. Action being an outcome of desires and opportunities, the co-variation of the latter two implies that we can also expect certain limits on what actions will be observed.

In Tocqueville's work, desires and opportunities co-vary because they have a common cause. If the common cause P is a necessary condition of Q and a sufficient condition of R, it follows that Q will always be accompanied by R. In most cases, the common cause is the democratic organization of society (*l'état social démocratique*), by which Tocqueville meant a society with equal access to political power, the absence of legal privileges, and high rates

---

40 I am indebted to Robert Goodin for constructive comments on an earlier version of this typology.
41 See ch. III of Elster (1983b). This chapter also includes a brief comment on case G ("counteradaptive preferences"). To my knowledge the only passage in which Tocqueville mentions this possibility occurs at the end of *Democracy*, when he observes that in democracies men "get tired of the duration even of the state they have chosen" (DA, p. 702).
42 See Elster (1984), ch. II.

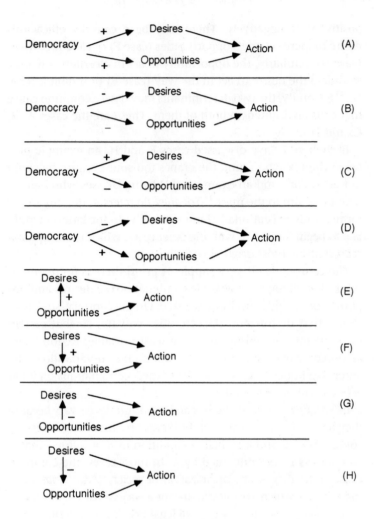

Figure 4.2.

of social mobility.[43] With respect to a given action X, the common cause can act in four different ways, corresponding to cases A through D. It can have a negative or a positive influence both on the desire to do X and on the opportunities for doing X.

Tocqueville does not often refer to case A. Here is a rare example, which occurs in the context of a discussion of military advancement in wartime:

> Officers whose minds and bodies have grown old in peacetime are eliminated, retire, or die. In their place a multitude of young men, already toughened by war, press forward with ambitious hopes aflame. They want promotion at any price, and continual promotion. They are followed by others with the same passions and desires, and then by more still after these, the size of the army itself being the only limit. Equality allows every man to be ambitious, and death provides chances for every ambition. (DA, p. 657)

Thus war is the common cause which both kindles the ambitions of the military – which, as we shall see, lie dormant in peacetime – and creates the opportunity to satisfy them.

By contrast, there are numerous arguments of type B, often recognizable by Tocqueville's use of the phrase "not only." A famous example is the following: "Thus the law of inheritances not only makes it difficult for families to retain the same domains intact, but takes away their wish to try to do so" (DA, p. 53). An apparently similar example refers to the poor conditions for the "labors of the mind" in America: "Both the will and the power to engage in such work are lacking" (DA, p. 56). On closer inspection, however, this example turns out to rest on a combination of cases C and D: "In America most rich men began by being poor; almost all men of leisure were busy in their youth; as a result, at the age when one might have a taste for

---

43 It is often, but wrongly, assumed that Tocqueville also stipulated equality of income or wealth at each point of time as part of the democratic social state. Although some of his arguments do indeed presuppose this view, his more explicit statements (DA, p. 50) devalue the importance of equality and emphasize that of mobility.

study, one has not the time; and when time is available, the taste has gone" (DA, p. 55).

Another famous example concerns the impact of slavery on slaveowners. In the first place, slavery is unprofitable, compared to free labor.

> The free worker receives wages, the slave receives an upbringing, food, medicine, and clothes; the master spends his money little by little in small sums to support the slave; he scarcely notices. The workman's wages are paid all at once and seem only to enrich the man who receives them; but in fact the slave has cost more than the free man, and his labor is less productive (DA, pp. 346–7).

But "the influence of slavery extends even further, penetrating the master's soul and giving a particular turn to his ideas and tastes" (DA, p. 347). Because work is associated with slavery, the Southern whites scorn "not only work itself but also enterprises in which work is necessary to success" (ibid.). They lack both the opportunities and the desire to get rich: "Slavery . . . not only prevents the white men from making their fortunes but even diverts them from wishing to do so." (ibid.) If Tocqueville is right, the classic debate over the economic stagnation of slave societies is spurious. There is no need to ask whether lack of investment desires or lack of investment opportunities provides the correct explanation: Both sides could be right.[44]

A similar instance of explanatory overdetermination occurs in Tocqueville's discussion of why American democracy fails to select good leaders. On the one hand, he argues, most people do not have the intellectual discernment and skill which is needed to assess the character of politicians. On the other hand, being under the sway of the "democratic sentiment of envy," they may deliberately prefer mediocre to outstanding leaders. Once

44 As I explained in Chapter 1, Genovese, following Hegel, argued that the psychology of the slaveowner channeled his desires toward conspicuous consumption and, by implication, away from investment. Marx asserted that the psychology of slaves, which makes them treat tools and instruments badly, destroyed any investment opportunities for the slaveowner. For a fuller discussion, see Elster (1985a), pp. 275ff.

again, "it is not always ability to choose men of merit which democracy lacks; sometimes it has neither desire nor taste to do so" (DA, p. 198). Strictly speaking, to lack the ability to select the best is not exactly the same as lacking the opportunity to select them. The latter idea, which would presuppose that the best fail to stand for election, is also asserted by Tocqueville. Politics is both too dirty (DA, p. 198) and too trivial (DA, p. 205) to attract the best minds. The best don't stand; if they did, the electorate wouldn't recognize them; and if it did, it wouldn't vote for them.

A further example with the same structure occurs in Tocqueville's discussion of the fate of an occupied country under a democratic regime. Because individual citizens in a democracy are powerless and isolated, "none of them can either defend himself or offer a rallying point to others" (DA, p. 662). Moreover, they do not really have an interest in defending their country: "each citizen has but a small share of political power and often none at all; on the other hand, all are independent and have property to lose; as a result, they are much less afraid of conquest and much more afraid of war than the inhabitants of an aristocratic land" (DA, pp. 662–3). Hence he concludes, "not only will the population be unable to continue the war, but, I fear, they will not even want to try" (ibid.).

I now turn to case C. I have already cited an example to the effect that Americans never have the time to study at the age when they desire to do so. Much more important is the following text, which summarizes one of the most central ideas in *Democracy*:

> The same equality which allows each man to entertain vast hopes makes each by himself weak. His power is limited on every side, though his longings may wander where they will. . . . This constant strife between the desires inspired by equality and the means it supplies to satisfy them harasses and wearies the mind. One can imagine men who have found a degree of liberty completely satisfactory to them. In that case they will enjoy their independence without anxiety or excitement. But men will never establish an equality which will content them. (DA, p. 537).

This passage suggests that *anomie* is a permanent and inevitable feature of democratic societies. Elsewhere, however, Tocqueville seems to tell us that anomie is a purely transitional feature of democracies:

> [A]mbitions are on the grand scale while the democratic revolution lasts; that will no longer be true some considerable time after it has finished. Men do not in one day forget the memory of extraordinary events which they have witnessed; and the passions roused by revolution by no means vanish at its close. A sense of instability is perpetuated amid order. . . . Longings on a vast scale remain, though the means to satisfy them become daily less. The taste for huge fortunes persists, though such fortunes in fact become rare, and on all sides there are those who eat out their hearts in secret, consumed by inordinate and frustrated ambition. (DA, p. 628).

Later I shall cite the continuation of this passage, where Tocqueville asserts that in the democratic equilibrium desires and opportunities are once more in harmony with each other, an argument that seems to contradict the central Tocquevillian idea that frustration and restlessness are constant features of democratic societies.

A more special case of anomie is found in the army:

> Desire for promotion is almost universal in democratic armies; it is eager, tenacious and continual. All other desires serve to feed it, and it is only quenched with life itself. It is therefore easy to see that promotion in times of peace must be slower in democratic armies than in other armies in the world. As the number of commissions is naturally limited, while the number of competitors is almost innumerable, and they are all subject to the unbending rule of equality, no one can make rapid progress, and many can make no progress at all. Thus the desire for promotion is greater and the opportunities for it are fewer than elsewhere. (DA, p. 647)

On this point, too, we shall see later that Tocqueville also asserts the opposite conclusion: Officers end up adapting to the lack of possibility of advancement. In this case the possibility of permanent and constitutive *anomie* is, in fact, less plausible. I shall return to this question.

Case D is also exemplifed by the statement that Americans have no taste for studies when they finally acquire the means to do so. A structurally similar argument is advanced to explain the lack of ambitions in democratic societies:

> From hatred of privilege and embarrassment in choosing, all men, whatever their capacities, are finally forced through the same sieve, and all without discrimination are made to pass a host of petty preliminary tests, wasting their youth and suffocating their imagination. So they come to despair of ever fully enjoying the good things proffered, and when at last they reach a position in which they could do something out of the ordinary, the taste for it has left them. (DA, p. 630)

Another argument of the same general form has a central place in Tocqueville's explanation of the stability of democratic societies: "while the law allows the American people to do everything, there are things which religion prevents them from imagining and forbids them to dare" (DA, p. 292). To see that the opportunity for violent or licentious behavior and the lack of any desire to behave in such ways have the same cause, it suffices to observe that for Tocqueville religion is an endogenous product of democracy. In a passage already quoted, and worth quoting again, he says that "For my part, I doubt whether man can support complete religious independence and entire political liberty at the same time. I am led to think that if he has no faith he must obey, and if he is free he must believe" (DA, 444). Once again, the ills or dangers of democracy are cured or neutralized by democracy itself.

Among the four cases I have been discussing, case C stands out because of its potential dangers. As Tocqueville explains in *The Old Regime*, social stability is threatened by a gap between aspirations and the opportunity to satisfy them, not by limited opportunities in themselves. In *Democracy* the same point is made to explain why noncommissioned officers are a great danger to democratic institutions. Whereas regular officers after a while tend to adjust their ambitions to their opportunities and take consolation in the standing they have achieved, NCO's live in a state of constant uncertainty and frustration to which they can never adapt themselves. To realize their goals of promotion they are irresistibly tempted to create more opportunities, by provoking a war or a revolution.

Thus, to reduce the likelihood of insubordinate or rebellious behavior, it is more effective to reduce men's desire to engage in it than to limit their opportunity to do so. Tocqueville himself makes this distinction in his remarkable discussion of slavery. "In antiquity men sought to prevent the slave from breaking his bonds; nowadays the attempt is made to stop him wishing to do so" (DA, p. 361). The crucial difference between the two regimes lay in their attitudes toward emancipation and manumission:

> The ancients bound the slave's body but left his spirit free and allowed him to educate himself. In this way they were acting consistently; at that time there was a natural way out of slavery: from one day to the next the slave could become free and equal to his master. The Americans of the South, who do not think that at any time the Negroes can mingle with them, have forbidden teaching them to read or write under severe penalties. Not wishing to raise them to their own level, they keep them as close to the beasts as possible. . . . The Americans of the South have realized that emancipation always presented dangers, when the freed slave could not succeed in assimilating himself to his master. To give a man liberty but to leave him in ignominious misery, what was that but to prepare a leader for some future slave rebellion? Moreover, it had long been noticed that the presence of a free Negro vaguely disturbs the minds of those not free, infecting them with some glimmering notion of their rights. In most cases the Americans of the South have deprived the masters of the right to emancipate. (DA, pp. 361–2)

The argument goes as follows. Individual slaveowners might want to emancipate their slaves. The slave states forbid them from doing so because of the consequences that might ensue.

172

First, in the newly emancipated slaves the gap between the desire for material well-being suggested to them by their freedom and the lack of opportunities for satisfying that desire would lead to discontent. Secondly, in the unemancipated slaves the presence of free blacks would create a desire for freedom that, once again, would not be matched by opportunities. One day potential leaders and potential followers would join in a slave rebellion. Instead of using force against the slaves to limit their opportunities for rebellion, the American slaveholding states used the law against the slaveowners to limit the desire of the slaves for rebellion.

Destabilizing frustration disappears when men adapt and adjust to their fate, corresponding to case E in Figure 4.2. The adjustment of desires to opportunities is in fact a constant theme in *Democracy*. An important special case is resignation and adaptation to oppression: "nothing comes more natural to man than to recognize the superior wisdom of his oppressor" (DA, p. 436). Tocqueville often applies this argument to the old regime, as in the following passage:

> Having never conceived the possibility of a social state other
> than the one they knew, and never expecting to become equal
> to their leaders, the people accepted benefits from their hands
> and did not question their rights. They loved them when they
> were just and merciful and felt neither repugnance nor
> degradation in submitting to their severities, which seemed
> inevitable ills sent by God. (DA, pp. 13–14)

A similar comment on American slavery is preceded by a general observation:

> Should I call it a blessing of God, or a last malediction of His
> anger, this disposition of the soul that makes men insensible
> to extreme misery and often gives them a sort of depraved
> taste for the cause of their afflictions? Plunged in this abyss of
> wretchedness, the Negro hardly notices his ill fortune; he was
> reduced to slavery by violence, and the habit of servitude has
> given him the thoughts and ambitions of a slave; he admires
> his tyrants even more than he hates them and finds his joy
> and pride in a servile imitation of his oppressors. (DA, p. 317)

The opening statement, already cited in the previous chapter, nicely captures the ambiguity of adaptive preferences. Do they add to or detract from misery? On the one hand, by lowering frustration they are conducive to happiness. On the other hand, they undermine the autonomy and dignity of the slave. It is not clear, however, that rebellious slaves are more autonomous. Recall the passage cited in Chapter 3, to the effect that to go against the current a man must have "something of violence and adventure in his character." Tocqueville goes on to add: "That, one may say in passing, is the reason why, even in the case of the most necessary and hallowed revolutions, one seldom finds revolutionaries who are moderate and honest" (DA, p. 597). If the normal response to oppression is to accept it as just, only unbalanced individuals will take to arms against it.

In the New World, people adapt to other aspects of their environment. American women, for example, show a remarkable flexibility: "In no country of the world are private fortunes more unstable than in the United States. It is not exceptional for one man in his lifetime to work up through every stage from poverty to opulence and then come down again. American women face such upheavals with quiet, indomitable energy. Their desires seem to contract with their fortune as easily as they expand." (DA, 593) A similar although more painful process of adjustment is observed among commissioned officers:

> I have pointed out the extreme slowness of promotion in democratic armies in times of peace. At first the officers are impatient of this state of affairs; they grow agitated, restless and despairing; but in the long run most of them become resigned to this. Those of most ambition and resources leave the army; the others, finally adapting their tastes and desires to their humdrum lot, come in the end to look on a military career from a civilian point of view. What they value most is the comfort and the security that goes with it. They base their vision of the future on the assurance of a small competence, and they ask no more than to be allowed to enjoy it in peace. So not only does a long peace fill democratic armies with

aging officers, but it often gives even those men who are still
in the vigor of their years the instincts of old men. (DA, p. 656)

These examples allow us to state what may be the most difficult
problem that faces the reader of *Democracy in America*. How can
mechanisms C and E coexist? How can there be both chronic
(nontransitional) anomie[45] *and* a tendency to adapt to circumstances? In the continuation of a passage I cited earlier, Tocqueville
affirms that in steady-state democracies, as distinct from what
happens in the transition to democracy, adaptation is the rule:

> Little by little the last traces of the battle are wiped out and
> the relics of aristocracy finally vanish. The great events which
> accompanied its fall are forgotten. Peace follows war, and
> order again prevails in a new world. Longings once more
> become proportionate to the available means. Wants, ideas,
> and feelings again learn their limits. Men find their level, and
> democratic society is finally firmly established. (DA, p. 628)

On the other hand, Tocqueville says over and over again that
men in democratic societies are characterized by frustration,
constant restlessness, and unsatisfied ambitions. In addition to
the passage from the second volume (DA, p. 537) cited earlier,
the following excerpt from the first volume is quite unambiguous:

> One must not blind oneself to the fact that democratic
> institutions most successfully develop sentiments of envy in
> the human heart. This is not because they provide the means
> for everybody to rise to the level of everyone else but because
> these means are constantly proving inadequate in the hands of
> those using them. Democratic institutions awaken and flatter
> the passion for equality without ever being able to satisfy it
> entirely. This complete equality is always slipping through the
> people's fingers at the moment when they think to grasp it,
> fleeing, as Pascal says, in an eternal flight; the people grow
> heated in search of this blessing, all the more precious because
> it is near enough to be seen but too far off to be tasted. They

45 For an account of Durkheim's theory of chronic anomie, see Besnard (1987),
    pp. 100ff.

are excited by the chance and irritated by the uncertainty of success; the excitement is followed by weariness and then by bitterness. (DA, p. 198)

In these two passages Tocqueville finds the source of frustration in envy. Because democracy induces people to search for positional goods, they can never reach a durable satisfaction. As soon as they have reached the equality or eminence they sought for, others may leave them behind again. Another source of frustration is the high degree of social mobility in democratic societies. "In democratic countries, no matter how rich a man is, he is almost always dissatisfied with his fortune, because he finds that he is less wealthy than his father was and he is afraid that his son will be less wealthy than he." (DA, p. 552). Or again:

There are always plenty of citizens in any democracy whose patrimonies are being divided up and diminished. These still have the tastes acquired in their time of prosperity without the means to indulge them, and they are anxiously on the lookout for some roundabout way of doing so. There are, too, in any democracy men whose fortunes are on the increase but whose desires increase much more quickly than their wealth, so that their eyes devour the good things wealth will one day provide long before they can afford them. . . . These two elements always provide democracies with a crowd of citizens whose desires outrun their means and who will gladly agree to put up with an imperfect substitute rather than do without the object of their desire altogether. (DA, p. 466)

I believe it is possible to reconcile these statements with the assertion that in stable democracies men adjust their desires to their means. After a violent transition, democracy becomes established in its steady-state form. As people realize that the time of revolution is past, the Napoleonic ambitions of a Julien Sorel become rare. At a less lofty level, however, life is constantly changing, too rapidly for adaptation to be possible. Democratic citizens tend to be frustrated because the process of adaptation is slow compared to the rate of social mobility. This rapid metabolism is an endogenous feature of steady-state democracy, as Tocqueville himself tells us. "One must make a clear distinction between the sort of permanent agitation characteristic of a peaceful and well-established democracy, and the tumultuous revolutionary movements that almost always go with the birth and development of a democracy" (DA, p. 460). The ambitions of a Rastignac, the rise and fall of a Lucien de Rubempré, are normal features of a well-established democracy.

What, then, about American women? How can they adapt to the waxing and waning fortunes of their husbands? Tocqueville does not offer an answer, and any response must be conjectural. One crucial difference is that women, in the case he is referring to, *react* to circumstances, whereas men are in part responsible for them. To adopt a Stoic outlook is easier when circumstances are wholly beyond one's influence than when they are partly under one's own control. The famous prayer of the Stoa runs, "God grant us the serenity to accept the things we cannot change, courage to change the things we can and wisdom to know the difference." It is much easier to grant this wish to those who are obviously unable to effect any changes.

Let me finally consider case H, in which the desires are involved in shaping the opportunities. I limit myself to the case in which the agent *intentionally* tries to *limit* his opportunities. Cases in which desires influence opportunities by causal, nonintentional mechanisms may have some importance in politics, but I shall not treat them here.[46] Also I shall not discuss the practically

46 An example is Tocqueville's observation that "nothing makes for success more than not desiring it too ardently" (Tocqueville 1970, p. 88). One can imagine at least two mechanisms to sustain this assertion. First, the desire for success may detract one's attention and energy from the practical tasks that have to be solved as a precondition for success. This mechanism is one by which the desire to succeed affects the *ability* to succeed rather than the *opportunity* to do so, analogously to the case in which a strong desire to hit a target makes the rifleman so nervous that it affects his ability to hit it. Second, a person who desires success too strongly may not be perceived as trustworthy by others, who may block some of his opportunities of success. As briefly indicated in the previous chapter, this mechanism may well describe Tocqueville's own career under the July Monarchy. A related mechanism is described elsewhere in the *Recollections* (Tocqueville 1970, p. 189): A

important but theoretically trivial case F of agents trying to expand their opportunity set.

Why would anyone want to throw away some of his options? I can see four main reasons. First, one may tie one hand behind one's back so as to make the success appear more striking. Thus in mathematics it is considered more elegant to prove theorems in number theory by arguments that appeal to real numbers only than to invoke complex numbers. Secondly, one may deliberately constrain one's options so as to facilitate meaningful choices within the constraints. This argument has always been offered as a main reason for conventions in art.[47] Thirdly, one may burn one's bridges or otherwise constrain oneself to obtain a strategic advantage.[48] Finally, one may follow Ulysses and bind oneself to limit the effects of predictable weakness of will. This is the only case considered by Tocqueville.

It is, however, a case to which he accords very little importance. To my knowledge there is only one passage that refers to individual efforts of self-control. It is, moreover, heavily ironical:

> A single fact is enough to show that the stage is not very popular in America. The Americans, whose laws allow the utmost freedom, and even license, of language in other respects, nevertheless subject the drama to a sort of censorship. Plays can only be performed by permission of the municipal authorities. This illustrates how like communities are to individuals: without a thought they give way to their chief passions, and then take great care not to be carried away by tastes they do not possess. (DA, p. 493)

This idea – that individuals, like communities, are unable to exercise self-control when it is most needed – supports my claim that Tocqueville's view of individual psychology lacks a strategic dimension. One might expect, perhaps, Tocqueville to refer to the need for collective self-control in democracies. I have given

person who is too confident that he will get a huge majority of the votes may alienate others and incline them to vote against him.

47 For a fuller discussion, see ch. II. 7 of Elster (1983b).
48 See notably Schelling (1960), ch. 5.

several instances of Tocqueville's argument that the dangers of democracy are reduced by democracy itself, adding that he also believed that some ills of democracy must be cured by imposing constraints on the democratic process, such as bicameralism and indirect elections. He never argues, however, that these constraints are democratically chosen by the people to protect itself against its own tendencies towards impulsive behavior. Rather, they are imposed from outside: They have their source in the wisdom of the framers, not in the popular will.

Let me pursue this theme, using the example of monetary policy, which is often analyzed in terms of Ulysses and the Sirens.[49] The argument is sometimes made that it is in the interest of politicians to abdicate their right to intervene in monetary policy, to protect themselves against popular demands that otherwise might be irresistible. Tocqueville's view is rather different:

> The Bank of the United States always has in its hands a large number of notes of provincial banks; any day it could force the latter to repay these notes in cash. But it has no fear of a similar danger to itself; the extent of its available resources enables it to face all demands. With their existence thus threatened, the provincial banks are obliged to exercise restraint and to keep their notes in circulation proportionate to their capital. The provincial banks are impatient at this salutary control. The newspapers that they have bought up, and the President, whose interest makes him their mouthpiece, therefore attack the bank with the greatest vehemence. They rouse local passions and the blind democratic instincts of the country against it. According to them, the directors of the bank constitute a permanent aristocratic body whose influence is bound to make itself felt on the government and will sooner or later change the principles of equality in which American society rests. (DA, p. 389)

In Tocqueville's view, individuals or societies never bind themselves to control their weakness of will. In fact, as I argued above, he did not even believe in the existence of any weakness of will to be controlled.

49 See for instance Nordhaus (1975) and Elster (1984), ch. II. 4.

SPILLOVER, COMPENSATION, AND CROWDING-OUT EFFECTS

I shall conclude by considering Tocqueville's views on intrapsychic causality in the formation of beliefs and desires. Before proceeding to an analysis of these views, however, I shall comment on some mechanisms by which the external environment may impinge on the same process. One important effect is the adaptation of desires to opportunities (case E above). Tocqueville also stresses another kind of adaptation – conformity – that is especially important in democracies. However, he offers no less than four different explanations of the fact that people's opinions are more similar to each other in democracies than in other societies.

In the first place, people always need some authorities, since otherwise they would be condemned to the impossible task of making up their own mind from scratch on all matters.

> So somewhere and somehow authority is always bound to
> play a part in intellectual and moral life. The part may vary,
> but some part there must be. . . . Thus men who live in times
> of equality find it hard to place the intellectual authority to
> which they submit, beyond and outside humanity. Generally
> speaking, they look into themselves or into their fellows for
> the source of truth. (DA, pp. 434–5)

In the further development of this idea, there occurs an astonishing non sequitur. Tocqueville first asserts that the appeal to authority is justified because it leaves men time for important matters: "it is a salutary bondage which allows him to make good use of freedom" (DA, p. 434). This is the Cartesian idea from *Discourse on Method*: when in Rome, do as the Romans, to economize on the costs of decision-making. As the passage goes on, however, public opinion is said to be "mistress of the world. Not only is public opinion the only guide left to aid private judgment, but its power is infinitely greater in democracies than elsewhere" (DA, p. 435). By a sleight of hand, the voluntarily assumed "salutary bondage" has been transformed into a degrading and servile condition.

Secondly, men living in democracies have similar ideas in so far as their circumstances are alike. Similar causes produce similar effects. "Men with equal rights, education, and wealth, that is to say, men who are in just the same condition, must have very similar needs, habits, and tastes" (DA, pp. 640–1). Or again, "When equality is complete and old-established, all men, having roughly the same ideas and doing roughly the same things, do not need to come to an understanding or to copy each other in order to behave and talk in the same way; one sees a lot of petty variations in their manners but no great difference. They are never exactly alike, since they do not copy one pattern; they are never very unequal, because they have the same social condition" (DA, p. 607). Because the similarity of ideas is not maintained by a mechanism that penalizes deviants, there is no reason to expect complete conformity.

Thirdly, in a democracy men have similar opinions because of a fear of social sanctions. "In America the majority has enclosed thought within a formidable fence. A writer is free inside that area, but woe to the man who goes beyond it. Not that he stands in fear of an *auto-da-fé*, but he must face all kinds of unpleasantness and everyday persecution" (DA, p. 255). Or again, "in democracies . . . public favor seems as necessary as the air they breathe, and to be out of harmony with the mass is, if one may put it so, no life at all. The mass has no need of laws to bend those who do not agree to its will. Its disapproval is enough" (DA, p. 643). This is a mechanism that accounts for conformity in action and overt expression, but not necessarily that of the mind. The mental state is one of hypocrisy rather than of inner acquiescence.

Finally, there is inner conformity, the *sincere* adoption of generally held opinions simply because they are generally held. "The majority is invested with both physical and moral authority, which acts as much upon the will as upon behavior and at the same moment prevents both the act and the desire to do it" (DA, p. 254). Or again, "One finds governments striving to protect mores by condemning the authors of licentious books.

No one in the United States is condemned for works of that sort, but no one is tempted to write them" (DA, p. 256: compare also case D in Figure 4.2). And finally, "In times of equality men, being so like each other, have no confidence in others, but this same likeness leads them to place almost unlimited confidence in the judgment of the public. For they think it not unreasonable that, all having the same means of knowledge, truth will be found on the side of the majority" (DA, p. 435).

These passages pose a dilemma. Either similar ideas come from similar conditions, in which case neither hypocrisy nor inner conformity are needed to keep them similar. Or these corrective mechanisms are in fact indispensable, but then we have to ask about the origin of these ideas that everybody is supposed to conform to. Perhaps the problem can be settled as follows. Initially, opinions and habits are externally generated, being the product of similar social conditions. Once established, however, they can be maintained by inner or other conformity, in the way just explained.

> When an opinion has taken root in a democracy and
> established itself in the minds of the majority, it afterward
> persists by itself, needing no effort to maintain it since no one
> attacks it. Those who at first rejected it as false come in the
> end to adopt it as accepted, and even those who still at the
> bottom of their hearts oppose it keep their views to
> themselves, taking great care to avoid a dangerous and futile
> contest. (DA, pp. 643–4)

Two implications follow. First, over time the similarity should increase and take on a more systematic form as social sanctions screen out deviants. Second, the similarity can maintain itself, perhaps in an ever more rigorous form, even when the initial similarity of conditions ceases to obtain. One may then observe a *false conformity* that Tocqueville analyses in a remarkable passage:

> Sometimes, though no change may be visible from the
> outside, it does happen that time, circumstances, and the
> lonely workings of each man's thought do, little by little, in
> the end shake or destroy some belief. It has not been openly

attacked. No meetings have been held to fight against it. But one by one its supporters quietly drop it, so that finally these small continual defections leave it with but a few upholders. In such conditions it still prevails. As its opponents still hold their peace or only stealthily exchange their thoughts, they are themselves long unsure that a great revolution has taken place, and when in doubt, they take no action. They watch and keep quiet. The majority no longer believes, but it looks as if it did believe, and this empty ghost of public opinion is enough to chill the innovators and make them maintain their silent respect. (DA, p. 644)

One cannot blame Tocqueville for not having foreseen the opinion polls that tend to unravel these ghost opinions. Nor did he seem to anticipate the possibility of a more malignant and paradoxical form of false conformity, which for a long time dominated in the Communist world. In "mature" communism it was true, roughly speaking, that everybody knew that nobody believed in the tenets of the official ideology, and yet everybody was compelled to talk as if they did.[50] This system of open lies can be explained by its repressive efficacy.[51] The reason why the leaders forced people to make absurd statements in public was not to make them believe in what they said, but to induce a state of complicity and guilt that undermined their morality and ability to resist. Moreover, the tendency toward dissonance reduction may even induce a sort of semibelief in the indefinitely repeated absurdities, a belief that, while not sufficient to induce action, may at least prevent other beliefs from taking their place.

We have seen that mental events – desires, beliefs, tastes, habits – can be accounted for in terms of a *reaction to external circumstances*, as when we adapt our desires to the means available for achieving them or adjust our beliefs to those of others. I now discuss attitude formation that takes place as a reaction *to internal circumstances*, the action of one mental fact on another. Habits and desires can reinforce each other, compensate for each other and limit each other by means of three mechanisms that

50 See for instance Walder (1986), pp. 156–7.
51 This is the explanation offered in Kolakowski (1978), vol. 3, pp. 83–91.

I propose to call the *spillover effect*, the *compensation effect*, and the *crowding-out effect*. The spillover effect says that if a person follows a certain pattern of behavior P in one sphere of his life, X, he will also follow P in sphere Y. The compensation effect says that if he does not follow P in X, he will, if he can, do so in Y. The crowding-out effect says that if he does follow P in X, he will not do so in Y.

The compensation and crowding-out effects, if conjoined, imply a *zero-sum effect*, which is also present in what has been called "the hydraulic model" of the mind. Some of Freud's early work, for instance, was based on the assumption that there is a constant amount of psychic energy. In his later writings, Tocqueville dissociated himself from hydraulic reasoning:

> It would seem that civilized people, when restrained from
> political action, should turn with that much more interest to
> the literary pleasures. Yet nothing of the sort happens.
> Literature remains as insensitive and fruitless as politics. Those
> who believe that by making people withdraw from greater
> objects they will devote more energy to those activities that
> are still allowed to them treat the human mind along false and
> mechanical laws. In a steam engine or a hydraulic machine
> smaller wheels will turn smoother and quicker as power to
> them is diverted from the larger wheels. But such mechanical
> rules do not apply to the human spirit.[52]

I believe that Tocqueville here betrays poor understanding of his own method. The *theory* of the mind as a zero-sum system is indeed unacceptable, but the idea of a zero-sum *mechanism* is not. In any given case, that mechanism belongs to the repertoire of possible causal accounts. The presence of a pattern P in sphere Y may turn out to be explicable in terms of its absence in X – or in terms of its presence in X. The presence of P in X may serve to explain its presence in Y – or its absence in Y. A priori, we cannot tell whether the spillover effect, the compensation effect, the crowding-out effect, or the latter two combined in a zero-sum effect, will be observed.

52 Tocqueville (1986), p. 168.

Tocqueville's Psychology II

The spillover effect

At the cost of some repetition, let me reproduce here the main passages in *Democracy in America* that invoke this mechanism. They can often be identified by the occurrence of the verb "transporter," usually translated as "carry over," "transfer" or "pass on." When he uses different language, the identification of the effect may be more controversial:

> Every citizen in the United States may be said to transfer the concern inspired in him by his little republic into his love of the common motherland. (DA, p. 162)

> That constantly renewed agitation introduced by democratic government into political life passes . . . into civil society. Perhaps, taking everything into consideration, that is the greatest advantage of democratic government, and I praise it much more on account of what it causes to be done than for what it does. (DA, p. 243)

> Juries, especially civil juries, instill some of the habits of the judicial mind into every citizen, and just those habits are the very best way of preparing people to be free. It spreads respect for the courts' decisions and for the idea of right throughout all classes. (DA, p. 274)

> The passions that stir the Americans most deeply are commercial and not political ones, or rather they carry a trader's habit over into the business of politics. (DA, p. 285)

> The American derives from his home that love of order which he carries over into affairs of state. (DA, p. 292)

> In Europe we often carry the ideas and habits of private life over into public life. . . . But the Americans almost always carry the habits of public life over into their private lives. (DA, p. 305)

> It is through political associations that Americans of every station, outlook, and age day by day acquire a general taste for association and get familiar with the way to use the same. Through them large numbers see, speak, listen, and stimulate each other to carry out all sorts of undertakings in common. Then they carry these conceptions with them into the affairs of civil life and put them to a thousand uses. (DA, p. 524)

If . . . a man believes in the religion that he professes, it will hardly cost him anything to submit to such restrictions as it imposes. Reason itself advises him to do so, and habits already formed make it easy. (DA, p. 529)

Religions instill a general habit of behaving with the future in view. In this respect they work as much in favor of happiness in this world as of felicity in the next (DA, p. 547)

Once men have become accustomed to foresee from afar what is likely to befall them in this world and to feed upon hopes, they can hardly keep their thoughts always confined within the precise limits of this life and will always be ready to break out through these limits and consider what is beyond. (DA, p. 549)

The Americans carry over into agriculture the spirit of a trading venture. (DA, p. 554)

The inhabitants of democracies love their country after the same fashion as they love themselves, and what is habitual in their private vanity is carried over into national pride. (DA, p. 613)

As [men in democratic societies] usually aspire to none but facile and immediate pleasures, they rush straight at the object of any of their desires, and the slightest delay exasperates them. This temperament, which they carry with them into political life, makes them impatient of the formalities which daily hold up or prevent one or another of their designs. (DA, p. 698)

It is clear from these passages, I believe, that the spillover effect was a major conceptual tool, perhaps the most important single tool, in Tocqueville's analysis of democracy. (As we shall see, he also appeals to this mechanism in *The Old Regime*, but much less frequently.) As observed in the Introduction, the spillover effect, if operating by itself, would make us expect much greater cross-situational consistency of behavior than is actually the case. However, the picture is blurred by the presence of two other effects.

The compensation effect

This mechanisms rests on the idea that desires or needs that are not satisfied in one arena seek an outlet in others. People have certain basic needs, which seek satisfaction one way or another. Here are two examples, which invoke the compensation effect to explain the emergence of religion in, respectively, aristocratic and democratic societies. The first explanation is of the "opium of the people" variety, whereas the second belongs to the "fear of freedom" category.

> In nations where an aristocracy dominates . . . the poor are driven to dwell in imagination on the next world; it is closed in by the wretchedness of the actual world but escapes therefrom and seeks for joys beyond. (DA, p. 531)
>
> For my part, I doubt whether man can support complete religious independence and entire political liberty at the same time. I am led to think that if he has no faith he must obey, and if he is free he must believe. (DA, p. 444)[53]

The relationship between private and public life is also subject to the compensation effect. For an American, "To take a hand in the government of society and to talk about it is his most important business and, so to say, the only pleasure he knows. . . . But if an American should be reduced to occupying himself with his own affairs, at that moment half his existence would be snatched away from him; he would feel it as a vast void in his life and would become incredibly unhappy" (DA, p. 243). The European, somewhat similarly, "tries to escape his sorrows at home by troubling society" (DA, pp. 291–2). In both cases,

---

53 A similar compensation effect is also asserted in *The Old Regime*: "Even in our own time we find men who seek to compensate for their groveling servility to the meanest jack-in-office by declaiming against God and who, while going back on all that was freest, noblest, most inspiring in the revolutionary ideal, pride themselves on keeping faith with its true spirit by remaining hostile to religion" (Tocqueville 1955, p. 5). Whereas the presence of religion in democracy is explained by the need for having some authority in one's life, the turning away from religion in authoritarian societies is explained by the need for having some independence.

although more ambiguously in the latter,[54] public life fills a need left unsatisfied by commercial or domestic activities.

The compensation effect also shows itself in times of war. "War, having destroyed every industry, in the end becomes itself the one great industry, and every eager and ambitious desire sprung from equality is focused on it" (DA, p. 657). This is *not* a spillover effect. One might imagine that in a democracy men would transfer their private passions onto political and military matters, but Tocqueville tells us that in normal times this does not happen. "Violent political passions have little hold on men whose whole thoughts are bent on the pursuit of well-being. Their excitement about small matters makes them calm about great ones" (DA, p. 638). It is only when the normal, peaceful outlet for their energy is blocked that they turn to warfare.

The crowding-out effect

In the two passages just cited, the compensation effect is accompanied by a crowding-out effect. The former derives from the need to have some great passion, the latter from the fact that one cannot have more than one. The amount of ardor is, as it were, limited. "In times of democracy, private life is so active and agitated, so full of desires and labor, that each individual has scarcely any leisure or energy left for political life" (DA, p. 671). A similar mechanism ensures that there will not be much adultery in democratic societies: there simply is no time for it (DA, p. 598). Nor does their busy life leave democratic citizens with any leisure for examining their opinions (DA, p. 643).

In a remarkable passage we can see Tocqueville affirming both the spillover effect and the crowding-out effect:

> The governments of today . . . bear a natural good will toward
> civil associations because they easily see that they, far from

---

54 In fact, as we have seen, Tocqueville also explains the relation between private and public life in Europe by means of the spillover effect.

directing public attention to public affairs, serve to turn men's minds away therefrom, and getting them more and more occupied with projects for which public tranquility is essential, discourage thoughts of revolution. But they do not take the point that the multiplication of political associations is an immense help for civil associations and that in avoiding one dangerous ill they deprive themselves of an efficacious remedy. (DA, p. 523)

On the one hand, then, civil associations limit political activity, by the crowding-out effect, while on the other political associations induce citizens to come together in civil life, by the spillover effect. I now turn to a discussion of such complex cases.

Interaction effects

Sometimes, we may ask whether two domains are linked by a spillover effect or a crowding-out effect. Consider, for instance, the relation between economic and political democracy. Many writers from John Stuart Mill to Carole Pateman have argued that participation in the small community – at the workplace or in the local community – creates a mental habit that will also favor participation in the larger political community. Against this, we may set Oscar Wilde's observation that even under socialism, there will only be seven evenings in the week. In analytical terms, the first view argues for decreasing direct costs of participation, by virtue of some kind of learning process, and the latter for increasing opportunity costs. Although thus stated the two views are fully compatible, they tend to generate different political recommendations.

Tocqueville's views of the relation between public and private life involve all three effects in a causal sequence rather than, as in the previous paragraph, in simultaneous operation. First, the void in the private life of the Americans makes them seek an outlet for their energy in politics: This is the compensation effect. Next, the habit of forming political associations facilitates the formation of associations in civil life: This is the spillover effect.

Finally, the proliferation of civil associations distracts the attention and energy of the citizens from political participation: This is the crowding-out effect.[55] As elsewhere in this chapter, my concern here is not with the greater or lesser plausibility of this scheme. Rather, I want to emphasize how the micropatterns identified by Tocqueville can be combined so as to generate a larger social dynamic. Independently of the substantive assertions made, I believe this is a model that social scientists would do well to pursue.

In *The Old Regime* Tocqueville plays on both the compensation effect and the spillover effect in this explanation of the radical character of the French Revolution. Because of the lack of political freedom under the old regime, "the political ferment was canalized (*refoulé*) into literature, the result being that our writers now became the leaders of public opinion and played for a while the part which normally, in free countries, falls to the professional politician":[56] This is the compensation effect. Later, "when the time came for action, these literary propensities were imported into the political arena":[57] This is the spillover effect.

The relation between political and religious authority is a central theme in *Democracy in America* and in *The Old Regime*. I have cited passages to the effect that this relation is shaped by the compensation effect. A much more common view, however, is probably that there is a spillover effect by which political freedom tends to undermine religion, bringing about a state in which man has "ni Dieu ni Maître." Tocqueville himself, as we saw in Chapter 3, was aware of the fact that the democratic disrespect for authority may also induce aversion to the idea of an authority "beyond and outside humanity" (DA, p. 435). In my view, it is very plausible that both effects operate; in fact, I find that their simultaneous operation offers a more compelling

55 Hirschman (1982) offers an alternative view of the cyclical swings from the private to public and back again.
56 Tocqueville (1955), p. 142.
57 Ibid., p. 147.

view of the relation between religion and politics than any other analysis I have come across.

The analysis of the three effects underlines what I said earlier, that Tocqueville, unlike Marx and Hegel, finds the link between different spheres of society in psychological attractions and repulsions rather than in functional necessities or contradictions. I am not saying that there is nothing of value in the structural–functionalist approach. A political system may shape or constrain economic activities (and vice versa) by providing incentives or disincentives to action, even assuming that motivations remain constant. However, I believe, somewhat tentatively, that in the long run the more important causal connections will be found in the realm of preference formation.

The previous chapter demonstrated, I hope, the arbitrary and speculative character of much of Tocqueville's thinking. We can now see that there is some method in his madness. In approaching social institutions and social change, he drew on a relatively small number of well-defined psychological mechanisms. These, rather than his hyperbolic and often inconsistent explanatory claims, constitute the reason for reading and rereading him today. Once we have accomplished this shift of perspective, his autistic outlook need not disturb us as much. I have said elsewhere that when reading Marx, one has the impression that his mind is guided by two premises: Whatever is desirable is possible, and whatever is desirable and possible will inevitably come to pass.[58] In reading Tocqueville, the underlying premise sometimes seems to be that whatever is intelligible is ipso facto true. This unnerving confusion of explanation and story telling[59] has no doubt led many readers who were initially struck by his brilliance, as I believe anyone must be, to turn away from his work. I hope I have been able to persuade some of them to take a second look.

58 Elster (1985a), p. 55.
59 Elster (1989a), ch. 1.

191

REFERENCES

Ackerman, B. 1991. *We the People*, vol. 1: *Foundations*, Cambridge, Mass.: Harvard University Press.

Ainslie, G. 1992. *Picoeconomics*. Cambridge University Press.

Alloy, L., and Abrahamson, L. 1979. Judgment of contingency in depressed and non-depressed students. *Journal of Experimental Psychology: General* 10:441–85.

Aronson, E. 1988. *The social animal*. New York: Freeman.

Asbjørnsen, P. C., and Moe, J., eds. 1957. Manndatteren og kjerringdatteren, in *Samlede Eventyr*, vol. 2. Oslo: Gyldendal.

Axelrod, R. 1984. *The evolution of cooperation*. New York: Basic.

Barry, B. 1978. *Sociologists, economists and democracy*, 2nd ed. Chicago: University of Chicago Press.

Becker, G. 1976. *The economic approach to human behavior*. Chicago: University of Chicago Press.

Bell, R., Raiffa, D. E., and Tversky, A., eds. 1988. *Decision Making*. Cambridge University Press.

Besnard, P. 1987. *L'Anomie*. Paris: PUF.

Boehm, C. 1984. *Blood revenge: The anthropology of feuding in Montenegro and other tribal societies*. Lawrence: University of Kansas Press.

Boudon, R. 1973. *Mathematical structures of social mobility*. Amsterdam: Elsevier.

1982. *The unintended consequences of social action*. London: Macmillan Press.

1986. *Theories of social change*. Oxford: Blackwell.

Bourdieu, P. 1979. *La distinction*. Paris: Editions de Minuit.

Bourdieu, P., and Passeron, J.-C. 1970. *La reproduction*. Paris: Editions de Minuit.

Bovens, L. 1992. Sour grapes and character planning. *Journal of Philosophy* 89:57–78.

Bryson, F. R. 1935. *The point of honor in sixteenth-century Italy*. New York: Publications of the Institute of French Studies, Columbia University.

Caro, R. 1974. *The power broker: Robert Moses and the fall of New York*. New York: Vintage Books.

Chen, Y. 1986. *Making revolution. The Communist movement in Eastern and Central China 1937–1945*. Berkeley and Los Angeles: University of California Press.

References

Cohen, G. A. 1978. *Karl Marx's theory of history: A defence.* Oxford University Press.

Condorcet, Marquis de (1947). Examen sur cette question: Est-il utile de diviser une assemblée nationale en plusieurs chambres. In *Oeuvres de Condorcet*, vol. 9, pp. 333–64. Paris: 1847.

Cyert, R. M., and de Groot, M. H. 1975. Adaptive utility. In R. H. Day and T. Groves, eds., *Adaptive economic models*, pp. 223–46. New York: Academic Press.

Davidson, D. 1980. *Essays on actions and events.* Oxford University Press.

1986. Deception and division. In J. Elster, ed., *The multiple self*, pp. 79–92.

Davies, N. 1982. *A History of Poland.* New York: Columbia University Press.

Descartes, R. 1897–1910. *Oeuvres complètes.* Paris: Vrin.

Dixit, A., and Nalebuff, B. 1991. Making strategies credible. In R. Zeckhauser, ed., *Strategy and Choice*, pp. 161–84. Cambridge, Mass.: MIT Press.

Egret, J. 1950. *La révolution des notables.* Paris: Armand Colin.

Elster, J. 1975. *Leibniz et la formation de l'esprit capitaliste.* Paris: Aubier-Montaigne.

1976. Some conceptual problems in political theory. In B. Barry, ed., *Power and political theory*, pp. 245–70.

1978. *Logic and society.* Chichester: Wiley.

1979. Risk, uncertainty and nuclear power. *Social Science Information* 18:371–400.

1983a. *Explaining technical change.* Cambridge University Press.

1983b. *Sour grapes.* Cambridge University Press.

1984. *Ulysses and the sirens*, rev. ed. Cambridge University Press.

1985a. *Making sense of Marx.* Cambridge University Press.

1985b. Sadder but wiser: Rationality and the emotions. *Social Science Information* 24:375–406.

1986a. Introduction to J. Elster, ed., *Rational choice*, pp. 1–33.

1986b. Self-realization in work and politics. *Social Philosophy and Policy* 3:97–126.

1988. Is there (or should there be) a right to work? In A. Guttman, ed., *Democracy and the welfare state*, pp. 53–78. Princeton, N.J.: Princeton University Press.

1989a. *Nuts and bolts for the social sciences.* Cambridge University Press.

1989b. *The cement of society.* Cambridge University Press.

1989c. Marxism and individualism. In M. Dascal and O. Gruengaard, eds., *Knowledge and Politics*, pp. 189–206. Boulder: Colo. Westview Press.

1989d. *Solomonic judgements.* Cambridge University Press.

1990a. Norms of revenge. *Ethics* 100:862–85.

1990b. When communism dissolves. *London Review of Books*, January 24.

References

1991a. Patterns of causal analysis in Tocqueville's *Democracy in America*. *Rationality and society* 3:277–97.

1991b. Arguing and bargaining in two constituent assemblies. The Storrs Lectures, Yale Law School.

1991c. Constitutionalism in Eastern Europe: An introduction. *University of Chicago Law Review* 58:447–82.

1991d. Envy in social life. In R. Zeckhauser, ed., *Strategy and choice*, pp. 49–82. Cambridge, Mass.: MIT Press.

ed. 1985. *The multiple self*. Cambridge University Press.

ed. 1986. *Rational choice*. Oxford: Blackwell.

Faia, M. A. 1986. *Dynamic functionalism: Strategy and tactics*. Cambridge University Press.

Farber, L. 1976. *Lying, despair, jealousy, envy, sex, suicide, drugs, and the good life*. New York: Basic.

Feller, W. 1968. *An introduction to probability theory and its applications*, vol. I, 3d. ed. New York: Wiley.

Festinger, L. 1957. *A theory of cognitive dissonance*. Stanford, Calif.: Stanford University Press.

1964. *Conflict, decision and dissonance*. Stanford, Calif.: Stanford University Press.

Fink, E. C. 1987. *Political rhetoric and strategic choice in the ratification conventions on the U.S. Constitution*. Ph.D. Diss., Department of Political Science, University of Rochester.

Finley, M. I. 1973. *Democracy: ancient and modern*. London: Chatto & Windus.

Fowles, J. 1963. *The collector*. London: Jonathan Cape.

Furet, F. 1988. *La révolution 1770–1870*. Paris: Hachette.

Gauchet, M. 1986. Le nominalisme historien. A propos de "Foucault révolutionne l'histoire" de Paul Veyne. *Information sur les Sciences Sociales* 25:401–19.

Genovese, E. 1974. *Roll, Jordan, roll*. New York: Pantheon.

Gilcher-Holtey, I. 1986. *Das Mandat des Intellektuellen*. Berlin: Siedler Verlag.

Goodin, R. 1978. Uncertainty as an excuse for cheating our children: The case of nuclear wastes. *Public Policy* 10:25–43.

Groh, D. 1973. *Negative Integration and revolutionärer Attentismus*, Frankfurt a.M.: Suhrkamp.

Gullestad, S., and Tschudi, F. 1982. Labelling theory of mental illness. *Psychiatry and Social Science* 2:213–26.

Habermas, J. 1984/1989. *The theory of communicative action*, vol. I (1984), vol. II (1989). Boston: Beacon.

1990. Discourse ethics. In *Moral consciousness and communicative action*, pp. 43–115. Cambridge, Mass.: MIT Press.

Hardin, R. 1982. *Collective action*. Baltimore: Johns Hopkins University Press.

Heckscher, E. 1955. *Mercantilism*. London: Allen & Unwin.

References

Hegel, G. W. F. 1977. *The phenomenology of spirit*. Oxford University Press.

Henry, C. 1974. Investment decisions under uncertainty: The 'irreversibility effect.' *American Economic Review* 64:1,006–12.

Hintikka, J. 1961. *Knowledge and belief*. Ithaca, N.Y.: Cornell University Press.

Hirschman, A. 1973. The changing tolerance for income inequality in the course of economic development. *Quarterly Journal of Economics* 87:544–65.

  1977. *The passions and the interests*. Princeton, N.J.: Princeton University Press.

  1982. *Shifting involvements*. Princeton, N.J.: Princeton University Press.

Hirshleifer, J. B. 1987. On the emotions as guarantors of threats and promises, in J. Dupré, ed., *The latest on the best*, pp. 307–26. Cambridge, Mass.: MIT Press.

Holmes, S. 1984. *Benjamin Constant and the making of modern liberalism*. New Haven, Conn.: Yale University Press.

  1988. Precommitment and the paradox of democracy. In J. Elster and R. Slagstad, eds., *Constitutionalism and democracy*, pp. 195–240. Cambridge University Press.

  1989. Destroyed by success: On Tocqueville's *Recollections* (Unpublished manuscript).

  1990. The secret history of self-interest. In J. Mansbridge, ed., *Beyond self-interest*, pp. 267–86. Chicago: University of Chicago Press.

Horn, L. R. 1989. *A natural history of negation*. Chicago: University of Chicago Press.

Hume, D. 1960. *A treatise of human nature*. Ed., Selby-Bigge. Oxford University Press.

  1963. *Essays: moral, political and literary*. New York: Oxford University Press.

Hungdad, C. 1987. Institutionalizing a new legal system in China. (Paper presented at a conference at Brown University, November 1987.)

Inhelder, P., and Piaget, J. 1959. *La genèse des structures logiques élémentaires*. Paris: PUF.

Jardin, A. 1984. *Tocqueville*. Paris: Hachette.

Jillson, C. C. 1988. *Constitution making: Conflict and consensus in the Federal Convention of 1787*. New York: Agathon Press.

Jones, R. A. 1977. *Self-fulfilling prophesies*. Hillsdale, N.J.: Lawrence Erlbaum.

Kahneman, D., Slovic, P., and Tversky, A., eds. 1982. *Judgment under uncertainty*. Cambridge University Press.

Kolakowski, L. 1978. *Main currents of Marxism*. Oxford University Press.

Kolm, S.-C. 1982. *Le bonheur-liberté*. Paris: PUF.

Kreps, D. M., and Wilson, R. 1982. Reputation and imperfect information. *Journal of Economic Theory* 27:253–79.

References

Langholm, S. 1984. *Elitenes valg*. Oslo: Universitetsforlaget.
Laplanche, J. 1970. *Vie et mort en psychanalyse*. Paris: Flammarion.
Leff, A. 19??. *Swindling and selling*. New York: Free Press.
Lerner, M. J. 1980. *The belief in a just world*. New York: Plenum.
Levenson, J. 1968. *Confucian China and its modern fate*. Berkeley and Los Angeles: University of California Press.
Levy, R. 1973. *The Tahitians*. Chicago: University of Chicago Press.
Lewinson, P., et al. 1980. Social competence and depression. *Journal of Abnormal Psychology* 89:203–12.
Lewis, A. 1982. *The psychology of taxation*. New York: St. Martin's.
Lovejoy, A. O. 1961. *Reflections on human nature*. Baltimore: Johns Hopkins University Press.
MacIntyre, A. 1962. A mistake about causality in the social sciences. In P. Laslett and W. Runciman, eds., *Philosophy, politics and society*, 2nd ser., pp. 48–70. Oxford: Blackwell.
March, J. 1966. The power of power. In D. Easton, ed., *Varieties of political theory*, pp. 39–70. Englewood Cliffs, N.J.: Prentice-Hall.
Marx, K. 1842. *Neue Rheinische Zeitung*, May 5, 1842.
    1981. *Capital*, vol. 3. London: Penguin.
Merton, R. 1957. *Social theory and social structure*. Glencoe, Ill.: Free Press.
Mischel, W. 1968. Personality and Assessment. New York: Wiley.
Mora, G. F. de la. 1987. *Envy*. New York: Paragon House.
Mounier, E. 1789. Exposé de ma conduite dans l'Assemblée Nationale. Reprinted in F. Furet and R. Halévi, eds., *Orateurs de la Révolution Française. I: Les constituants*, pp. 908–97. Paris: Gallimard 1989.
Nash, W. 1989. *Rhetoric: The wit of persuasion*. Oxford: Blackwell.
Needham, J. 1956. *Science and civilization in China*, vol. 2. Cambridge University Press.
Nisan, M. 1985. Limited morality. In M. W. Berkowitz and F. Oser, eds., *Moral education: Theory and practice*, pp. 403–20. Hillsdale, N.J.: Lawrence Erlbaum.
Nisbett, R., and Ross, L. 1980. *Human inference*. Englewood Cliffs, N.J.: Prentice-Hall.
Nordhaus, W. 1975. The political business cycle. *Review of Economic Studies* 42:169–90.
Olson, M. 1965. *The logic of collective action*. Cambridge, Mass.: Harvard University Press.
Parfit, D. 1984. *Reasons and persons*. Oxford University Press.
Parijs, P. van. 1981. *Evolutionary explanation in the social sciences*. Totowa, N.J.: Rowman and Littlefield.
Pears, D. 1984. *Motivated irrationality*. Oxford University Press.
Popkin, S. 1979. *The rational peasant*. Berkeley and Los Angeles: University of California Press.
Porter, J. 1978. The solitary life of the writer. In D. Winn, ed., *Murder ink: The mystery reader's companion*. Newton Abbot: Westbridge Books.

References

Proust, M. 1957. *The captive*. London: Chatto & Windus.

Pruyser, P. W. 1974. *Between belief and unbelief*. New York: Harper & Row.

Quattrone, G., and Tversky, A. 1986. Self-deception and the voter's illusion. In J. Elster, ed., *The multiple self*, pp. 35–58. Cambridge University Press.

Rakove, J. N. 1987. The Great compromise: Ideas, interests, and the politics of constitution making. *William and Mary Quarterly* 44:424–57.

Rapaczynski, A. 1991. Constitutional politics in Poland. *University of Chicago Law Review* 58:595–632.

Roemer, J. 1985. Rationalizing revolutionary ideology. *Econometrica* 53:85–108.

Russell, B. 1905. On denoting. *Mind* 14:479–93.

Samuelson, W., and Bazerman, M. 1985. The winner's curse in bilateral negotiations. *Research in experimental economics* 3:105–37.

Sartre, J.-P. 1968. *Being and nothingness*. London: Methuen.

Schelling, T. C. 1960. *The strategy of conflict*. Cambridge, Mass.: Harvard University Press.

Scocpol, T. 1983. *States and social revolutions*. Cambridge University Press.

Searle, J. 1969. *Speech acts*. Cambridge University Press.

1979. *Expression and meaning: Studies in the theory of speech acts*. Cambridge University Press.

Shepard, R. 1964. On subjectively optimum selection among multiattribute alternatives. In M. W. Shelley and G. L. Bryan, eds., *Human judgment and optimality*, pp. 257–80. New York: Wiley.

Simon, H. 1954. Bandwagon and underdog effects in election predictions. *Public Opinion Quarterly* 69:245–53.

Smullyan, R. 1978. *What's the name of this book?* Englewood Cliffs, N.J.: Prentice-Hall.

Snyder, D. P. 1971. *Modal logic*. New York: Van Nostrand Reinhold.

Stinchcombe, A. 1968. *Constructing social theories*. New York: Harcourt, Brace & World.

1976. Merton's theory of social structure. In L. Coser, ed., *The idea of social structure: Papers in honor of Robert Merton*, pp. 11–33. San Diego, Calif.: Harcourt Brace Jovanovich.

Stone, L. 1972. *The causes of the English revolution*. New York: Harper & Row.

Sunstein, C. 1991. Constitutionalism and secession. *University of Chicago Law Review* 58:633–70.

Suppes, P. 1970. *A probabalistic theory of causality*. Amsterdam: North Holland.

Sutton, J. 1986. Non-cooperative bargaining theory: An introduction. *Review of Economic Studies* 53:709–24.

Taylor, M. 1987. *The possibility of cooperation*. Cambridge University Press.

References

ed. 1988. *Rationality and revolution*. Cambridge University Press.

Thaler, R. 1980. Towards a positive theory of consumer choice. *Journal of Economic Behavior and Organization* 1:39–60.

1983. The mirages of public policy. *The Public Interest* 73:61–74.

1991. *Quasi-rational economics*. New York: Russell Sage.

1992. *The winner's curse*. New York: Free Press.

Thaler, R., and Shefrin, H. M. 1981. An economic theory of self-control. *Journal of Political Economy* 89:392–406.

Thomas, K. 1973. *Religion and the decline of magic*. Harmondsworth: Penguin Books.

Thomson, J. M. 1988. *Robespierre*. Oxford: Blackwell.

Tocqueville, A. de 1836. Political and social conditions of France. *The London and Westminster Review* vol. III and XXV:137–69.

1952. *L'ancien régime et la révolution*, vol. II, Part I of the *Oeuvres complètes*, Paris: Gallimard.

1953. *L'ancien régime et la révolution*, vol. II, Part II of the *Oeuvres complètes*, Paris: Gallimard.

1955. *The old regime and the revolution*. New York: Doubleday.

1970. *Recollections*. London: Macdonald.

1986. *The European revolution and correspondence with Gobineau*. Gloucester, Mass.: Peter Smith.

Tong, J. 1988. Rational outlaws: rebels and bandits in the Ming Dynasty, 1368–1644. In M. Taylor, ed., *Rationality and revolution*, pp. 98–128. Cambridge University Press.

Tumin, M. 1957. Some unapplauded consequences of social mobility in a mass society. *Social Forces* 15:32–37.

Tversky, A., and Kahneman, D. 1974. Judgment under uncertainty. *Science* 185:1,124–30.

1981. The framing of decisions and the psychology of choice. *Science* 211:453–8.

Veyne, P. 1983. *Les Grecs ont-ils cru à leurs mythes?* Paris: Editions du Seuil.

1984. *Writing history*. Middletown, Conn.: Wesleyan Press.

Walcot, P. 1978. *Envy and the Greeks*. Warminster: Avis & Philips.

Walder, A. 1986. *Communist neo-traditionalism*. Berkeley and Los Angeles: University of California Press.

Watzlawick, P. 1978. *The language of change*. New York: Basic.

Watzlawick, P., et al. 1974. *Change*. New York: Norton.

Whitaker, R. 1992. Reason, passion and interest: Pierre Trudeau's eternal triangle. In R. Whitaker, *A Sovereign Idea*, pp. 132–64. Montreal: McGill-Queen's University Press.

White, M. 1987. *Philosophy, "The Federalist," and the Constitution*. Oxford University Press.

Wittgenstein, L. 1978. *Philosophical investigations*. Oxford: Blackwell.

Zinoviev, A. 1990. *Les confessions d'un homme en trop*. Paris: Gallimard.

INDEX

absolute veto, 28, 28n
abstention from revolutions, 16
active indifference, 93
adaptive preferences
    and choice behavior, 54–7
    extremes in, 56–7
aftereffects, 106, 106n
agriculture in America, 131
alethic logic, 76, 95n
altruistic motivation
    democratic societies, 130
    as explanatory mechanism, 3–4
    in revolutionary movements, 19
ambition in democracies, 116–17,
    170–1
amorality, Zinoviev's sociology, 86,
    98
amour-propre, 27–8
ancient Rome
    contradiction in emperor system,
        66–9
    euergetism, 39–43, 47–8, 59
    function of collegia, 59
    ideology, 63
    oligarchy, 46–7
    social psychology, 48
anomie, 170–1, 175
arguing, and constitution making,
    24–5, 25n, 30
aristocracies
    compensation effect, 187
    durable passions in, 158–9
    honor in, 160
    love marriages in, Tocqueville,
        104–6
    social norms, 159–61
    Tocqueville's attitude, 107–10
armies
    anomie in, democracies, 170–1
    in democratic societies, 174–5
Assemblée Constituante in Paris,
    26–7, 30–1, 33

atheism, 80–1
attitudes toward death, 60–2
authoritarian regimes
    and dissonance theory, 54–5
    political typology, weaknesses,
        1–2
    threats to, 43–5
    upward mobility in, 45–6
    use of power, 97
authority
    compensation effect, 190
    in democratic societies, 180
    Veyne's interpretation, 43–6
banality of evil, 84
"bandwagon effect," 3
bankruptcies in America, 113–14, 161
bargaining
    in constitution making, 24–5, 30
    secrecy effect, 30
beliefs
    in America, Tocqueville, 126–7
    and cognitive dissonance, 12
    contradictions in, Veyne's analysis,
        60–2
    formation of, 11–15
    logic of, 76
    need for meaning origin, 14
Bourdieu, 142n, 159
Bread and Circuses (Veyne), 35–69

Catch 22 (Heller), 89
Catholicism, 129
charisma, 60
checks and balances, 33, 33n
Chinese legal system, 88n, 90, 90n
choice behavior
    cognitive dissonance theory, 54–6
    extremes in, 56–7
    and self-control need, 56
    Veyne's theory, 50–7
civil associations, 188–91

civil life, and religious life, 124–5
class structure, America, 130–1
cognition, 10–11
cognitive dissonance
  adaptation to authoritarianism,
    54–5
  in choice behavior, 54–7
  role in motivation, 12–13
Cold War, 80
commissioned officers, 171–2, 174
Communist regimes, 65, 183
compensation effect, 180–91
  as explanatory mechanisms, 4, 6
  in Tocqueville's writings, 187–8
compromise, 96–7
compulsory military service, 115,
  151
condemnation, 92
conditional altruism, 4
conformity
  in democracies, Tocqueville, 119,
    180–3
  and public opinion, 180–3
conscious motivation, 9–10
consciousness, Hegel's theory, 79
conscription in America, 115, 151
constitution making, 24–34
correlations, 5–6
credibility problem, revolutionary
  governments, 18
crowding-out effect, 180–91
  in Tocqueville's writings, 188–9
cult of the king, 42, 61, 65

death, attitudes toward, 60–2
delegated charisma, 60
delegation of power, 43
democracy, 101–91
  Assemblée Constituante opinion,
    31
  compensation effect, 187–8
  conformity in, 180–3
  crowding-out effect, 188–9
  desire and opportunity in, 162–79
  effect on ambition, 116–17, 170–
    1, 176
  impact on women, 104–6
  and instability of desire, 148
  love marriages in, 104–6
  political typology weaknesses, 1–2
  and religion, 118–19, 126–7, 171

selection of leaders, 168–9
  spillover effects, 185–6
  Tocqueville's writings, 101–91
Democracy in America (Tocqueville),
  101–91
  comparison to other works, 136
  contradictions in, 112–35
deontic logic, 76
desire
  adaptation to external
    circumstance, 180–3
  and cognitive dissonance, 12–13
  consciousness function, Hegel, 79
  formation of, 11–15
  logic of, 76
  and opportunities, democracies,
    162–79
  in times of equality, 148
  in Tocqueville, 147–9, 162–79
dialectics, in Zinoviev, 70–100
dignitas, 49n
display, 51–2
divinity of the emperor, 42, 62
duty, 20

economic rationality, 51–7
education, Zinoviev's sociology,
  87–8
emancipation of slaves, 172
emperor-subject dialectic, 67–9
enlightened self-interest, 144
envy
  consequence of equality, 151–3
  as explanatory mechanism, 4
  and promotion by merit system,
    45–6
  and selection of leaders,
    democracy, 168–9
  source of frustration, democracy,
    176
epistemic logic, 76, 95n
equality
  cause of envy in democracies,
    151–3
  and conformity, 180–2
  effect on desire, 169–71
  and instability, 148
  propensity in democracies, 142–3
  and self-interest, 145–7, 151
  Tocqueville's writings, 118–19,
    142–9, 167n

Index

equilibrium analysis, 101–2
euergetism
    in ancient Rome, 39–44, 47–8
    in *Bread and Circuses*, 35–43
    free rider problem, 48n
    functional explanations, 57–60
    in Greek democracy, 38–9
    interpretations, 44
    and public goods, 47–8
    excess of will, 52
    external negation, 70–100
    and Khrushchev's de-Stalinization
        failure, 94–5
    logic of, 73–8
    Zinoviev's understanding, 79n,
        82–8

false conformity, 182–3
family life, Tocqueville's view, 124
Federal Convention in Philadelphia
    (1787), 26–7, 30, 32
Festinger's theory, *see* cognitive
    dissonance
feudal honor, 160
feuds, 49n
floating capital, 157
free rider problem, 18, 48n, 144
freedom, and self-interest, 146
freedom of the press, 120
Freud's early work, 184

Genovese, Eugene, 67–8
Greek regime, *see* Hellenistic regime
guilt, Zinoviev's interpretation, 99

Hegel, internal negation theory, 79–
    80
Hegel-Sartre lineage, 71, 71n
Hegelian master-slave dialectic, 67–8
Hellenistic regime
    euergetism, 38–9, 55
    ideology, 63
    oligarchy, 46
    plebeian adaptation to, 55
honor, in ancient Rome, 48–9
"hydraulic model" of the mind, 184

ideology
    justification explanation, 63
    and passion, 64–6
    rationality in, 64–6

unconscious role, 63–4
Veyne's analysis, 60–6
    in Zinoviev's system, 97
    ignorance, and self-interest, 145–6
immigrants to America, 126
impulsive emotions, 156–7
incentives, in revolutionary
    movements, 17–18
independence, in democracies, 119
individual choice, *see* choice
    behavior
individual psychology, in
    Tocqueville, 136–8
industry in America, 131
informing, Zinoviev's sociology, 82–
    3, 97
inheritance laws, 122, 157, 167–8
inner conformity, 181–2
instinctive patriotism, 128–9
instrumental rationality, 50–1
intention
    logic of, 76
    and willed indifference, 92–3
    in Zinoviev's system, 98
internal negation, 70–100
    Hegel's view, 79–80
    Kant's treatise on, 78
    and Khrushchev's de-Stalinization
        failure, 94–5
    logic of, 73–8
    paradox of, 80–2
    role of education, 87–8
    Zinoviev's understanding, 79n,
        82–8
irrationality
    in revolutionary movements, 15–
        16, 19, 19n
    spontaneity in, 53–4
    Zinoviev's study, 70–100

"just world" theories, 14, 65

Kantian ideas, 11, 13, 20
Kant's negation treatise, 78
Khrushchev, Nikita, 94–5

lawyers
    and passions of democracy, 157–8
    Tocqueville's observations, 142–3,
        157–8
legal system, American democracy,
    121–3

201

Index

letter of the law, 90
liberty, and self-interest, 145–6
love marriages, and Tocqueville,
104–6

masculinity, Tocqueville's attitude,
107
mechanisms
and functionalism, 57–9
of revolutionary movements,
15–24
study of, 2–7
and theories of mind, 184
versus theory, 2–3, 7n, 8n
in Tocqueville's writings, 119,
135, 184
mediocrity, Zinoviev's sociology, 84–
5, 98
methodological individualism
and motivation, 8–10
reductionism in, 7–8
microeconomic illusion, 49
micropolitical illusion, 66
modal logic, 74–6
monarchy, Tocqueville's attitude,
107–10
morality, Zinoviev's sociology, 86,
98
mores, 121–3, 181–2
motivation
in constitution making, 24–34
formation of, 11–15
in methodological materialism,
8–10
and rational choice, 9–10, 138–9
in revolutionary movements,
17–20
and Tocqueville, 138–62
myopic behavior, in democracies,
146–9

need for meaning, 14, 57
negation, see external negation;
internal negation
newspapers in America, 114
noncommissioned officers, 171–2

Old Regime and the Revolution, The
(Tocqueville), 17, 101–2, 136–7,
187n, 190
oligarchy, comparative sociology,
46–7

opportunism, Zinoviev's sociology,
83–4

Le Pain et de Cirque (Veyne), 35–69
passions
in aristocracies, 158–9
in constitution making, 24–5, 25n,
30
in democratic societies, 150–9
and ideology, 64–6
promotion of self-interest, 156–7
and self-deception, 155
subversion of self-interest cause,
145–57
in Tocqueville, 143, 150–8
patriotism in America, 128–9
Phenomenology of Mind, The (Hegel),
79
philanthropy, 49
political associations, 189–90
political life, and family life, 124
poverty, and revolutionary
movements, 17, 17n
power, Zinoviev's system, 97–100
pride, 27–8
primitive mentality, 73–8
Principle of Contradiction, 74–6
Principle of the Excluded Middle,
74–6
Prisoner's Dilemma, 16; see also free
rider problem
promotion by merit, 45
propensities, Tocqueville's
observations, 142–3
Proust, 159
public opinion
and conformity, 180–93
in democracies, 118, 180–3

The Radiant Future (Zinoviev), 72, 83
rational behavior
and action, 9–10
and ideology, 64–6
in revolutionary movements,
15–17
and Tocqueville, 139
Veyne's theory, 50–7
rationalism, Veyne's criticism, 50–7
reason, in constitution making, 24–
5, 30–1
reciprocal causality, 125–6

Index

Recollections (Tocqueville), 102–3, 111, 137, 139, 177*n*
reductionism, 7–8
reflective patriotism, 128–9
religion
  civil life relationship, 124–5
  compensation effect, 187, 190
  contradictions in, 126–7, 129
  in democracies, Tocqueville, 118–19, 126–7, 171, 190
  spillover effect, 190
repressive regimes, 21
revenge, 162
revolutionaries, 174
revolutions, 15–24
  credibility problem, 18
  dynamics, 15–24
  motivations, 17–21
  rationalistic interpretation, 16–19
Rome, *see* ancient Rome

sampling effects, 106, 106*n*
self-control
  and choice behavior, 56
  in democracies, Tocqueville, 178–9
self-deception, 13, 53, 155
self-interest
  in constitution making, 24–5, 25*n*, 29–30, 32
  democratic societies, Tocqueville, 130, 143–50
  reasons for acting against, 145–55
  and will-power, democracies, 150
selfishness, democratic societies, 130
servility, 123
slavery
  adaptation to, 173
  effect on slaveowners, 168
  system in America, 67–8
  Tocqueville's interpretation, 109–11, 123, 168, 172–3
social mobility, democracies, 176–7
social norms
  in egalitarianism systems, 157
  feudal societies, 160–1
  in Tocqueville, 143, 156–7, 159–62
"sour grapes syndrome," 3, 66, 165
Soviet empire, internal negation, 80
spillover effect, 180–91

as explanatory mechanism, 4, 6
and Tocqueville, 124, 128, 185–6
spirit of the law, 90
spontaneous behavior, 53–4
Stalin, 84
statistical correlations, 5–6
submission, 66
suspensive veto, 28, 28*n*

theoretical constructions, 2–3, 7*n*, 8*n*
threat-based bargaining, 24–6, 30
Tocqueville, 101–91
  contradictions in writings, 112–35
  emotional and intellectual makeup of, 103–35
  equilibrium analysis framework, 101–2
  individual psychology of, 136–8, 178
  prejudice of, 111–12
  psychological universals, 140–1
  statement on revolutions, 15, 17
"Tocqueville effect," 137*n*
totalitarian regimes
  political typology weaknesses, 1–2
  use of power, 97

unconscious motivation
  cognitive dissonance effect, 12
  and human action, 9–10
  Veyne's view, 60, 60*n*
"underdog effect," 3
upward mobility, 45, 46, 46*n*
utilitarianism
  as explanatory mechanism, 4
  in revolutionary movements, 19

vanity, 27–8, 139
Veyne, Paul
  analysis of ideology, 60–6
  euergetism analysis, 35–69
  and functionalism, 57–60
  relationship to Tocqueville, 37
  theory of choice, 50–7
Vietnam revolutionary movement, 17
voluntary servitude, 109–11
voting, motivation for, 41, 41*n*
voting paradox, 41*n*

war, in democracies, 169
weakness of will, 52

will-power, 150, 178–9
"Winner's Curse," 69*n*
wishes, logic of, 76
women
    adaptation in American society,
        177
    Tocqueville's views, 111–12

Writing History (Veyne), 36*n*

Yawning Heights (Zinoviev), 71–2,
    82, 84, 96

Zero-sum effect, 184
Zinoviev, Alexander, 70–100